How Compat

How Compatible Are You?

*Reveal the Secrets of your Relationship
using Handwriting Analysis*

Miranda Cahn

BLOOMSBURY

The case studies that appear throughout this book are based on possible real-life situations, but they are not meant to be taken too seriously or to reflect the author's or the publisher's opinions on particular personality traits. Rather, they are intended to illustrate, in a light-hearted and accessible way, aspects of the personality that can be revealed through handwriting analysis.

First published 1997 by Bloomsbury Publishing Plc, 38 Soho Square, London W1V 5DF

Copyright © Miranda Cahn 1997

The moral right of the author has been asserted

A copy of the CIP entry for this book is available from the British Library

ISBN 0 7475 3229 X

10 9 8 7 6 5 4 3 2 1

Typeset by Hewer Text Composition Services, Edinburgh
Printed in Great Britain by Cox & Wyman Ltd, Reading

To my late grandparents. And with thanks to all who have provided such invaluable assistance and inspiration, in particular my parents, Juliette and Alistair, Jessica and Mark, Rufus Leonard, Tim Wong, Tony Freeman, Gnocchi, and most importantly of all, Harmen.

Contents

Introduction

- *Gain a better understanding of yourself and others.*
- *Discover your strengths and start using your special talents and skills.*
- *Confront your weaknesses and insecurities and then learn how to overcome them.*
- *Increase your self-confidence.*
- *Appreciate your own values and identify what is really important to you in your life.*
- *Save wasted time and emotions by changing or improving stagnant relationships.*
- *Find out the types of people with whom you are most compatible.*

What Will this Book Do for You?

In this book you will discover the amazing powers of handwriting analysis. Graphology, the scientific term for it, can show you how well matched you are with your partner and where -- if at all – you are likely to have problems in your relationship.

If you are already in a relationship, you will gain extraordinary insights into your own and your partner's personalities. Knowing why your partner thinks or acts in the way he or she does, and being able to anticipate his or her reactions, will help improve your relationship enormously. If you are single but would like to be half of a couple, graphology can help you discover the type of person with whom you are most compatible. If you are embarking on a new relationship, graphology can reveal the likelihood of its success. Single or attached, graphology can assist you to eliminate misunderstandings, make all of your relationships more rewarding and, ultimately, make you happier.

Most people, men and women alike, dream of stumbling across their soul-mate, falling in love and living happily ever after. Unfortunately the fairy tale often crumbles apart. Sometimes it never even gets started and the story remains a dream, hidden in the recesses of the brain, recalled in moments of sadness or introspection, happiness or hope.

These days divorce is rife. More and more people are living alone, their dreams shattered and their lives embittered by cynicism. The cement that used to bind two people together seems to have turned into a weak glue that easily comes unstuck. More and more relationships are failing. But why?

Much of this failure is due to poor communication, conflicting ambitions and goals, and differing reactions to the stress piled upon us in this fast-paced, modern world. But if we take the time to really understand ourselves and our partner, then our relationships need not fail.

This book will lead you through the basic steps of preparing a compatibility analysis. By the end of it you will have learned how to identify the signs in handwriting for many of the most important traits comprising the personality. However, you will need to pursue further study if you wish to be able to complete full analyses, or if you wish to become qualified or practise graphology professionally.

What is graphology?

When we write words on a page with a pen or pencil, signals are sent from our brain to our hand, which causes us to move the pen over the paper. These signals are electrical impulses, controlled by our neuromuscular system and drawing on both our conscious and unconscious mind. The result is writing, as unique to you as your fingerprints.

Think back to your early school days. All the children in your class were taught to write in the same way. But very quickly your writing would have taken on *your own* identity. As an adult, if you compare your writing to that of your ex-school mates, it is most unlikely that you will find any of the original similarity. In fact, it is highly unlikely that you will find any human being who has writing identical to your own. This is because you have a unique and dynamic personality, a uniqueness that is represented in your handwriting.

Many people state that their writing changes, certainly as they grow older from year to year, and sometimes more dramatically from day to day. How can you analyse handwriting based on that, they ask?

As we grow older we mature; our personalities develop and we change. Some characteristics are lost, others are gained. And all this is shown in our handwriting, the window to our personality. Those people who have moods that fluctuate strongly from day to day will find that their handwriting also changes. When in a good mood we tend to write larger, more boldly and more confidently.

Normally day-to-day changes in a person's handwriting are fairly minor. The personality does not alter dramatically and such changes frequently look greater to the untrained eye than they really are for the purposes of graphology.

Nevertheless, it is important to acknowledge the fact that our personalities are dynamic, so it is always preferable to use samples of handwriting gathered over a period of days, weeks or even months, should you require the most accurate analysis of an individual's personality.

The secrets of your personality

All elements of personality are revealed in the unique way that every person constructs the lines and strokes of his or her handwriting. So graphology can uncover numerous aspects of your character and personality. These are the traits that make up the real you – not the characteristics that you have developed as your façade to the outside world. Graphology uncovers what lies behind your surface personality, looking deeper than the initial impressions that you make on others. For instance, many people appear confident and self-assured, while in reality they are battling with fears inside, constantly fighting to maintain that confident image. Graphology strips away the façades, exposing the truth underneath. As a result, graphology analyses often provide you with lots of surprises!

We will be looking at all of the following:

- **Emotions** – your emotional make-up and feelings. We will consider whether or not you and your partner feel the same way.
- **Thought processes** – how your mind works and how you come to decisions. We will consider whether you and your partner think in the same way.
- **Sociability** – how well you get on with people and how they perceive you. We will find out whether you and your partner are equally sociable.
- **Fears** – conscious and unconscious fears and anxieties. We will uncover any hidden fears that you and your partner may have.
- **Reactions** – how you react to problems and difficulties. We will discover whether you and your partner react in a similar way.
- **Motivations** – what motivates you and how likely you are to achieve your aims. We will consider whether you and your partner want the same things out of life.
- **Integrity** – honesty, dignity and other important issues. We will find out whether or not you and your partner have the same standards.
- **Sexuality** – how important sex is to you, and what your preferences are. We will discover whether you and your partner are sexually compatible.

Everybody's personality is deeply complex, a mixture of characteristics that we are born with and those we have learned. Often it can take a lifetime to really understand a spouse, partner or best friend, but graphology can help you skip years of that learning process! And, by the end of this book, once you have analysed your own writing, you will understand yourself to a degree that many people never achieve.

What is graphology unable to do?
Handwriting analysis has nothing to do with the occult, magic, fortune telling or palm reading. It is not predictive. It cannot tell you what is going to happen to you or to others in the future, or

how you are going to develop and change. Graphology provides you with a snapshot of your personality as it is on the day that you write the writing that is being analysed. Based upon this snapshot it may be possible to *estimate* how you are likely to behave, but it is important to stress that graphology is not predictive. It is a scientific method of personality assessment based on over a hundred years of empirical and clinical research. It has no connection with anything paranormal.

A little bit of background!

Handwriting analysis has been officially practised since the beginning of the seventeenth century. The basics of modern analysis were formulated by the French during the nineteenth century. The Germans, Swiss and Americans then furthered these studies. However, for the last seventy years one of the most popular, scientifically proven methods of analysis has been *graphoanalysis*. Much of what is explained in this book has its roots in graphoanalysis.

What is a compatibility analysis?

A compatibility analysis compares the writing of two or more people to see how well they are likely to get on together. It particularly identifies how the individuals communicate their feelings in relationships. It highlights both partners' emotional and mental rapport, their energy levels and anxieties. The more personality traits that are uncovered, the more material there is with which to compare the two writers and estimate where problems are, or are likely to appear, in their relationship.

Whatever your 'relationship' status, a graphology analysis and a compatibility report will be of assistance to you in achieving a happy love life or partnership.

Read through the following stories of people with different relationship status and see how graphology can help you!

How Can Graphology Help?

The single person

Who is your perfect mate? Do you know what you are looking for in a potential mate? Do you know what characteristics you should be looking for to ensure compatibility?

❛ It was a glorious day, the sunlight glowed through the curtains and the birds seemed to be singing louder than normal. Kate felt doubly depressed. 'It should be raining,' she thought, 'in support of the misery of my birthday.'

Grabbing the three thick envelopes awaiting her on the doormat, she hurried to work in anticipation of burying her unhappiness in the monotony of routine. Parents, sister, aunt – she knew whom the birthday cards were from, and she didn't bother opening them.

Lunchtime. 'Kate, take that miserable expression off your face. You're coming to lunch with me!' Julia bounded across the office, thrust Kate her coat and propelled her down the stairs. 'So what's up with you then?' Julia asked.

'Oh, nothing much. It's just my birthday – not that I expect anyone to remember, and not that I mind being a year older. But it reminds me that I'm still single and not so young! Everyone I know seems to be married or living with someone, returning home to a warm bed, a shared meal or even an argument. To be honest, I'm lonely.'

'When was the last time you had a boyfriend?' Julia asked gently.

'I honestly can't remember. Three – four years ago.'

'But lots of guys are chasing you. You're attractive, bright, witty – what's the problem?'

'I scare them all off!' Kate replied. 'Half the time I don't know what I'm looking for. I'm scared of being hurt and don't want to take the risk, so I act cool and distant and we rarely get past the second date. The other half of the time I fall deeply in love with someone who either isn't available or isn't interested in me. I'm really not lucky in love! I think I'm destined for the single life.'

'Don't be ridiculous!' retorted Julia, moving closer and turning round to face Kate directly. 'Your problem is lack of confidence in yourself and not knowing what you really want. I've got an idea. A belated birthday present. Expect it next week!'

That evening Kate returned home to find six friends sitting on her doorstep. 'Happy birthday!' they yelled, thrusting brightly wrapped gifts into her arms. 'Surprise! You're coming out for dinner with us.'

Their kindness and their gifts warmed Kate's heart, she felt wanted and happy. But a week later it was her colleague Julia's gift that changed her life.

Julia had removed some handwritten memos from Kate's desk and sent them to a graphologist for analysis. The report, which was sent directly to Kate, outlined her full personality – talents that Kate never appreciated she had, fears she knew she had to face. It told her how other people perceived her and how those perceptions contrasted with her real self. It even explained to her the type of person with whom she would be most compatible. Many of the points confirmed things that Kate already knew; some simply amazed her.

Understanding herself allowed Kate to take steps to improve her self-confidence. The next time she met someone new she approached the friendship with a different attitude – as an adventure, not a threat. That friendship did not develop into a relationship, but the following one did. Birthdays are no longer days to dread. For Kate, loneliness is a thing of the past! ❜

The new relationship, perhaps?

Single, but not for long — you've met someone and this may be the start of a wonderful romance, but you're not quite sure? How well suited are you really? Have you met the partner of your dreams? How can you know for sure?

Unless you embark on a relationship, and it stands the test of time, you cannot know whether you have met your soulmate! Although graphology cannot predict what is going to happen in the future, it can let you know how well suited you and your potential partner are. Then it's up to you to decide whether or not to take that relationship further!

❛ Daniel met Zoë a week before he was meant to be going abroad on a six-month work secondment. The timing was unfortunate. He had been looking forward to half a year in the sun, playing hard, meeting lots of different girls and acting out his carefree dreams. Now he wasn't so sure.

They saw each other every night all that week.

Towards the end of the week Zoë plucked up sufficient courage to ask Daniel whether he thought there was any future in their relationship.

'Daniel, do you want me to wait for you? Can I come and visit you? Or is this the end?' Zoë asked, embarrassed.

'I honestly don't know.' Daniel lowered his eyes, ran his hand through his hair and, in confusion, stuttered again, 'I just don't know.'

He lay awake most of the night wondering what to do. He knew it wasn't fair to ask Zoë to wait for him until he returned home. She should be out having a fun time. On the other hand, he wanted to keep her for himself. He thought he loved her. But what if their relationship didn't work out? He kept on thinking of all the potential lost opportunities with those imaginary golden beach girls.

'You look awful!' his sister commented at the breakfast table the next morning.

'I didn't sleep very well,' Daniel admitted, and went on to tell Kelly his dilemma.

'Oh, that's no problem. Give me her writing and I'll prepare a compatibility analysis for you,' she replied, 'then you've got a better idea of how well matched you two are and whether there's long-term hope.'

'That takes all the romance out of it, doesn't it?' joked Daniel. Answering his own question, he carried on, 'Well, perhaps not, it just gives me a helping hand. Okay, Kelly, go ahead and analyse!' ❜

The couple

You are in a relationship. It's chugging along all right, but you do have your ups and downs. What does the future hold in store for the two of you? Are you really compatible? Is it worth while investing more energy in the relationship? What steps can you take to improve things?

Many people are in relationships that have become rather stagnant. One or both partners would like to spice things up, but often don't know how. Some people exist within relationships where communication has completely degenerated. They may feel quite miserable, but don't know how to improve things. Sometimes the partners are too scared to break free.

If you are in such a relationship, graphology can give you the tools to improve your life. By understanding yourself and your partner, and the differences between you, you can take the necessary steps to improve your happiness. Graphology allows you to see into your souls, to find out whether you are still right for each other.

❻ Philip and Stella met at school. They married. He became a truck driver and she qualified as a nurse. They both worked long hours and increasingly began to see less of each other. When Stella became pregnant for the first time she quit her job and concentrated for seven years on bringing up their two children. She prided herself on always being at home for Philip whenever he returned, ready with a hot meal, a clean house and two smiley, polite children awaiting a hug from their father.

When Philip lost his job, it seemed to Stella that their fragile marriage disintegrated instantaneously. Philip wandered around the house like a zombie, flinching from his wife's touch and answering her questions in monosyllables. Stella offered to look for a job to bring in some money. Philip flew into a rage at the prospect.

Stella was in despair. She thought she still loved her husband, although she wasn't too enamoured by the man he had recently become. She thought that Philip probably still loved her. Deep down she didn't want to end their marriage, but on the other hand she didn't know what to do to improve things. Graphology became her life-line.

The evening that Philip read the handwriting analysis report was the first time that the two of them had held a proper discussion since Philip's redundancy. He was awakened to the fact that he was losing a grip on his life and his marriage. They were both reminded of the reasons they had married in the first place, the things they loved and admired in each other. It was the first step forward although it took a long time to rebuild their broken life. ❾

The honeymoon couple!

You are in a happy, secure relationship that you hope has a long future. What can you do to make sure that the relationship stays as rosy as it is now? What problems might you have to face in the future, and what should you do to overcome them?

Most partners have differences of opinion, varying aspirations and opposite ways of feeling or seeing things, to a greater or lesser degree. Sometimes these differences may develop into the cause of future relationship problems. However, if you can assess now where any problems may arise, you will be able to nip them in the bud and ensure that your relationship remains as happy and successful as it is at the moment.

❢ Jack and Sue had a compatibility analysis prepared for them at the start of their relationship. Every few months it comes out of the cupboard and they read the report out loud, to remind each other where their differences of opinion lie and what they should be consciously doing to ensure that their relationship remains happy and smooth-running. It makes all the difference! ❡

What to Expect in this Book!

This book is divided into chapters each of which covers a different aspect of your own and your partner's personality. There may be some aspects of the personality that interest you more than other, and it will not upset your compatibility report if you skip to these first. Although it is not essential to follow the order of the chapters, those personality traits that are listed towards the start of the book do have an impact on the traits listed later on, and so this should be borne in mind.

Every chapter is divided into different personality traits. These traits are explained, and case studies are used to illustrate how these traits affect people such as you and me in real life. We then explain what to look for in handwriting to assess whether that characteristic is present in the writing. Next we consider the importance of this characteristic in relationships, and how people with different characteristics are likely to get on together.

The last chapter of the book comprises a sample compatibility chart and analysis, which should help you when compiling your own analyses.

If you wish to study handwriting analysis in depth you will need to be able to evaluate the impact that one personality trait has on another. Some characteristics strengthen other traits, some weaken them. Some characteristics are cancelled out altogether by another trait. This evaluation is complicated and detailed and lies beyond the scope of this book. It must be stressed, however, that if you wish to use handwriting analysis for anything other than your own curiosity and amusement, it is vital to learn how different personality traits impact upon each other. Please remember that a little knowledge can be dangerous.

How Do You Do a Compatibility Analysis?

Preparation
When preparing a compatibility analysis you need to analyse both your own and your partner's writing.

Select your favourite pen. Ideally this should be an ink pen or biro. A pencil or a pen with a very soft nib is not appropriate, as you will be unable to assess the pressure and other important elements of the handwriting.

Take two pages of plain, unlined paper and write anything that comes into your head. You will get a more accurate analysis if you write spontaneous thoughts, instead of copying text out of a book. You need to write in lower-case (small) letters. Sign your name with your normal signature when you have finished.

Then ask your partner to do the same.

The analysis
Once you have your writing samples you need to put aside time to prepare your analysis. Use a red biro to mark the writing you are analysing and keep some paper at hand to write notes on. Systematically go though the chapters of this book. You may find it useful to copy the format of the sample chapter at the end of this book.

When you are analysing the writing of a stranger, it will help if you know whether the writer is left- or right-handed and whether they are male or female. Other than that, you need know nothing about the writer.

Before you analyse someone's writing it is ethically correct to get their permission first. You may find yourself in all sorts of trouble if you analyse a person's writing behind his or her back. Remember that you will be uncovering many sensitive and personal issues – issues that are private to the writer. It is essential to treat these with tact and diplomacy. Never reveal someone's personal secrets without their permission. Never abuse the power that you have in knowing how to analyse writing.

It is possible to analyse the writing of someone who has written in another language, although the language must be based upon the Latin script. The principles you are being taught in this book will therefore apply to European languages but will not apply to scripts such as Russian, Hebrew, Chinese, Japanese and Arabic.

Can signatures be analysed?

Signatures are interesting, but not as important as a person's writing as a whole.

Most people have relatively short signatures; it is most unlikely that someone will sign his or her name using every letter of the alphabet. As a result there will be many vital personality traits and characteristics that you will be unable to check simply by looking at a signature.

We develop our signatures as our outside face to the world. Our signature is written for consumption by others and is the façade that we like to portray. It does not necessarily indicate our true personality. If your signature uses writing very similar to your normal writing, this indicates that you have little to hide. What you see is what you get. But if your signature looks little like your normal writing and perhaps is very hard to read, this indicates that you do not reveal your true self easily, but have developed a façade that needs to be broken down if others are to know the real you.

Many people have signatures that look scrawled, as if they have been written carelessly or in a hurry. People who have to sign their names many times each day learn to abbreviate, signing off with the least effort so as to speed up the writing.

So analysing signatures alone can be very dangerous indeed, for it is unlikely to give an accurate picture of the true personality. Used in conjunction with normal handwriting, a signature can, however, be very valuable.

Explanation of Terms

There are many terms that are used in graphology that may be unfamiliar to you. It is worth while familiarizing yourself with them now, before you embark on the route to self-discovery!

Baseline

The baseline is an imaginary line upon which the writing sits. If you are writing on lined paper, you would normally sit your letters on the line. If you are writing on plain paper, imagine where the line would have been and you will have found the baseline.

Circle letters

Letters that are made with circles. These are a, b, d, e, g, o, p and q. All of these letters have complete circle formations within them.

Downstroke

These are the lines that are drawn downwards on the page. For instance, most people write the letter l starting with a down-stroke – a line that starts at the top of the letter and moves downwards.

Emotional slant chart

This is the tool that we use to measure emotional slant in handwriting. It looks rather like a protractor and its use is explained fully in Chapter 1.

Evaluate

This word is used when we assess the impact of one trait upon another.

Lower loop or stem

The loops or stems (single lines, drawn straight up and down, as opposed to looped) that descend from the baseline into the lower zone. Letters that have lower loops or stems are f, g, j, p, q and y.

Personal pronoun

Sometimes known as PPI, this is the personal pronoun I, as in 'I am', 'I have'. The letter I is studied in depth in more advanced graphology courses or books.

Pressure

The pressure of writing is the amount of force that the writer uses when writing on the page. The greater the pressure, the more heavily the page will be indented, and this can be felt on the reverse of the sheet. Often pressure can be gauged by the width of the lines drawn in the writing.

Retracing
This occurs when a downstroke retraces an upstroke. Retracing is not present when an upstroke retraces a downstroke. If you are unsure whether a stroke is an upstroke or a downstroke, take a pen and retrace the movements that the writer would have made.

Slant
The direction in which the majority of the upstrokes are leaning.

Stroke endings
These are the ends of strokes, where the line finishes. Some of these endings are finished bluntly, some taper off and others are made with force.

Stroke
These are the small lines that are made when writing a letter. For instance, when writing a capital T, most people use two strokes – a vertical line with a horizontal line on top of it.

T-bar
The t-bar is the horizontal line that crosses through the letter t. If the letter t is a tree, the t-bar would be a branch.

T-stem
The t-stem is the vertical section of the letter t. Imagine that the t is a tree – the t-stem would be the trunk.

Traits
These are the individual personality characteristics that are studied in graphology. Some traits can be evaluated in writing by studying various stroke formations. Other traits are made up of a number of different traits and cannot be evidenced so easily.

Upper loop or stem
The loops or stems that reach into the upper zone. Letters that have upper loops or stems are b, d, h, k, l and t.

Upstrokes
These are the lines that are drawn upwards on the page. For instance, when writing the letter w, most people will write the first line coming down, the next line going up in an upstroke, the next line coming down and the last line going up.

Zones

In graphology we divide letters up into three sections – the upper zone, the middle or mundane zone and the lower zone. This is best explained in diagram form:

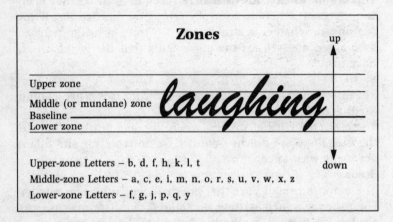

Lower zone

The lower zone incorporates the lower third of all long, downward-pointing letters – the loops and sticks of f, g, j, p, q and y that descend downwards.

Middle zone

The middle, or mundane, zone incorporates the middle third of all letters. Letters such as a, c, e, i, o, u, m, n, r, s, v, w, x and z fit completely into the middle zone.

Upper zone

The upper zone incorporates the top third of all tall, upward-pointing letters – the tops of b, d, f, h, k, l and t – the sticks or loops that reach upwards.

1

Do You Both Feel the Same Way?

- *Are you the emotional type, quick to feel strong emotions? Or are you cool and collected, rarely showing your feelings? Does your partner react in a similar way?*
- *How long do you remember your feelings? Do you both forgive and forget, or do your emotions smoulder on and on, losing little of their original intensity?*

Our emotions, otherwise known as our feelings, affect everything we do, say and think. And no one – not even the coldest, most heartless person you know – exists without emotions. In this chapter we will consider the importance of emotion in relationships.

The way we feel, how long we sense those feelings and the way we express them hold the key to your own and your partner's personality. It is our emotions that allow us to experience happiness and sadness, warmth and coolness, anger and love, and every other feeling that you can imagine.

Everyone's emotions are unique to themselves. We don't honestly know how someone else is feeling, or the effect that an emotion will have on them in the long term. All we can do is guess, based upon our own experiences. Quite often we guess wrongly. Sometimes we are simply incapable of understanding how or why someone is feeling the way they are. Misjudging, or not understanding a partner's emotions or feelings, is the greatest single cause of the breakdown of relationships.

Let's take a quick look at an example of how people differ in their emotional reactions.

❢ Six friends got together one evening to have a drink, eat a Chinese take-away and watch television. The film that Annie, Charles, Erica, Frank, Debbie and Brian saw was a real-life documentary about famine in Africa. The pictures were horrifying: starving children were dying in their parents' arms; disease-ridden adults were appealing for aid; people were herded together like animals off to the slaughter-house. Without exception, all six friends felt upset and bewildered by the programme. But their real feelings and subsequent actions were quite different.

Annie is intensely emotional. To begin with she started crying and couldn't eat her food, and then she told everyone that they should eat every morsel, as there were too many people starving out there to waste food. She didn't sleep that night. Images of dying people were constantly flashing in and out of her mind. The next day she called an international aid charity and asked for information on how she could go to Africa to help out.

Erica is also quite emotional. She felt dreadful about the programme and kept on imagining what she would do if her baby was starving. The next day she drew some money out of her building account and sent it to the charity.

Charles shows the way he feels by the way he acts. He was also put off his food, but he was more objective about it all. He felt saddened that evening, but after a good night's sleep the images had faded from his mind.

Frank felt sickened by the programme but was able to finish his meal, enjoying the food at the same time as feeling upset. He was sympathetic to Annie and Erica, who were obviously deeply moved by what they saw, but he himself seemed quite in control of his own emotions.

Debbie sat through the programme quite calmly. It wasn't that she didn't feel upset – in fact she was very disturbed, but she felt able to detach herself from what she saw. Famine wasn't affecting her or her family and, besides donating money to charity, she felt there was little she could do to change what was going on in Africa. She explained to the others that famines had happened throughout history and that they were the natural way of keeping birth rates in check. Four of her friends shouted at her for being so callous.

Brian didn't shout at Debbie because he agreed with her. He is the 'cold fish' of the group and shows no emotions about anything – especially something as remote as a television documentary about distant Africa. He watched the film but was really more interested in making sure that the food didn't get cold and that everyone's wine glasses were refilled. By the time he went home he had totally disassociated himself from the film and never thought of it again. ❣

You can see from the reactions of this group of friends that we all feel things very differently. Some people would remember the images of the film for days, feeling almost as devastated by it as if it were happening to them in real life. Other people would be upset at the time but would be able to disassociate themselves from it once the film had finished. These people are not callous or unfeeling, they can simply cut themselves off from things that do not affect them personally.

In graphology, the first thing we look for in handwriting is emotion. This is because our emotional reactions affect practically everything we do – the way we think, the way we interact with other people and how other people perceive us. As a general rule, the more the writing slants to the right, the more the writer lets his or her feelings affect his or her life – but this is explained much more towards the end of this chapter.

The tale of the six friends gives you an idea of the different emotional feelings. But it is important that we study these variances in feelings in greater depth, because differences in emotional feelings will have a crucial role to play when assessing compatibility.

❝ Adrienne Baloise is a Parisienne. Her shiny black hair is shaped into a neat bob, accentuating her strong cheekbones, pale blue eyes and bright red lips. She wears Hermes scarves, carries Louis Vuitton bags and strides around in high-heeled crocodile shoes and short, short skirts. Adrienne is perfectly poised and constantly calm. She is what graphologists call an *upright writer* and this shows in the way she conducts her business and her love affairs.

Adrienne runs an interior design boutique frequented by the rich and famous European ladies normally seen smiling out of the social pages of *Tatler*, *Hello!* or *Paris Match*. She only ever stocks the latest fabrics and wallpapers after she has fully analysed whether or not they are suitable for her clients. Her personal likes or dislikes do not come into play.

Recently, when one of her designers became sick, Adrienne posted her a cheque for a very large amount of money, sent her a bouquet of flowers and told her that 'There may or may not be a job awaiting you when you get better.'

'I have to make money,' she tells me in her husky, heavy French accent, 'I cannot let my heart rule my head!'

Adrienne faces crises calmly. She tilts her head to one side, weighs up the pros and cons of the actions she could take and then comes to a decision. Rarely does Adrienne make a bad move.

Many people are wary of Adrienne because she often appears distant and rather calculating. 'It is unusual for a French lady to be so reserved,' stated a well-known polo-playing, sports-car-driving gentleman. Adrienne is an excellent business person because she ensures that any moves she makes are based on reason, as opposed to emotion. Both her social life and her business life are ruled by her diary, her many point plans and the questions that she poses on every issue. Will it work? Will it pay? What will the consequences be? Adrienne cannot remember the last time she allowed emotions or feelings to enter into her mind when she made a decision or resolved upon a course of action.

Being a business lady and quite a socialite, Adrienne meets many different people each week. Over the years she has had a few affairs of the heart, and she was happy to show the handwriting of some of her lovers and to explain a little about her intimate relationships – several failures and one noticeable success.

'Charles is an Englishman I met in London. An important businessman and rather handsome. We saw each other many times, but the story did not work out. He was very into himself and never opened up to me. We got on well as friends but not as lovers. He was too worried, I think, about being hurt emotionally.'

Charles' writing shows him to be a left-slanting writer, and at times far left-slanting. Like Adrienne, his head rules his heart at all times, but he is more self-interested than an upright writer like Adrienne. He always assesses how actions will affect him personally and never lets anyone close to him emotionally. He is not selfish, but concerned with protecting his own inner feelings. Left-slanting writers are often perceived as rather introverted and are frequently insecure, hiding their emotions not only from others but from themselves as well.

'Antoine was a socialite. I was young when I met him and he took me to many parties and introduced me to exciting important people. He was romantic. Bah! Too romantic for me. He loved whisking me away on surprise weekends, which was bad for my business planning. He sent me flowers every day. Antoine asked me to marry him exactly one month after we met. It was too, too soon for me. He married my friend Corinne six months later. He is a nice man but too emotional for me. Poor Antoine has failed in business so many times I don't remember! You see, he lets his heart rule his head. Quel idiot!'

Antoine's writing falls into the right-slanting categories. He is fundamentally an emotional person and shows the way he feels by the way he acts. People can read him like an open book. He generally finds it hard to be objective and allows himself to be carried away by his feelings. If Antoine had other characteristics, such as determination, strong analytical powers or even pride, he might have been able to keep his emotions in check and have developed better business skills. Unfortunately he had little in his personality that kept control of his emotions.

'Daniel was the most exciting of my lovers. But he was not good for me. He was even more impulsive than Antoine. Mon Dieu, did I choose them! Daniel is an artist. You may know him, for he is very famous and popular now. When he painted me it was terrible. One day he was happy and he painted me in shades of yellows and oranges. The next day he would be in a bad mood. He would shout at me and repaint the portrait in black and grey. Then he would sulk until I said sorry even when it was not my fault! Everything was dramatic and everything was emotional for Daniel. I was obsessed by him for a long time.' Adrienne's voice trailed off wistfully and then returned strongly. 'But we were totally incompatible him and me!'

Daniel's writing slopes incredibly far to the right, so that it falls within the very far right-slanting category. He is intensely emotional and impulsive, reacting to whatever feeling prevails at that moment. For him, everything in life is an emotional experience. Unlike his predecessor Antoine, Daniel has developed mechanisms to control his intense emotionality. He is a proud man and, unless he is very close to someone, generally does not like people to see how emotional he really is. However, it is important that someone like Daniel does not repress his emotions too much, because if he was placed under considerable emotional strain he could burst, have a nervous breakdown or do something out of character.

Adrienne then went on to discuss her present lover, whom she will be marrying at the end of this year. She talked a lot about him for she is clearly in love, so we will print only a part of what she said.

'Pierre is wonderful! He is handsome and clever and kind, and a wonderful lover. You know, I am so lucky to have found someone that makes me so happy. I think he is a more friendly, sympathetic person than me, but he is still, as they say, level headed! He combines a clever, rational brain with a kind and gentle heart! It is not surprising that he is successful in business and has lots of friends. You must meet him!' Just as Adrienne was opening her wallet to show me a photograph of her handsome Pierre, the doorbell rang and in he strode carrying a fine bottle of claret and a single blue iris. 'To match her eyes!' he said, winking at me.

Pierre's writing shows him to be a slightly right-slanting writer. This type of person responds to emotional situations but is not swayed by them. For instance, he may feel saddened by someone else's loss, but that in itself isn't going to change his mind about doing something. Pierre, typically of right-slanting writers, is friendly and sympathetic but not in the extreme. He is well composed and other people will never see him out of control or stepping out of line.

It is not surprising that Adrienne and Pierre are so compatible. They understand each other well, both relying on their heads first and their hearts second. Pierre, no doubt, is viewed as the more kindly of the couple, as he will appear to others to be the most emotional. Neither of them will rush into decisions or actions. It is rather typical of upright and slightly right-slanting writers that they have been together for three years before deciding to commit to marriage! It is highly likely that theirs will be a successful, long-lasting partnership as neither of them is likely to rush off and do anything rash that they might later regret. **9**

Before we study how to measure each of the slants, how to assess what they mean and how compatible different slant types are with each other, we should consider one more slant type: the variable slant.

Many people have slants that fall into different categories. Typical is someone who has 20 per cent of their writing right-slanting, 60 per cent far right-slanting and 20 per cent very far right-slanting. This type of person would first and foremost be an emotional 'animal' but would at times be able to temper their emotionality with some objectivity. Such a variation in slant is normal, especially if it covers two or three consecutive slant types.

However, if someone's writing falls into four or more of the different slant types, or if the slant types vary from one end of the spectrum to the other – very far left-slanting to very far right-slanting – there could be a problem! Such a person is likely to be rather unbalanced and would certainly act in an unpredictable manner.

> ❝ Janice had the most dreadful mood swings. One moment she would be happy, singing and dancing; the next moment she would be slumped in a black depression. She had few friends because people would never know where they stood with her. Sometimes she would welcome them as her best friend, at other times she would walk past them in the street as if they were strangers. Janice's mood swings became so out of control that she lost her job. Eventually she was helped with both medication and counselling.
>
> As you can imagine, Janice's writing slanted all over the place. In the way that her behaviour was irrational, so was her writing. ❞

Being in a relationship with a person who is so irrational can cause enormous heartache. You simply never know where you stand with them. If the writing shows great slant variations, the chances are that that person needs some kind of help.

Emotional Slant

What do the slants mean and how well can you expect to get on with people within other slant categories?

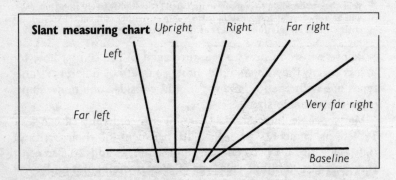

The case studies of Adrienne and her lovers and the six friends should have given you some insight into what the various slants mean. In the rest of this chapter the different emotional reactions are set out in depth.

First of all, check your own handwriting and decide which slant you have most of, then look at the following pages to learn more about yourself and the types of people you are most likely to get on with. If you have a partner, check his or her writing and then read on to see how compatible you are likely to be.

What to look for?
How to measure writing to check emotions:
- *Take your ruler and draw a line through the bottom of the letters, under the middle zone.*

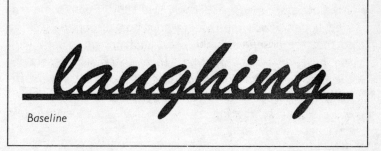

Baseline

- *Take a pen and copy the movements that the writer would have gone through to write the letters.*

- *Whenever the writer has made a stroke going upwards, stop. Take your pen and ruler and line it up so that you draw a straight line between the baseline you have drawn and the top of the upstroke.*

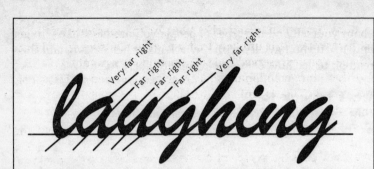

- *Take the slant-measuring chart and copy it onto some tracing paper. Place the tracing paper on top of the writing so that the baseline on the chart matches up exactly with the baseline on the writing. Then check which sections the lines you have drawn fall into. If you don't have sufficient time (or patience!) to do this, you can make an estimate simply by looking at the writing – but beware, this isn't necessarily so accurate.*

Upright Writers

What does the writing look like?
If you are an upright writer your writing will look quite vertical, with most of your letters going straight up and down the page, as in this typed text.

Samples of upright writing

lolloping   still undecided

the attention

What does upright writing mean?
You are normally cool, calm and collected. You are naturally objective and do not allow your feelings to affect your decisions and

actions. You will ask yourself, 'What are the consequences . . .?', 'Will it work?' It is unlikely that you are impulsive or rush into things. You are reserved and face emotional crises calmly.

Other more emotional people may perceive you as being cold or distant. This is unlikely to be the case. Just because you do not let your emotions run away with you does not mean that you don't feel them strongly.

As an upright writer, how compatible are you likely to be with other slant writers?

Upright and left-slanting

Such a relationship should work well, as each partner has similar cool judgement and a reserved outlook. However, both parties need to understand the differences in each other's emotional make-up. The upright partner will seem more outgoing and will find it easier to show his or her emotions, whereas the left-slanting writer will not be expressive and may be harder to get to know.

Upright and upright

This is an excellent combination for a successful relationship. Both parties will understand the way each other feels. Both will be rational. Don't expect any impulsive behaviour in this partnership – no surprise weekends to some romantic hideaway! And certainly no hysterical outbursts! Everything will be carefully slotted into place.

Upright and right-slanting

There is every chance that this will be a successful relationship. Neither party will get out of hand emotionally, although the right-slanting writer may appear more sympathetic than the upright writer. Assuming that there are no other outstanding characteristics in either individual that would negate this, such a partnership could prove highly successful. This couple is likely to be successful on a business as well as a personal level, as intuition, sympathy and level-headedness will be brought into the equation.

Upright and far right-slanting

This relationship can work so long as each writer understands the emotional differences of his or her partner. Problems could arise if the right-slanting writer feels unloved by his rather more distant partner. The upright partner may despair of the far right-slanting partner, who tends to rush head-long into things and does not stand back and evaluate his or her actions until it is too late. On the other hand, with one partner being rather rational and objective, and the other being more emotional and impulsive, this could prove to be a thriving partnership, with each partner complementing the other.

Upright and very far right-slanting
Such a relationship will work only if great understanding and patience are developed by both parties. Such people are fundamentally incompatible, as one partner always puts his head before his heart and the other partner her heart before her head. But, as they say, 'opposites attract' and this combination is really quite commonplace. Often the partner with the cool head gives objectivity to the highly emotional partner, and the very far right-slanting writer brings a bit of impulsiveness and crazy emotion into the life of the upright writer. Nevertheless this partnership will require hard work, excellent communication and patience to succeed in the long term.

Right-slanting Writers
What does the writing look like?
The writing will slant slightly to the right. However, on first glance, without measuring it, it may appear quite upright.

Samples of right-slanting writing

made one

end up doing   *the Kitchen*

What does right-slanting writing mean?

Right-slanting writers react to emotional situations but are not unduly swayed by them. You are likely to be seen as friendly and sympathetic, but you will rarely get out of line by showing excessive displays of emotion.

The more your writing slants to the right, the more emotional you are likely to be – although within this category of slant you will usually maintain some objectivity. Occasionally you may be indecisive, because you can get caught between logic and feelings. On the one hand you know what you should do, but that may run contrary to the way you are feeling.

As a right-slanting writer, how compatible are you likely to be with other slant writers?

Right-slanting and left-slanting

Such a relationship will work only if both parties understand the differences in each other's emotional make-up. The right-slanting partner is fundamentally an emotional person and will seem more outgoing, whereas the left-slanting writer will be considerably less expressive. Communication, patience and understanding will ensure the success of such a relationship.

Right-slanting and upright

There is every chance that this will be a successful relationship. Neither party will get out of hand emotionally, although the right-slanting writer may appear more sympathetic than the upright writer. Assuming that there are no other outstanding characteristics in either individual that would negate this, such a partnership could prove highly successful. This couple is likely to be successful on a business as well as a personal level, as intuition, sympathy and level-headedness will be brought into the equation.

Right-slanting and right-slanting

There is every chance that this will be an excellent relationship. Both partners will have the same emotional reactions and will understand each other on this level. Both have the capacity for feeling and showing emotions, but neither is likely to get out of control.

Right-slanting and far right-slanting
There is a good chance of a successful relationship. The right-slanting writer will understand the feelings of his or her far right-slanting partner, but will be able to bring some objectivity and perspective to the relationship.

Right-slanting and very far right-slanting
Such a relationship can work so long as both parties recognize the differences in their emotional response to situations. Emotions will certainly run high and, depending upon other characteristics, this could be a stormy relationship, as both partners have the capacity to be carried away by their feelings.

Far Right-slanting Writers

What does the writing look like?
The writing will slant to the right, and this will be noticeable at a glance. It will seem as if your letters are leaning forwards, trying to follow the pen as you write from left to right across the page.

Samples of far right-slanting writing

advantage

Management

ideas

What does far right-slanting writing mean?
If your writing slopes far to the right it means that you are strongly affected by emotions, perhaps to the degree that your

thinking is never completely free from the influence of your feelings. From time to time you tend to act before thinking, and you show the way you feel in your expression, manner, voice and action.

You lean towards people, and are quick to make decisions influenced by your likes and dislikes. You also have the capacity to arouse emotional feelings in other people.

As a far right-slanting writer, how compatible are you likely to be with other slant writers?

Far right-slanting and left-slanting
As both these partners have totally different approaches to emotions, a considerable amount of work will need to be undertaken after the initial 'honeymoon' period has worn off. It is possible that the far right-slanting partner will feel that the relationship is 'one-sided', as the left-slanting partner will not visibly be giving so much emotionally. Each partner takes a very different approach to everyday life and it will be hard for them to understand what makes the other tick.

Far right-slanting and upright
This relationship can work so long as each writer understands the emotional differences of his or her partner. Problems could arise if the right-slanting writer feels unloved by his or her rather more distant partner. The upright partner may despair of the far right-slanting partner, who tends to rush headlong into things and sometimes doesn't stand back and evaluate his or her actions until it is too late. On the other hand, with one rather rational objective partner, and the other more emotional and impulsive, this could be an excellent partnership, with each complementing the other.

Far right-slanting and right-slanting
There is a good chance of a successful relationship. The right-slanting writer will understand the feelings of his or her far right-slanting partner, but will be able to bring some objectivity and perspective to the relationship.

Far right-slanting and far right-slanting

In theory there is every chance that this should be a successful relationship, as both partners will understand each other on an emotional level. However, it is likely to be a volatile relationship as both parties tend to have strong emotional responses to situations. Mood swings by both partners are likely to be an integral part of this relationship, and if both coincide on a low, it could be rough-going.

Far right-slanting and very far right-slanting

This relationship could work well, as the partners have fundamentally the same emotional outlook and reactions. However, this could also be a volatile relationship, for emotion, as opposed to rationality, will rule over both – and especially the very far right-slanting writer's – lives. Both partners are highly emotional animals and neither will find it easy to listen to reason.

Very Far Right-slanting Writers

What does the writing look like?

The writing will slant dramatically towards the right, even to the extent that in some cases, it looks as if it is lying down on its stomach!

Samples of very far right-slanting writing

the time

pleasure

What does very far right-slanting writing mean?

If your writing slopes very far to the right this indicates that you are completely absorbed and influenced by your emotions. Everything in life becomes an emotional experience and you react strongly and often quickly. You find it extremely hard to be objective and you cannot distance yourself easily. You are impulsive and tend to jump to conclusions. This makes you easily influenced by your likes and dislikes.

Having such intense emotions means that you may, at times, have inexplicable mood swings. If you have not developed strong controls to stop your emotions (such as pride – you don't like other people seeing how emotional you really are; or caution – you like to be sure before you make a move), then you react like a bomb when your emotions are triggered, exploding without warning.

As a very far right-slanting writer, how compatible are you likely to be with other slant writers?

Very far right-slanting and left-slanting
There is little basis for compatibility in this partnership. If other traits in both personalities are strongly compatible, then this fundamental incompatibility could, possibly, be overcome. Both partners would need to make considerable efforts to maintain consistent and clear communication and then the relationship might be able to be sustained.

Very far right-slanting and upright
Such a relationship could work only if great understanding has been developed by both parties. Such people are fundamentally incompatible, as one partner always puts his head before his heart and the other partner her heart before her head. But, as they say, 'opposites attract' and this combination is really quite commonplace. Often the partner with the cool head gives objectivity to the highly emotional partner, and the very far right-slanting writer brings a bit of impulsiveness and crazy emotion into the life of the upright writer. Nevertheless this partnership will require hard work, excellent communication and patience to succeed in the long term.

Very far right-slanting and right-slanting
Such a relationship can work as long as both parties recognize the differences in their emotional response to situations. Emotions will certainly run high and, depending upon other characteristics, this could be a stormy relationship as both partners have the capacity to be carried away by their feelings.

Very far right-slanting and far right-slanting
This relationship could work well, as both partners have fundamentally the same emotional outlook and reactions. However, this could also be a volatile relationship, for emotion, as opposed to rationality, will rule over both – and especially the very far right-slanting writer's – lives. Both partners are highly emotional animals and neither will find it easy to listen to reason.

Very far right-slanting and very far right-slanting
Although both partners have the same emotional responses, this is likely to be a highly volatile relationship, with major ups and down, as both partners are so quick to react emotionally. Friends are likely to get fed up with such a couple. When things are good they will be brilliant company and when bad, they will be catastrophic. And these ups and downs will be frequent and unpredictable. If such a relationship broke down it might be hard to resolve it, as neither party would find it easy to take an objective view.

Left-slanting Writers

What does the writing look like?
Left-sloping writing normally looks as if it is sloping slightly backwards. On occasions it may simply look vertical, with the left slant only apparent in the upstrokes.

Samples of left-slanting writing

Jarmul   *Cant think*

all the best

What does left-slanting writing mean?

If you have left-slanting writing you will no doubt have been told that this means you are an introvert. To an extent this is correct, but it does *not* mean that you don't like people, or that you dislike socializing.

You often appear aloof and unfriendly because you like to keep an emotional distance from others. You do not show your feelings and find it hard to share them with others. Generally you are self-interested and cautious in your approach, asking yourself questions such as 'Will this work for me?' This does not mean that you are selfish, simply concerned with protecting yourself. You do respond to emotions, but you turn the reaction inwards, burying it within yourself and not showing your emotional response to anybody. It is possible that you have been hurt in the past by showing your emotions, and as a result you now hide them to protect yourself.

As a left-slanting writer, how compatible are you likely to be with other slant writers?

Left-slanting and upright

Such a relationship should work well, as both partners have similar cool judgement and a reserved outlook. However, both parties need to understand the differences in each other's emotional make-up. The upright partner will seem more outgoing and will find it easier to show his or her emotions, whereas the left-slanting writer will not be expressive and may be harder to get to know.

Left-slanting and left-slanting

This relationship should work well, as both partners have the same emotional reaction. It is likely that the relationship will develop slowly, as neither party will wish to show their inner feelings to the other until real trust has been built up. If both are quite far left-slanting writers, then the relationship could become emotionally sterile, as neither is able to give to each other emotionally.

Left-slanting and right-slanting

Such a relationship will work only if both parties understand the differences in each other's emotional make-up. The right-slanting partner is fundamentally an emotional person and will appear more outgoing, whereas the left-slanting writer will be less expressive. Communication, patience and understanding will ensure the success of such a relationship.

Left-slanting and far right-slanting

As both these partners have totally different approaches to emotion, a considerable amount of work will have to be undertaken after the initial 'honeymoon' period has worn off. It is possible that the far right-slanting partner will feel that the relationship is 'one-sided', as the left-slanting partner will not visibly be giving so much emotionally. Each partner's approach to everyday life will be very different and it will be hard for each of them to understand what makes the other tick.

Left-slanting and very far right-slanting

There is little basis for compatibility in this partnership. If other traits in both personalities are strongly compatible, then this fundamental incompatibility could, just possibly, be overcome. Both partners would need to make considerable efforts to maintain consistent and clear communication in order to sustain the relationship.

Far Left-slanting Writers

What does the writing look like?

The writing will slope sharply to the left, so that the letters look as if they are toppling backwards. Beware! Some writing looks

like this, but when you actually measure it, it is not left-slanting at all. Remember you are only looking at the 'upstrokes'.

Samples of far left-slanting writing

What does far left-slanting writing mean?
You are likely to have deep-rooted inner fears and to have withdrawn your emotions. You have a strong need for security and
as a result have hidden your emotions inside yourself, and do
not show them to anyone – normally not even yourself. You
are extremely withdrawn and probably prefer to be alone
rather than with others.

As a far left-slanting writer, how likely are you to be compatible with other slant writers?
You will not let anyone get close to you, and you will scare
people off by being so cold and distant. So long as you internalize your feelings in the way that you are currently doing,
you will find it difficult, if not impossible, to maintain a close
relationship. As with very varied slant writing (see overleaf),
there is little point in studying how well you will get on with
writers of different slants. As the saying goes, 'You must learn
to love yourself' before you can love others or expect them to
love you.

Both very varied slant and far left-slanting writing indicate
that the writer will find it extremely hard to make and maintain
relationships with other people. Both types of writing are rare
and it is most unlikely that you will find them in the course
of your analysis. Should you think that your writing – or the
writing of your existing or potential partner – fits either of these

categories, then it may be a good idea to get the writing checked by a professional graphologist.

Very Varied Slant Writers

What does the writing look like?
The writing will slope backwards and forwards. There will be little, if any, consistency to the writing and it will look messy on the page.

Samples of very varied slant-writing

What does varied slant writing mean?
You are likely to have dramatic mood swings and to demonstrate irrational behaviour. One minute you will be on top of the world, the next minute in a dark depression – for no obvious reason. You could be feeling ill or very confused and unhappy. Do get some help – it doesn't have to be like this.

As a very varied slant writer, how likely are you to be compatible with other slant writers?
There is little point in studying how well you are likely to get on with other slant writers. The chances are that the last thing in the world you want, or could cope with right now, is a relationship. Very varied slant writers are so confused within themselves that it is unlikely they can develop strong, lasting relationships. Upright writers will quickly lose patience with varied slant writers, and far right-slanting writers will be deeply hurt by them.

Emotional Depth

There is another aspect of emotion that it is vital to consider – and this concerns the length of time that we feel or remember our emotions for.

❛ When Clive was eighteen his best friend Tom ran off with Clive's then girlfriend, Moira. Clive was devastated and angry. He refused to talk to Tom ever again.

Twenty years later Clive was at a business conference when he heard this familiar voice shouting, 'Clive, is it really you?' Clive recognized the voice and carried on walking in the opposite direction until he was swallowed up by the crowd. He felt anger and betrayal rise up inside him and swore that he would carry on avoiding Tom for the rest of his life.

Clive is, of course, at one end of the emotional spectrum, and most of us do not remember our emotions in that way for such an incredibly long time.

Clive and Moira would never have developed a successful relationship, even if they had met when they were ten years older. Moira is the sort of person who feels intensely about something one day and then has forgotten that feeling, or transferred it elsewhere, by the next day. That is precisely what she did at the age of eighteen. One week she told all her friends that she was madly in love with Clive, and by the next week she was madly in love with Tom. ❜

What to look for?

In order to tell how long people remember their emotional experiences we have to look at the pressure of their writing. The stronger the pressure, or the more heavily the person writes on the page, the more lasting are that person's feelings.

Heavy Writers

Heavy writing indicates that your feelings are strong and lasting. Emotionally secure, you will be greatly influenced by past emotions and are not the kind of person who can forgive and forget easily. Likely to be energetic, you enjoy the good life. The chances are that you love colours, and have a strong sense of taste, smell and touch. You may have a tendency to be insensitive to other people's feelings, more influenced by the strong emotions that you have yourself.

Samples of heavy writing

lucky

NRoosevelt   *So agreed*

Light Writers

People who write with light pressure tend to feel emotions immediately but then quickly forget them and move on to the next emotion. If your writing is like this, the chances are that you are emotionally delicate and like to be told that you are loved a great deal. You are easily influenced. Sensitive to your environment, you tend to be strongly aware of other people's feelings.

If your writing is very light you may tire easily, for you have little emotional stamina and need a lot of rest.

Samples of light writing

starts

that has

I have always

Moderate Writers

People who write with moderate pressure generally hold on to feelings for an average length of time and do not become obsessed by them.

Samples of moderate writing

I fancy

living room

well not

Varied Writers

Occasionally you will come across writing that is light in some places and heavy in others. If this is strongly evident it indicates emotional imbalance and erratic feelings.

Samples of varied writing

thank you very much

afterwards

How compatible are writers of different pressures likely to be with each other?

Heavy writer with a light writer

It will be difficult to make this relationship work as the heavy writer will remember emotions for a long time, whereas the light writer will quickly forget them. It is probable that both partners will have widely differing energy levels, which will affect both the social and sexual elements of their relationship.

Heavy writer with a moderate writer

This relationship should work, as long as each partner is aware of the other's different emotional memory. The moderate writer may feel inspired by the heavy writer, and attracted by his or her strength of feelings.

Heavy writer with a heavy writer
This is likely to be a strong and probably passionate relationship.

Light writer with a moderate writer
The light writer will require reassurances of affection and security from the moderate writer, who in turn may become fed up with the flightiness of the light writer. If these differences are discussed and worked out, then this relationship should work.

Light writer with a light writer
As both writers are somewhat flighty – people who easily transfer their feelings of affection – such a relationship could be hard to sustain, and lacking in permanence. On the other hand, both partners will understand each other and may find it easy to come to some agreement. Having similar energy levels will certainly help the relationship.

Moderate writer with a moderate writer
This should be a most successful combination, as both parties absorb and remember emotions in moderation and have similar energy levels.

How do emotional slant and emotional depth affect each other?
The amount of emotion, and the length of time a person feels emotions, intensifies the emotional slant.

❦ Stephanie is a far right-slanting writer. A warm-natured girl, she feels emotions strongly. She also finds it hard to make decisions that are not influenced by her emotions. However, her strongly felt emotions are quickly dissipated. This is indicated by the fact that Stephanie writes with a very light pressure.

Julie, her girlfriend, is also a far right-slanting writer, although she writes with heavy pressure. She remembers all her emotions for a long time and becomes utterly absorbed in them. She is very impulsive and quite prejudiced. If she doesn't regularly find an outlet for her emotions, some small trigger can make her go wild! She has a rather well-known temper and the neighbours regularly hear plates being smashed. Stephanie, being light-hearted, thinks Julie's behaviour is a bit of a laugh, and they generally get on fine together.

Andrew is a light writer. Typical of many light writers, he is more of the home-body type, preferring routine and coping rather badly with stress. His slant is backward. Although he hides his emotions inside himself, he doesn't remember the emotions themselves for long, so there is little unhealthy build-up of repressed emotions.

Andrew's spinster aunt tragically committed suicide. Like her nephew, she had a backward slant, but unlike him she absorbed emotions and remembered them intensely for a long time. These feelings became more and more repressed until she couldn't cope with them any longer. Jilted by a lover, she took her own life when her emotions became totally out of hand. 〞

It is very rare for something like this to happen. However, backward-slanting writers with heavy writing do need to develop an outlet for their emotions – perhaps through a creative hobby if not through other people, otherwise their emotions can build up inside them, crashing out as the result of some relatively minor trigger.

2

Do You Think in the Same Way?

- What makes you and your partner tick?
- Do you both think along the same lines, or are you bewildered at how differently your minds work?
- Are you really aware of how important it is to the success of your relationship that you appreciate how each other's minds work?

Appreciating how someone's mind works and the way in which that person processes information is vital to understanding what makes him or her tick. However, graphologists generally agree that it is not possible to assess intelligence through handwriting analysis. On the other hand, if you understand how a person's mind works you can make a fair judgement about how clever they are likely to be.

We all think and come to decisions in different ways. Some people like to have all the facts in front of them and reach conclusions slowly and accurately. Other people make snap judgements based upon their gut reaction. Some people have to find out everything for themselves. It is never good enough for them to have been told something or to have read it in a book. They have to experience it for real.

The way in which we think is an often forgotten, but vital, ingredient in the recipe for a successful relationship. If two people's minds work in different ways, so that they process information and reach decisions using different means, the chances are that they will never fully understand each other.

By using our rational understanding we can accept the fact that our partner may be jealous, highly emotional or shy.

We may be the opposite, but we can take these things on board, understand and even help our partner overcome them in order to make a happy relationship. Unfortunately, it is almost impossible to change the way someone uses their mind. This is likely to be set in stone for the rest of their lives. So either we try to understand and accept the differences in thinking, or the relationship quite simply will not work.

In this book you will find each of these mental processes listed and explained separately. When analysing writing, you may find that two or more of the mental processes are evident in the writing sample. Normally one is predominant, and that is the one to concentrate on when doing your analysis. It is worth while remembering that the most mentally agile and clever people often use two or more mental processes. This makes them particularly well equipped to solve a variety of different problems.

Slow and Careful Thinkers

The slow and careful thinker is often described as methodical. Such a person likes to have all the facts in front of him or her and then build them up logically until he or she can come to a conclusion. The slow and careful thinker approaches problems step-by-step, building up thoughts rather as a brick layer builds his wall brick-by-brick. Careful thinkers often remember things much better than other types of thinker.

This type of person is frequently considered to be slow and may in fact lack a certain spontaneity. Such slowness is exacerbated by the fact that their writing often looks as if it has been written slowly. A slow thinker may be slow in coming to decisions, but he or she is not unintelligent. Speed of thinking is not related to intelligence. In fact, a slow, careful thinker is substantially more likely to come to a correct conclusion than many other types of thinker. Some of the greatest inventors – such as Thomas Edison, who invented the light bulb – were slow and careful writers.

Slow and careful writers are rarely the questioning type. They are generally conservative in attitude, accepting of what other people tell them. They tend to have good social behaviour and learn best by doing. They are frequently highly creative, often able to use their hands to great effect.

❝ Alison is typical of slow and careful writers. Her handwriting looks rather like the type of rounded writing we were taught to write at school.

However, Alison looks back on her school days with regret. She was always considered the dunce in her class, never putting her hand up in time to answer the teacher's questions. She was discouraged from pursuing further academic education as her teachers told her parents that she simply wasn't clever enough. Alison strongly denies this. As she explains, the difference was that she took longer to answer questions and didn't perform well under the pressure of exams. Luckily this matters little to her nowadays, for she is a famous sculptor, renowned throughout Europe.

'I am the type of person who absorbs ideas slowly. I guess I am not very questioning. If someone tells me something I will believe them. But I never jump to conclusions by myself.'

A few years after she left school, Alison won a national sculpture competition and her work was reviewed across Europe. It was a dream come true, and the break that she had never imagined would become a reality. Several galleries approached her, offering to exhibit her work. The one that Alison chose first was run by a handsome man called Paul. Whenever Alison visited the gallery, which was sited in the finest art area of London's West End, Paul was talking down several phone lines at once, wheeling and dealing, conversing in short, sharp sentences, using his arm to wipe his floppy blond hair out of his eyes, and using his feet to open drawers and doors. He became highly animated and excited whenever he discussed any of his projects. And Alison fell for him immediately.

'He's so good looking. And so interested in me,' she told her girlfriends. 'When he looks at me it's as if there is no one else in the room, as if no one else in the world interests him except me.'

Alison and Paul started going out together shortly before her first exhibition. The show went well and so did the relationship. After three months Paul whisked Alison off to the registry office and they were married, witnessed by a couple of strangers whom Paul had stopped on the street. That first year was difficult for Alison. The pace of her husband's life was so different from what she was used to. Deep down, she knew that the relationship probably couldn't last, but she found it impossible to put her finger on the problem. In retrospect, having been to a graphologist, she can now appreciate where the real problems lay, and it is now easy for her to identify the event that was the final straw in the breakdown of their marriage.

She explained what happened. 'Paul, my ex-husband, managed to use his contacts to get me an exhibition in the South of France. He needed a definitive answer as to whether or not I wanted to attend within twenty-four hours. I can't come to a decision like that. When I'm deciding whether or not to exhibit I need to weigh up all the advantages – the opportunity to get new clientele, the benefits of international exposure, the chance to have a great holiday, etc., against all the disadvantages – the expenses of getting the sculptures over there, the extra work-load, the stress, and much more. All day he nagged me, saying you must go, think of the fame it would bring you. I just couldn't decide. I took Vodka, my dog, out for a long walk in the park. I sat on a bench and wrote down all the pros and cons. Eventually I decided that

I couldn't cope with the extra work-load, that such an exhibition was too soon for me.

'When I got home, Paul had a big grin all over his face. "Darling, South of France is on next month, and not only that, but I've just been rung by further galleries in Berlin and Copenhagen. We'll be exhibiting there the month after. I took the decision for you as you weren't here."

'I sat down and cried. I didn't want Paul to take all the decisions for me, especially as he didn't seem to take into account my thoughts and feelings. It was easy for him to make snap decisions, but he couldn't appreciate that my mind doesn't work like that. These differences undermined every aspect of our relationship. In the end I knew that I had to leave him for my own peace of mind.' **9**

Artists and creative people are normally careful thinkers. Such types are often good with their hands and have an excellent sense of colour. They build up pictures or write musical compositions piece-by-piece, until they are happy with the whole of their masterpiece.

What to look for?

Slow and careful writing often looks quite rounded and similar to the sort of writing that we are taught as children. Normally each letter looks as if it has been carefully and slowly constructed.

The best places to look for slow and careful writing are in the letters m, n, and r. The m and n should have rounded tops. The r should have a wide, flat top. Circle letters, such as a, o, and e are normally broad in size. The majority of connections between the letters are made with convex arch forms. Look at the samples below to understand this fully.

Samples of slow and careful writing

making me   m n r

Three months

seem even loose

Quick Thinkers

Quick thinkers, as their name implies, understand new ideas and grasp new concepts rapidly. They come to conclusions quickly, as their thought processes are instinctual. Such people need few explanations when they are taught new things. Normally it is difficult, if not impossible, to trace the steps by which a quick thinker arrives at his or her decisions. Thinking seems easy to them and such people are often viewed as particularly intelligent. However, being a quick thinker is not all plain sailing!

Quick thinkers learn fast, but they tend to forget quite quickly too. They frequently rely on immediate impressions without having all the facts in front of them. Consequently they may jump to the wrong conclusions. The most intelligent people are those who are quick thinkers but have their impulsiveness tempered by one or more of the other types of thought process.

Quick thinkers have an instinctive understanding of people and can rapidly appreciate new situations. As a consequence they normally find it easy to relate to others and they like people. They are often caring and open-hearted, as well as strongly sympathetic towards others. All the same, it is worth noting that their mothering type of nature can be manipulative.

There are two types of quick thinker. First, there are those who think deeply, are contemplative and have the ability to grasp the most complex ideas on a philosophical and material level. Second, there are those who think rather more superficially, and who are often easy-going and laid back. They make quick superficial decisions, based on a limited understanding, and may reach incorrect conclusions. They are curious, but not deeply interested. The difference between the two types is shown by the depth of the quick thinker's stroke. You will see what this means in the section 'What to look for?'

❜ Charles was a politician. At thirty-three he was the youngest minister in the British parliament. Nowadays the general public knows about him for a rather different reason.

As a student Charles excelled. He raced through university, gaining a first-class degree in law. Although he was involved in numerous social activities, thespian groups and drinking and dining clubs, he had few friends that he could call his own. Most of his acquaintances were made through his girlfriend Ursula.

Ursula is extraordinarily bright. One of the highest scorers of Mensa, she arrived at the university at sixteen years of age. By the time Charles met her she was studying for her doctorate in law, whilst he was just an undergraduate. She helped him in his studies and he fell in love with her. Ursula's and Charles' minds work in a similar way; they both find it easy to grasp the most complex of conundrums. However, Charles never studies things in the depth that Ursula does. He prefers to gloss over the surface, making quick decisions, sometimes without having undertaken the necessary research first.

As a student this didn't matter. But as an adult quick thinking would complicate matters for Charles. When they left university the couple got married. Charles put his first foot on the political ladder, helped by his politician father. Ursula became a university professor, assisting Charles on the more complicated governmental cases that were presented to him. When they met their voting public, she was the one who presented the caring, sympathetic, confidence-inspiring face. Charles concentrated on manipulating his way up the political hierarchy.

Before long, Charles found himself spending very little time with his wife. She was based in the university town, whereas he spent most evenings in London. Their love life was non-existent, but on the occasions they saw each other, they both relished the other's company, taking pleasure in debating legal and political problems.

Shortly afterwards Charles had his first affair. It lasted a week. It was easy, exciting and nobody noticed. He then had another, and several more. He received a word of warning from his under-secretary. 'Be shrewd, not lewd!' But then Charles fell for Gail, a politician in the opposition party. He knew it was crazy and dangerous, not only for his own political career, but also for the reputation of his party. But Charles pushed the fears out of his mind and embarked on a passionate affair.

One evening his mistress explained a change that her party intended to make to the controversial Child Care Bill. Charles knew little about it, for his specialization lay in taxation, but they ended up having a heated argument, at the end of which his mistress stormed out of the flat.

The next day Charles got up to speak in the House of Commons. To his surprise he was asked a question by Gail, his mistress, the Member of Parliament on the opposing side. She asked him to explain his thoughts on the very issue that they had been arguing about the night before.

'In my opinion, women who are unfaithful to their husbands should automatically lose access rights to their children and should be forced to pay maintenance to their husbands. In section 4.5 of the 1982 Bill . . .' The laughter, jeering and shouting grew so loud that Charles could not finish his sentence.

'What on earth do you know about that?' shouted one Member of Parliament.

'Quite a lot actually,' said Charles, sitting down despondently.

The next day his photograph was plastered across the front pages of all the national newspapers. 'Hypocrite and fool!' claimed one headline.

Charles had to resign, and Ursula left him. Gail claimed their affair had never happened. At the age of thirty-three Charles was ruined, for jumping to a conclusion, for talking about something he knew nothing about, for being too impulsive and hypocritical.

Charles has a very bright mind, he can quickly grasp and solve problems. But unlike his ex-wife Ursula, he is happy skimming the surface of issues. This was his downfall. If he had not jumped to conclusions on issues he knew little about, he might have maintained his position. Most people say he deserved what he got for cheating on his wife. **❯**

What to look for?

Quick thinkers have plenty of needle-like points in their writing. The connections between letters are rounded at the base and the letters m and n resemble the letter u. In graphology this type of writing is normally described as being written in a garland form. Those who think deeply make needle-like points that rise above the top of the other middle-zone letters. Those who think more superficially make points that are short in height.

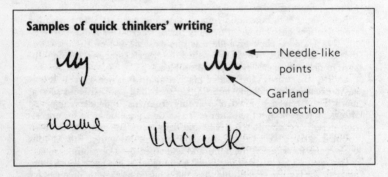

Samples of quick thinkers' writing

Needle-like points

Garland connection

Curious Thinkers

Curious thinkers are questioning types. They want to know things, and often need to find out things for themselves. Their minds work in a logical manner. They have the need to uncover the facts before making up their minds, but at the same time they must be convinced that the facts are correct, that the why's, where's, when's and how's are proven.

Curious thinkers tend to prefer argument to compromise. They may take a somewhat inflexible, mechanical approach to life – uncompromising and tireless. When writers have no other thinking types except curiosity, other people may view them as being cold. Curious thinkers instinctively need to compete and can be viewed as aggressive.

There are two types of curious thinker. We will call them curious and very curious thinkers. All curious thinkers like to uncover facts for themselves. They enjoy problem-solving. However, curious thinkers, although they have the urge to uncover information, are willing to accept information second-hand rather than go to the source of it themselves. They are content to read about far-flung lands as opposed to actually visiting them.

Very curious thinkers not only want to delve into the unknown but want to explore it for themselves. They need to find out everything for themselves. If a very curious thinker sees a wet-paint sign attached to a wall, he or she will touch the wall to check whether or not it really is wet! Such people are willing to go to great lengths to uncover what is not already known.

❦ Walter is a microbiologist. He works in a laboratory, undertaking research work on behalf of a massive pharmaceutical company.

Walter met Vivian at work. They quickly learned that they had a lot in common. Both were eager to find a cure for a horrific flesh-eating disease spreading to epidemic levels in a far-flung part of Africa. Both loved travelling and were addicted to crossword puzzles. They seemed to have an instinctual understanding of each other. Not surprisingly, both are curious-type thinkers.

They rapidly became best friends, seeing each other after work most evenings. But the relationship didn't progress any further. 'I love him dearly as my closest friend,' Vivian explained to her sister. 'But I don't think I could go out with him. I really don't fancy him at all!' Being fundamentally shy, and sensing Vivian's slight distance, Walter never made a move.

One afternoon in the laboratory Vivian rushed up to Walter, grabbed his arm and excitedly motioned for him to go outside with her. Checking that their boss wasn't watching, they slipped out into the corridor.

'I think I'm on to something!' She jumped up and down. 'In fact, I know I am. When we go back, look at the cells and you will see what I'm talking about. Walter, the next step now is for me to go out to Africa and see for my own eyes what is happening. I think I've got the cure.'

'Don't be ridiculous, there's no need for you to go to Africa. And anyway, they'll never send you. You're too junior.'

Walter was full of mixed emotions. On the one hand, he was proud of Vivian that she had made a major breakthrough. On the other hand, he was envious that it wasn't himself who had succeeded. He certainly didn't want her going out to Africa. For his part, he couldn't imagine the desire to want to go anyway. For him it was quite sufficient trying out the tests in the lab.

Over the next few days Vivian shocked Walter. She told the company that she needed a two-month sabbatical and if they would not give it to her she would resign. She booked a flight to Africa and the next thing Walter knew, he was hugging her goodbye at the airport. He tried every argument in the book to try and convince her not to go. They had screaming fights, and harsh words were flung between them. They simply could not understand each other.

Walter missed Vivian dreadfully. He began chastizing himself that he had never made a romantic move. Late at night he began to wonder whether he should go and join her. In the cold light of day he quickly dismissed the idea.

A month after she had left, Walter was summoned to see his senior manager. 'Walter, sit down. I have some rather difficult news to tell you.' Walter's heart sank. 'I know you are very close to Vivian, so I wanted to let you know what has happened before we tell anyone else in the lab. Vivian told us where she was going, and as a precautionary measure we asked the British consul to keep an eye on her out there. Last night we received an emergency call to say that Vivian is very ill. We think she may have the disease. I am afraid they are not sure that she will make the trip home. Walter, we are offering to pay your flight to go and visit her. As you know, it may be too late.' His voice trailed off.

Rarely an emotional person, at this point Walter put his head in his hands and wailed. Shock gave way to panic, which gave way to numbness. Before he fully appreciated what was happening, he found himself on a plane to Africa.

Fifteen hours later Walter was met at the airport by a car. The air was hot and rancid and the noise was overwhelming. He tried to make conversation with the driver. 'My friend, Vivian, do you know if she is okay?' he asked.

'Many people dead,' the driver replied. 'Your friend I think dead too.'

Tears ran down Walter's face. He felt lost, frightened and quite desperate. Minutes later they arrived at the British consulate. He was ushered inside and handed a coat, gloves and a mask. Hastily putting them on, he was led upstairs to a small room at the back of the big house. Inside lay Vivian, white-faced and seemingly unconscious. She was being attended by two nurses covered from head to toe in protective clothing.

'She is alive!' Walter gasped. He turned to one of the nurses and said, 'I am going to give her this pill. It is her only chance, please let me. I brought it all the way from England.' The nurse shrugged her shoulders. 'Good luck to you!' she muttered under her breath.

It took Vivian weeks to recover, and she wasn't strong enough to return to England for two months. Walter had had to return long before. But when they were eventually reunited their relationship rapidly grew from good friends to lovers. Today they are planning their wedding.

Walter still finds it hard to forgive Vivian for being too curious. She is not content with learning about things second-hand, but has to try things out for herself. She is a true explorer at heart, but rather more cautious these days. **9**

What to look for?

Curious thinkers make upward-pointing angles throughout their writing. The letters m and n resemble an upside-down v. The writing looks angular, sharp and sometimes rigid.

Curious thinkers
Their angles tend to be shallow. They do not rise above the middle-zone height. The angles are less pronounced.

Very curious thinkers
Their angles are particularly sharp and extend above the middle-zone letters into the upper zone.

Samples of curious thinkers' writing

Upside-down v formations

Curious writing   Very curious writing

Questioning Thinkers

Questioning thinkers have an analytical mind. They weigh up all information that is given to them, evaluating which is of use and which is of no relevance, sifting out whatever information is not needed and then coming to a decision. Questioning thinkers are not easily fooled as they check out matters for themselves. They have the ability to evaluate what is essential.

❝ Sasha began to have doubts about Harry around the time that all her friends began telling her how wonderful they thought he was. Harry is a big talker, claims to be successful, to have travelled the world and to be friends with lots of famous people. Sasha is no fool. She realized that the stories didn't add up and she started to do her own investigating.

Sasha has a questioning type of mind. When Harry gave her fifty pounds that he claimed to have won on the lottery, Sasha asked to see Harry's winning ticket. When he started travelling a lot on business, she found out the name of the travel agent and checked up to see whether he was on the flights he said he was on. Once he was, twice he was not. When he called her one evening from abroad, she rang the operator to find out where the call had come from – the other side of the city, not a different country!

Few people can fool Sasha. She is a bright girl with a keen mind. At work she is a key problem-solver, finding it easy to sort out the facts from the rubbish, and coming to the correct conclusions rather more often than her boss! **9**

What to look for?
Questioning writing is made up of downward-pointing angles – plenty of v-formations linking letters.

Samples of questioning thinkers' writing

Downward pointing angles

game badminton

Superficial Thinkers

Superficial thinkers tend to rely on surface knowledge. They skim along, only extracting the things that are of most importance to them. The problem is that they often face the danger of not understanding the wider ramifications of the issues that they are dealing with, because they haven't studied them in sufficient detail. Sometimes these individuals have ambitions that extend far beyond their capabilities.

Superficial thinkers are frequently unpredictable, inconsistent and unstable in the extreme. They have a tendency to be evasive and to change their attitudes and opinions at the drop of a hat. Certainly such writers are malleable and opportunistic.

When the superficial writing appears towards the ends of words, or in the writing of a successful leader, intellectual or business person, this indicates a degree of impatience in getting rid of obstacles so that the writer can complete the job in hand. Where a person has to write fast, his or her writing may fade into superficiality. This is often evident in doctors' prescriptions. It indicates speed rather than superficiality. It is therefore important to evaluate the whole of the writing, otherwise a wrong conclusion may be reached.

What to look for?

Superficial writing has a thready look to it, sometimes representing an unwinding coil. Often some of the letters are so flattened that they have become illegible. The writing may look irregular or poorly formed.

It is important to check where in the writing the thready forms appear. If they are in the middle of words, or consistently throughout the writing, then this is representative of a typical superficial type writer. If the threads appear at the ends of words, then the writer may simply have been in a hurry and this is not indicative of real superficial thinking.

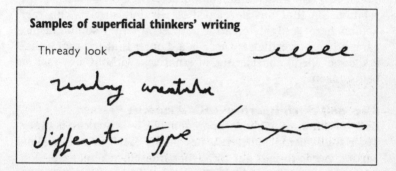

Samples of superficial thinkers' writing

Thready look

A Combination of Thought Processes

As mentioned earlier in this chapter, many people's writing indicates that they possess several different thought processes. This is quite normal and equips individuals well in solving problems. These types of people find it easier to understand other types of thinker, as they practise a number of the thought processes themselves.

Only infrequently will you find writing that has different thought processes indicated in equal amounts. Normally there will be one thought process that dominates.

Samples of a combination of thought processes

When the wind it may

How do the different types of thinker get on with each other?

Two slow and careful thinkers together
These two will understand each other. Theirs will have been a relationship that has developed slowly but surely – no rash actions here! A highly creative partnership, they should inspire each other. Nevertheless there is a danger that too much time could be spent considering alternatives without any action being taken.

Slow and careful partner with a curious partner
Both of these individuals approach life in a logical manner. Their fundamental difference lies in the fact that the curious partner needs to find out things for himself, whereas the slow and careful partner is happy to rely on facts given to him by others. Their minds work in different ways, but they may find that they are complementing each other.

Slow and careful partner with a questioning partner
The fundamental difference between these two partners lies in the fact that the questioning partner will always be analytical, checking things out for himself, whereas the slow and careful partner will not. These two thought processes can work well together.

Slow and careful partner with a quick partner
These partners are very different indeed. The quick partner comes to instantaneous decisions based almost on gut reaction, whereas

the slow and careful partner takes considerable time when think-ing. The quick partner may become frustrated and impatient with the slow and careful partner, who in return could feel flustered and insecure. Such a relationship is likely to need considerable work and patience for success.

Slow and careful partner with a superficial partner
Slow and careful thinkers are by their very nature secure and consistent. Superficial thinkers tend to be the opposite. Unfortunately, such a relationship does not bode well.

Two quick thinkers together
Thinking along the same wave-lengths, these two are likely to understand and appreciate each other. With fast and agile minds, this couple will be more successful on a personal than a business level. If working together, they will need a slow and careful thinker or a questioning thinker to ground them, ensuring that they do not rush off, acting upon impulsive ideas.

Quick partner with a curious partner
This combination has the potential for being successful. Never-theless the curious partner may become frustrated with the quick, and sometimes unfounded, decisions that his or her quick partner makes. These two make an intelligent couple.

Quick partner with a questioning partner
Quick and questioning partners should complement each other, with the questioning partner weighing up the information and analysing the facts, while the quick partner comes to a conclu-sion based on gut reaction. However, these two are very differ-ent and may find they cannot get to grips with how their partner thinks.

Quick partner with a superficial partner
On a superficial level, these two may seem rather similar. How-ever, the quick partner is often quick due to intelligence and the superficial partner is frequently quick due to laziness. These two will find it hard to understand each other.

Two questioning thinkers together
These partners think along the same lines and consequently will understand each other. Their mental processes should help their mutual appreciation.

Questioning partner with a curious partner
These two partners are well suited. Their thought processes complement each other. Both take a factual approach. The curious partner likes to unearth the facts and the questioning partner has the ability to evaluate those facts, sifting the information and sorting the trivia from the relevant facts. It is important that they each appreciate the way their own and their partner's minds work, and then there is no reason why this relationship should not be a success.

Questioning partner with a superficial partner
The questioning and the superficial-type thinkers are fundamentally different. One seeks the facts, the other glosses over them. It is unlikely that these two will ever get to grips with how their partner thinks. Considerable work would be needed for such a relationship to thrive.

Two superficial thinkers together
These two are similar and will understand each other. This will not be a dynamic relationship, but nevertheless it should work.

Superficial partner with a curious partner
Unfortunately some problems await this partnership. Both think along opposing lines. One likes argument, the other will adopt a *laissez-faire* attitude. If one partner's writing strongly shows superficiality and the other strongly shows curiosity, eventually it is possible that each will frustrate the other to such an extent that the relationship will probably break down.

Two curious thinkers together
These two think along the same lines and should understand each other. Nevertheless both are fundamentally argumentative and theirs is likely to be a fiery and dynamic relationship.

Optimism and Pessimism

Do you look on the bright side? Optimistic people see good in everything. They tend to be positive thinkers, eager to believe that things will turn out well. Optimistic types are often energetic and cheerful. Optimism spurs people on to success, as they put failure down to experience and persist, sure that they can succeed next time. The most powerful part of optimism is that it dispels fear. Fear is what holds us back. If we are fearful, we will not try anything new. If we are optimistic, we will feel confident and positive and the fear will evaporate. Optimism is a strong antidote to any of the insecurities or fears that you may find in a person's handwriting.

Optimism breeds optimism in other people, and such types are frequently well liked, good companions and strong leaders. Occasionally you may come across an overly optimistic person. Such an individual will be living in his or her own dream world, with their head in the clouds, feeling sure that everything will work out well, far beyond the hopes of reality. Overly optimistic people kid themselves that everything is fine. They are ridiculously over-cheerful and view the world through rose-tinted spectacles, believing that the sun shines every day, that every human being has a heart of gold and that they themselves are capable of achieving what other people would realize is impossible.

The extreme opposite of this is pessimism. Pessimistic people expect the worst. They have a negative approach to life, feeling sure that things will go wrong. Pessimistic types are often troubled and unhappy, will rarely show enthusiasm and people will not want to spend too much time around them.

Pessimistic people frequently 'cross bridges before they come to them'. Sure that the worst possible outcome will materialize, they tend to act or talk themselves into such a position where the worst really does become reality.

Pessimism is an indicator of fear and insecurity. The pessimistic person views the world through dark glasses and constantly fears the worst. Consequently he or she will never realize their maximum potential, as they will believe that the odds are weighted against them, even before they begin trying.

Pessimism can bring people down, and if it grows it leads to depression. Where writing slants very heavily down the page, you may be studying the writing of a depressive. Pessimism may be the result of illness, tiredness or grief, and if so it may be only temporary, existing until the writer regains a balanced view of life. Of course there are some people who have been pessimistic for so long that the original cause of their pessimism can no longer be identified.

> ❛ Pete's philosophy of life is to look on the bright side. A couple of years ago he was made redundant. Never one to wallow in self-pity, he went straight to the local job centre and applied for twenty vacancies that very day! 'Sure, it's tough,' he told the interviewer, 'but the way I see it, redundancy is a big challenge. I always believe that good comes out of bad.'
>
> That night Pete saw Sally, his girlfriend. Sally wailed at Pete, 'You'll never get another job in this market. And that means that now we can't afford to buy a flat. Why us? Things always go wrong for us! I knew you'd lose your job, you should never have taken it in the first place. Next week it'll be me out of work, and then what will we do?' She put her face in her hands and cried her eyes out.
>
> Sally is one of life's pessimists. She assumes the worst is going to happen. Instead of being positive and supporting Pete in his search for a job, she became increasingly depressed and convinced that more and more things would go wrong. After a month of this black attitude, Pete finished the relationship. 'I just couldn't cope with Sally's negative frame of mind. She brought me down,' he said.
>
> With his optimistic and confident personality back on course once again, Pete soon found another job and he is now earning considerably more money than before. ❜

Optimism breeds self-confidence, which in turn enables the optimist to develop an inner strength. This results in the optimist being able to achieve more than the average person. In contrast, pessimistic people allow their self-confidence to be further and further eroded, to the extent that they will settle for very little, in the belief that they cannot achieve and do not deserve any more.

What to look for?

Optimism

Optimism is evident in handwriting when the writing slopes upwards, as if the writing is being pulled up to the top right of the page. The lines should slant upwards, but individual letter forms or words can do so as well.

Excessive optimism
If the lines slant dramatically upwards, then this indicates that the writer is overly optimistic, seeing the world through rose-tinted glasses.

Pessimism
Pessimism is evident in handwriting when the writing slopes downwards and seems to be sliding downhill towards the bottom right of the page.

Depression
If the lines slant dramatically downhill, then it is likely that the writer is suffering from depression. If severe, this is a medical condition that needs help.

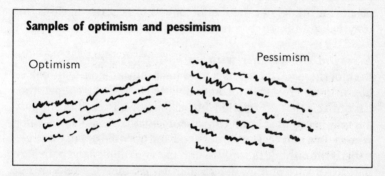

Samples of optimism and pessimism

Optimism

Pessimism

How do optimism and pessimism affect compatibility in a relationship?
Both optimism and pessimism have a major effect on a couple, for both, in time, are infectious. As can be expected, optimism – so long as it is not excessive and unrealistic – will have a positive effect on a relationship, and pessimism a negative effect. The majority of people have writing that flows straight across the page, so their writing shows neither optimism nor pessimism. Although they may occasionally feel optimistic or pessimistic, these traits are not strong enough to affect their personality on a regular basis. Where one partner has optimism or pessimism in his or her writing, but the other partner has neither, the latter partner will be strongly affected by his or her optimistic or pessimistic partner, and in time may gain the same trait.

Two optimistic people together

This will probably be a happy, successful couple, who find it easy to attract and keep friends. With both partners looking on the bright side, they will propel each other along, adding to each other's motivation. Such a relationship can be very powerful.

Two pessimistic people together

This will not be an easy or healthy relationship. Each pessimistic partner will bring down the other even more. Each will accentuate the other's fears. They are likely to make a very morose, insular couple with few friends. It is probable that one or both partners could end up depressed. What they both need is a boost to their self-confidence and encouragement to adopt a positive attitude, not the reinforcement of negative feelings that they will find in such a relationship.

A pessimistic partner with an optimistic partner

Each of these partners has a fundamentally different outlook on life. If there are other incompatibilities facing the couple, then it is unlikely that the relationship will survive. The optimistic partner may become fed up and impatient with the pessimistic partner, who in turn may feel misunderstood and imposed upon. However, if this is the only, or the only major, incompatibility and both partners are aware of their differing attitudes, then the relationship can develop. It is possible that the optimistic partner can change the attitude of the pessimistic partner. By communicating their hopes and fears, they can gain an understanding of their differing outlooks and learn to be patient with each other.

Individuals who are overly optimistic or at the opposite extreme, depressive will find it very hard to maintain any form of long-lasting, mature relationship.

Broad-mindedness and Narrow-mindedness

Are you open to everything or just won't listen? Broad-minded types are willing to accept other people's ideas. They are interested in human beings and are eager to learn about friends' or colleagues' experiences. Being broad-minded is highly beneficial, for it ensures that the person has an open mind and is not prejudiced. It helps people achieve success – they are good listeners and find it easy to accept advice.

Broad-minded people make successful employees and first-class managers. On the social scene, broad-minded individuals are popular and make excellent friends. They not only deal with others sympathetically and warmly, but are considerate and willing to accept new ideas or try out new things. They are normally considered to be good sports, and friends and colleagues will quickly warm to them.

Broad-mindedness in moderation is an excellent trait to possess. It is a wonderful ingredient to add to any relationship. However, in excess it can be rather dangerous. If someone is too broad-minded they will adopt the attitude that 'anything goes'. As a result, they will become very permissive both of themselves and of other people. They will not develop a strong conscience and will be too forgiving. People who are overly broad-minded may be lacking in morals – acting in a way that society considers unacceptable.

❝ Simone had her first baby when she was sixteen. She decided that being a single mother was not going to affect her life. She would still behave like a teenager, go out clubbing and have fun. Simone's morals left plenty to be desired. She slept with many different men and indulged in rather dubious sexual pursuits. When she got involved with a young man who shoplifted as a 'career', she was forgiving. 'Each to their own,' she would say. 'If that's what he wants to do, who am I to stop him!' Her broad-minded attitude allowed her to be much too easy on herself and on others. Throughout her life Simone got into trouble. Men used and abused her. On a couple of occasions she even ended up in prison.

When her daughter reached twelve years old, she was allowed to bring boys back to stay, smoked at home with her mother and knew every swear word in the English language. Simone failed to give her daughter any standards of morality, and from an early age it was obvious that the child would follow in her mother's footsteps. Her school friends were envious that she had such a cool mum, but in fact her mother's extreme broad-mindedness was a burden to her daughter, not a gift. ❞

If someone is the opposite of broad-minded, they are narrow-minded. This means that they are totally unreceptive to other people's ideas or opinions. Narrow-minded people do not listen to others, but insist that their own opinion is the only one that counts.

Narrow-mindedness has a negative impact on relationships.

On a social level it can result in a person being cut off and isolated from others. He or she is not interested in friends' opinions or experiences. Such a person may only want to talk about himself or herself, and could be considered a 'stick-in-the-mud', never wanting to share new experiences. This type of narrow-minded person may find it difficult to make friends. They will appear cold and aloof.

On the work front, narrow-mindedness is likely to be a severe restraint on success. The narrow-minded person will be unwilling to listen to colleagues, will probably be a poor manager and unable to accept innovative ideas from other people. Equally dangerous is the fact that a narrow-minded person is likely to be prejudiced in his or her outlook. As he or she is unwilling to listen to other people's opinions, such an individual will make a decision without weighing up all the facts objectively. To have a narrow-minded boss can be the ultimate nightmare. He or she will feel frightened by your good ideas and will either refuse to acknowledge them or become domineering or threatening. Equally, such problems will adversely affect a social relationship. Narrow-minded people are fearful, and this fear will show itself in a particularly unpleasant manner.

Many of us are broad-minded about some things but narrow-minded about others. For instance, we may be tolerant with friends and colleagues with regard to almost everything, but when it comes to discussing politics we may refuse to take other people's opinions on board. Most people have their own personal intolerances.

❝ Myra, a qualified graphologist, will refuse to accept that some people do not believe in handwriting analysis. Instead of listening to them and logically counteracting their negative opinions, she gets angry and quickly changes the subject. On other issues, about which she feels less emotive, she is open-minded and an excellent listener. ❞

Some people are generally broad-minded but when they are very busy they become narrow-minded, not listening to others' opinions simply because they do not have time to consider them.

❝ Simon runs a leading computer hardware corporation. Highly intelligent himself, he rarely listens to other people's views on computers, other than to those of a handful of senior staff carefully selected by him. His wife recently had some excellent ideas for the business. As Simon wouldn't listen to her ideas, she went to Simon's key business adviser and told him, who then passed on the ideas to Simon as if they were his own. Simon loved the new concept and immediately implemented it. He wasn't impressed when he found out that the idea had come from his wife in the first place. Although he is generally an open-minded person, Simon has developed this narrow-mindedness about his products – an intolerance to save him time from listening to what are generally useless ideas. Of course he is now considerably more receptive to his wife's opinions! **❥**

Narrow-mindedness and broad-mindedness both have dramatic effects on relationships. Although it is unlikely that one or the other is going to make or break a relationship by itself, they will both play a key role in compatibility and the long-term outlook of a partnership.

❦ Ken was on the wrong side of middle age and had never married. It wasn't that he was particularly unattractive or even shy – in fact, he rather liked the ladies! So his friends and family found it quite a mystery that he had never settled down. Ken was a senior accountant in a provincial firm where he made a good living. No one at work knew what his hobbies were, he just got on with his work and minded his own business.

In fact, Ken was quite obsessed with photography, particularly wildlife photography. He spent his evenings in his dark room and his weekends out taking photos in the countryside. One summer he went on a week's photographic holiday, and it was here that he met Dot. She was a spindly little lady and a widow of many years. She was also obsessed with photography. They pointed their lenses at each other and fell in love! Stranger things do happen.

Dot's son was delighted when his mother married Ken. He explained why the two had clicked. Ken, he said, had been a real 'bottom pincher' in his younger days, but as soon as a relationship began to get serious he would back off. He was extremely narrow-minded and refused to accept anyone's opinions unless they matched his own. Over the years he began to assume that people would act and think in a certain way, just based upon their appearance. 'Wouldn't trust a woman in heels or a woman that wore a red coat!' he told his neighbour. 'Would never do business with a person of a different race!' And he wasn't joking. He lost many friends, and those that he kept were, on the whole, superficial acquaintances.

Dot was the complete opposite. She never stopped talking and had time for everyone. She had loved the Sixties and the permissiveness of society and tried to maintain that attitude throughout her life. Her friends described her as the one with the 'big heart, little body'. She loved photography because it gave her an insight into other people's lives. Whereas Ken photographed wildlife, Dot photographed people. She was typical of a broad-minded person. She listened to other people's opinions even if she did not agree, and adopted a 'live and let live' attitude. She accepted people for their good qualities, whatever their position, colour or creed. And people loved her for it.

Luckily Dot's appearance met with Ken's approval in the first instance. And she was such a strong character that she brought out the best in him, forcing him to become more open-minded. For his part, Ken restrained Dot's open-mindedness, making sure that people didn't take advantage of her. They are the first to admit that they make an unlikely match. For sure, their cameras were very important that summer. They were both looking through rose-tinted lenses!

Incidentally, after a year or so of marriage Ken's writing was noticeably different. The middle-zone letters had spread slightly wider and his letter e relaxed, showing a small loop. **❯**

What to look for?

Both broad- and narrow-mindedness show up in the letter e. You need to look at the width of the loop of the e.

Broad-minded

The loop of the letter e is well rounded, as are many of the other circle letters. If the loop of the e is very wide, especially in proportion to other middle-zone letters, then the writer is likely to be too broad-minded.

Narrow-minded

The loop of the letter e is very narrow or tightly closed. The writer is a little narrow-minded if the loop is more like an oval than a round, and is extremely narrow-minded if the e is retraced so that it looks more like an i.

Look at the examples below to understand the difference between broad-minded and narrow-minded e's.

Samples of narrow- and broad-mindedness

Broad minded

e meat

zippedee

Narrow minded

e meet the

concentrate

How do narrow- and broad-mindedness affect compatibility in a relationship?

Narrow-mindedness in one or both partners is likely to cause problems in a relationship, whereas broad-mindedness is going to enhance compatibility. Where one or both partners are narrow-minded about some issues and broad-minded about others, this will only invoke discord in the relationship if the area of narrow-mindedness is not appreciated by the other partner. The relationship may be made more stormy, but in itself it should not ruin the chances for a perfectly happy and successful partnership.

Two narrow-minded partners together

This will be a very difficult combination as neither partner will be prepared to listen to, or accept, the ideas of the other. Communication will be limited and tolerance will be close to zero. Of course, if both partners are narrow-minded about the same things in life and have the same opinions, then the relationship will be fine, albeit rather insular. Unfortunately, this is rather unlikely to be the case.

Two broad-minded partners together

Such a relationship will be easy-going, relaxed and, all other things being equal, successful. Communication will be good and both partners will find it easy to listen to, and accept, the opinions of the other. As a couple they will have plenty of friends and will be liked and admired by all acquaintances.

A narrow-minded partner with a broad-minded partner

This couple are fundamentally different in attitude. The broad-minded individual will try to be accepting and patient with his or her narrow-minded partner but may eventually give up, tired of the uncompromising attitude of the other. The narrow-minded partner will simply be unable to accept the easy-going nature of his or her partner. Such a relationship will require a great deal of work. Arguments and differences of opinion will be rife; life will not be easy!

Decisiveness and Indecision

Can you make up your mind? Decisive people make a quick and firm choice between possible courses of action. They do not change their mind but stick resolutely to what they have decided. Being decisive is generally considered to be positive. The decisive person is able to take a stance on an issue, not worrying what other people think or worrying unduly about the consequences if they have made the wrong decision. Other people know where they stand with a decisive person.

To be a strong leader and a good manager it is vital to be decisive, to have the ability to make up your own mind. Such a person weighs up the alternatives and then decides which way to go, planning a course of action and sticking by it. When asked a question, a decisive person answers 'yes' or 'no', not 'perhaps', 'maybe' or 'I'm not sure'. They are fundamentally confident people.

Although indecision is obviously the opposite of decisiveness, the implications of being indecisive are more far-reaching than those of being decisive. Indecision has a negative effect on more areas of the personality and hinders success in relationships and achievements at work.

An indecisive person finds it impossible to make a decision. He or she prefers to vacillate between one opinion and another, rather than take a firm stance one way or the other. Indecisive people have a fear of finality. They prefer to prevaricate than take what seems to them irrevocable action. Instinctively they feel that any decision is too final, offering them no escape route. They are fearful of taking the wrong decision and so would rather take none at all.

Indecisive people easily become confused – they have too many options to deal with. Others perceive them as weak and vague; they become ineffectual in all aspects of their life. In order to achieve, we need to weigh up the options, make a decision and then take action. If someone cannot make a decision, then it follows that they will not take action. They will miss opportunities in every sphere of their life. Indecisive people miss out on the chance of being happy, as they are consumed with self-doubt and unable to deal with life's hurdles confidently and strongly. They are fearful of failure and of disapproval by others. Indecisive people are incapable of taking risks – risks that must be taken if a person is to mature, learn and progress in life.

It has been proven that indecision weakens the whole personality. Indecisive people tend to be more prejudiced, they are unable to think clearly, and their desire and ability to achieve are dramatically impaired. As they vacillate between one school of thought and another, constantly wanting to be on the side of the majority, they lessen their integrity and lose the respect of those very friends and colleagues from whom they are trying so desperately to gain approval. Indecision is very much a problem trait, one that will have a considerable negative effect on relationships.

❝ Geoffrey had his own business manufacturing wellington boots. He employed a handful of people and had done pretty well over a couple of years. The trouble was that Geoffrey only had one client – a big international company. On the work front, all his eggs were in one basket. If the client had decided to take its business elsewhere, Geoffrey would have had no business at all.

To compound this potential problem, Geoffrey was having an affair with Linda, a key manager working for the client company. It all seemed hunky-dory for a while, as she passed more and more work his way and his business thrived. But then the relationship started to go sour. Linda was tired of being Geoffrey's mistress. She wanted him to divorce his wife so that the two of them could settle down together. When it became clear that Geoffrey still hadn't told his wife about his affair with Linda, she got angry.

'I'm sick and tired of making all your business decisions for you,' she told Geoffrey. 'I put so much business your way and all you do is spend the money on your wife. You keep on telling me that you love me and want to marry me, but where's the evidence? I just don't believe you any more!'

Geoffrey started panicking. If he left his wife he wouldn't get to see the children. He would probably have to relinquish half his business to her and he would certainly lose his home and all the security he had built up over the last twelve years. If he finished with his mistress he might lose all the work he had. He wouldn't have anyone to guide him and his business would surely go down the drain. He would probably end up bankrupt. Certainly he would lose a lot of the excitement in his life. Geoffrey just didn't know what to do. One day he told his wife he loved her and they should try to mend their marriage. The next day he told his mistress he loved her and that he intended to marry her.

While all this trauma was raging in his personal life, a new manager called Mark joined Geoffrey's company. Geoffrey had told Mark that he had a free rein to do whatever he wanted with the company as he, Geoffrey, wished to retire slowly from the business.

Mark produced a business plan and outlines of how he wanted to expand the company. Geoffrey took one quick look at them and put them at the bottom of his in-tray. Naturally, Mark started pestering him for some decisions. Geoffrey's typical answer was, 'Well, what do you think?' Mark proceeded to tell him what he thought, but Geoffrey simply said, 'I don't know.'

Mark was getting nowhere. By this time he had realized that Geoffrey was sleeping with his main client. Mark didn't care, but he was concerned that the company had all its eggs in one basket. So he decided to grab the bull by the horns and started to develop business in Holland. He spent a lot of time in Rotterdam, doing his homework, meeting potential clients, finding an office and staff. There was very little financial risk for Geoffrey's company, as Mark already had commitment from several major clients. Delighted, he returned to Manchester to present his findings to Geoffrey.

Geoffrey sat with a glum expression and then tilted back in his chair, placing his large hands over his face. He let out a pathetic moan. 'I just don't know what to do,' he said. 'Frankly, I don't know if I can be bothered to expand this business. I just don't know what to do.'

A month later Mark left Geoffrey's firm and set up his own business in Holland. 'To hell with Geoffrey,' he said. 'I'm sick and tired of mollycoddling a grown man. If he can't make his own decisions and won't let other people make them for him, what am I expected to do?'

Two months later Geoffrey's wife filed for a divorce and told him to get out of the family house. Three months later Geoffrey's mistress told him their affair was over; she wanted a younger, more dynamic man. Four months later Geoffrey's only client, his mistress' company, took its account away and gave it to another firm. Three of Geoffrey's staff walked out. At this point Geoffrey had no wife, no relationship, no staff and no work.

'What have I done to deserve all of this?' he cried.

Geoffrey's story clearly demonstrates that he is a weak person. Of course, you may say that he got what he deserved. But over and above that, he has one major problem that hinders every aspect of his life – indecision. Geoffrey is incapable of making a decision. He is terrified of being wrong, so instead he does nothing! And the result of doing nothing can be that, as happened to Geoffrey, your life falls around your feet. **9**

What to look for?

Indecision and decisiveness are apparent in the endings of letters and words. They are particularly visible in the endings of t-bars.

Decisiveness

This is shown when endings are made with blunt or thick points. All endings are firm; some may increase in weight, some may end in a blob, others may just remain firm until the end.

Indecision

This is shown when endings taper off, are weak, dwindle into thinner lines or fade out into nothing.

Samples of decisive and indecisive writing

Decisive

Indecisive

further on towards

happily touching

finished

I guess

How do decisiveness and indecision affect compatibility in a relationship?

Indecision in either partner is bound to have a negative effect on an otherwise healthy relationship.

Two indecisive partners together

Nothing will ever be achieved in this relationship. The fact that these two actually got together in the first place is quite remarkable, for they were committing to something that they would normally shy away from. They will not have many friends, as people will steer clear of a couple with vacillating opinions. These two are compatible, but both have considerable problems of their own. The relationship will not have a strong foundation.

Two decisive partners together

Assuming there are no other incompatibilities and fears evident in their writing, both partners are secure in themselves and will be capable of building a strong relationship. Obviously the chemistry must be right and other elements of their personality compatible or complementary. In the long term being decisive will help their relationship.

An indecisive partner with a decisive partner

It is almost impossible for an indecisive person to get on well in the long term with a decisive person unless, of course, the decisive person has infinite patience! Decisive people tend to see things in black and white. They want to move fast, and are not scared of taking risks. They know what has to be done and they go out and do it. On the contrary, indecisive people hesitate; they keep on changing their minds, not sure which course of action to take. They would rather do nothing than be wrong. They will be totally led by their decisive partner, dumping all decisions to be made on them, abdicating all responsibility. The decisive partner is likely eventually to become completely fed up at having to make all the decisions in the relationship.

3
Are You Equally Sociable?

- Do you and your partner like people? Are you most happy when surrounded by friends? Or do you prefer to be alone, just the two of you together?
- Do people like you? Are you easy to get along with? And how about your partner? Do your friends like him or her?
- Are you a chatter-box, or do you like to keep your thoughts to yourself? Is your partner the same? Or perhaps you haven't yet found out!

Sociable individuals like other people. Typically, they are friendly and easy-going. If you are sociable, the chances are that you have many friends, enjoy going out and probably talk more than average! You enjoy involving yourself in other people's interests and in turn enjoy having others share in your own life.

Many sociable people also have social presence. This is the ability to handle yourself well in a social situation. It may be an ability that is learned or one that comes naturally. If you have both sociability – you like being with other people – and social presence, you will be the type of person who makes friends very easily. People are attracted to you and your friends will define you as having charisma. No doubt at school you were the most popular child in the class.

The word unsociable commonly has negative connotations. People do not like to be defined as unsociable. In today's society it has become a prerequisite to be sociable if you are to be popular and well thought of. However, in this chapter it is vital that you do *not* think of the word unsociable as being negative. *Some people are sociable, some are unsociable — neither type of person is superior to the other.*

Unsociable people frequently appear detached, withdrawn, quiet and unobtrusive. In social situations they may seem awkward or ill at ease. Typically their behaviour is conventional — they would rather slip into the background than be noticed. However, although unsociable people may seem cold and aloof, this is often a façade. They feel strongly and deeply inside, but simply don't want to show their real emotions.

Sociability is undermined by fears and insecurities. The more fears and hang-ups a person has, the more likely he or she is to shun people and feel most comfortable with their own company. Generally speaking, if you are analysing writing that reveals many fears (see Chapter 4) then you can assume that the writer is not a social animal!

Of course there are some people who are sociable — they love going out and meeting people — but who are not socially effective, so they don't have many friends. This means that they don't know how to make a good impression on other people, or are unable to win other people's respect and admiration. Perhaps they are the type of person who tries too hard or has some characteristics that stop others wanting to get too close to them.

Sociability affects your lifestyle. So if one partner is the sociable sort and the other isn't, someone is going to have to compromise. For an easy life, it is definitely preferable to have a relationship with someone who has similar attitudes towards sociability.

Your handwriting reveals a number of characteristics that will show how well you get on with other people and how they are likely to relate to you.

In this chapter we will look at different elements of sociability. To start with, we will look at overall sociability. How do you and your partner get on with other people? Are you an introvert or an extrovert? We will then consider how people view you. Do they perceive you as sympathetic and friendly, or cool and distant?

How do you choose your friends? Do you have lots of them or just a select few? These are the next points we will cover. Then of course there is the issue of talking. Are you talkative or do you keep things to yourself and only speak when really necessary? Finally we will consider your sense of humour – the characteristic most often placed at the top of the list when defining our ideal partner.

Sociability

Are you and your partner extrovert or introvert? Unsociable people are typically introverts. They tend to be quiet and reserved, preferring their own company to spending lots of time with other people. Introverts can feel lonely even when they are among large groups of friends or acquaintances. When among strangers they may even feel a sense of isolation and disconnectedness. Some introverts enjoy interacting with other people but easily become drained by doing so. One thing all introverts have in common is that they need to recharge their batteries by being alone – they get energy from within themselves.

Extroverts, on the other hand, get their batteries recharged and their energy increased by being around other people. They are sociable and need to talk or be with others to feel at their best. When not in contact with other human beings they feel lonely. Extroverts are fundamentally sociable people.

Let's have a look at how sociable and unsociable people react in different ways.

6 Duke is tall, blond and tanned with beautifully toned muscles. Most mornings he can be found tangled between the arms and legs of some stunning girl. Come lunchtime, he bids them farewell and saunters off to the beach to ride the waves. Duke starts work at six in the evenings. 'Can't really call it work, can you, mate! We're paid to have fun!' he laughs, running to join the other Aussie guys.

Duke works in a holiday camp. His job is to organize entertainment, barbecues, anything to keep the guests amused well into the early hours of the morning. It's his ideal job. Duke just loves people – any type of person.

The guests at the holiday camp all fall in love with Duke. He charms them, whatever their age, for he is always checking to make sure that they're having a good time. He just loves to be surrounded by people and is genuinely concerned about how they are and what's happening to them. By two in the morning when 'work' is finished, he's charged up and raring to go to the next party. It is unusual to find a party in the area that Duke hasn't popped into.

Duke is one of life's extroverts. He doesn't like to go surfing for too long each day, because – he'd never admit it, of course – he gets a bit lonely. He just has to be around people as much as possible.

Tabitha split up with her boyfriend and didn't have anyone to go on holiday with. She had already made a provisional reservation for two at the holiday camp near Melbourne where Duke worked, and she desperately wanted to go. So she took her colleague and friend Cara out for lunch and, after much persuasion, got Cara to agree to join her.

In the weeks before the holiday Cara had major reservations about going. Coming from a sheep-farming family near Auckland, wild parties and gregarious guys were not really her scene. She preferred to holiday alone with the family dog Leo up at her parents' cabin in the Bay of Islands.

Cara and Tabitha worked together in the secretarial pool of an insurance company. If they hadn't both joined the firm on the same day and ended up working for the same monster of a boss, they might never have become friends. Tabitha partied most nights and came into the office each morning with large black rings under her eyes. Cara occasionally went out for a bite to eat with a couple of old school friends or went to the cinema with one of the many guys who chased her. She had a handful of people she was really close to and tended to feel most comfortable with country folks like herself.

The camp was heaving with holidaymakers when they arrived, and live music was blaring out of loudspeakers and tannoys positioned everywhere, from the toilets to the beach! Cara felt uneasy. When she saw her room she wanted to cry. It was the size of a shoe-box, and she had to share a bunk-bed with Tabitha. 'Hey, how cool,' screamed Tabitha, 'I've always wanted to sleep in a bunk-bed. Come on, let's dump the gear and get down partying!'

'I think I'll just stay here for a moment and put my feet up for a while,' murmured Cara.

'As you like,' said Tabitha and she rushed off to join in the fun.

Well, that was pretty much the pattern for the rest of the holiday. Cara simply wasn't cut out to spend lots of time with other people. She needed her own space. Half an hour into a party she normally felt ready to go home, needing to recharge her batteries in isolation. Being around so many strangers made her feel isolated in a bizarre way. As she wrote in a card to her gran, 'It's a fun place but weird. I feel lonely even though I'm among so many people.'

On her second to last evening, early on just as the sun was setting, Duke asked her to dance. Her first reaction was to say no, but looking at his dark blue eyes and lazy smile she felt compelled to go along with him. They swayed around the pool for about an hour before Duke led her by the hand down to the beach front and gave her a long, lingering kiss. 'Okay, you beauty,' he said, 'we're off to party now.'

It was a typical Duke party, full of different types. Cara hung onto Duke's arm. 'Please don't leave me,' she murmured.

Later that night, under much duress from Tabitha, Cara gave her friend the full run-down on the evening.

'So when are you going to see him again?' nagged Tabitha.

'I'm not,' retorted Cara. 'I just hate his lifestyle, I've got nothing to say to his friends and anyway we're going home the day after tomorrow.'

'Weirdo,' said Tabitha, 'why don't you run with a bit of passion for a change! I just don't understand you, girl!' Cara lay awake most of the night feeling miserable.

Although they never dated, Tabitha and Duke would have been rather compatible. Both are extroverts, party animals and relish being around lots of people. Their only danger would have been not having enough time for each other.

On the other hand, Cara has less interest in, or need of, people. She is choosy in her friendships, selecting friends if they have similar interests to herself or similar standards to her own. She is conservative and shy. Cara also fears criticism, and feels safer with friends cast in a similar mould to herself, as they are less likely to be critical of her. **'**

What to look for?

There are a number of different signs that indicate if you and your partner are the sociable, extrovert types or more introvert and less outgoing.

1. The slant indicates extrovertism – where you get your energy from
2. Spacing between letters indicates social abilities
3. Spacing between words indicates how close you wish to get to others
4. Size of writing indicates how expressive you are to other people.

SLANT – extrovert or introvert?
Measure the emotional slant of your writing, following the steps set out in Chapter 1.

Left and upward-slanting writing
These writers are likely to be reserved, not expressing their emotional feelings.
Right-slanting writing
Generally speaking, the more the writing slants to the right, the more extrovert and outwardly sympathetic the writer is.

BEWARE – if the writing is left- or upward- slanting but is *also* big, heavy or appears to move hurriedly forwards across the page, the writer may appear extrovert to others but in fact is really an introvert.

Samples of extrovert and introvert writing

Extrovert   Introvert

SPACING BETWEEN LETTERS – how socially adept are you?
Are people drawn to you?

Decide if your letters are cramped closely together or are quite wide apart. Look at the samples below and then compare them to your own writing.

Closely spaced letters

These writers tend to be reserved and finds it hard to express inner feelings. Such people often find it difficult to relate or get close to other people and sharing does not come easily to them. Such writers will find it difficult to attract many friends.

Widely spaced letters

These writers are more relaxed, expressive and accepting. They find it easier to share themselves and their belongings with others. Such people will find it easier to make friends.

Samples of spacing between letters

Closely spaced   Widely spaced

SPACING BETWEEN WORDS – *how close do you let others get to you?*

Decide if the spaces between your words are wide or narrow, even or uneven. Look at the samples below and then compare to your own writing.

Even spacing

The writer shows respect for social boundaries. He or she likes stability and reliability in his or her relationships.

Uneven spacing

Sometimes the writer will want to be close to you, at other times distant. Such a person will seem unreliable.

Narrow spacing

The writer likes to be close to other people. He or she is the type of person who is happy to sit close to somebody else on the train. This type of person may fear independence and could become clingy to the person or people they are closest to.

Wide spacing

This person likes to keep others at a distance – both emotionally and physically. He or she prefers space and needs solitude, even if he or she has an outgoing nature. Sometimes such a person dislikes being touched.

Very wide spacing

Such writing shows isolation, fear of contact and intimate conversation. Such a person has difficulty establishing close relationships due to fear of losing his or her own identity.

Samples of spacing between words

Even

Again I picked

Narrow

When I shall be

Uneven

go with his friends

Wide

eye , make a men

SIZE OF THE WRITING – *how open and expressive are you to others?*

First decide if the middle zone of your writing is large or small. Do this by looking at the middle zone of your letters and comparing them to the upper and lower zones.

If the middle zone is substantially larger (taller and wider) than either the upper or lower zone, then the writing is large. If the upper and lower zones dwarf the middle zone, the writing is small. If all three zones are balanced, then the writing is average. Look at the samples below to decide if your middle-zone writing is large, small, varied or average.

Large writing

The larger the writing, the more outgoing, socially active and expressive the writer. This person lives for today and likes to enjoy relationship experiences without reflecting too much on the past or future.

Small writing

The smaller the writing, the more modest, reserved and quiet the writer is likely to be. Such people tend not to express themselves well in group situations. They are often perceptive about the outside world but find it hard to understand their own emotions.

Varied-sized writing

This person is likely to be moody – sometimes outgoing and sometimes insular and private. An emotional balance has not been achieved and the writer may be facing relationship problems.

Average writing

This person is socially self-confident and well adjusted in everyday life.

Samples of size of writing

Large

girlfriend

Average

a wonderful view

Small

after that

Varied

Sometimes never

Once you have considered all four of the above factors, you can decide how sociable and how socially adept you and your partner are.

How does sociability affect compatibility in a relationship?

How sociable, extrovert or introvert you are will have a profound effect on your relationship. Look at both of your writings and decide whether you are each sociable or unsociable, extrovert or introvert. Then decide which of the following categories you fall into.

Both partners are sociable

Your life together will be party, party, party! Constantly surrounded by friends, you are no doubt living in the fast lane. You are well suited to each other, as you both draw your energy from the same source – being around others. Both of you find it easy to express your emotions. This will help considerably in any long-term relationship.

Both partners are unsociable

Your life together will be quiet. Both of you will be happy just being alone together, and neither of you will want to spend too much time socializing. You are both fundamentally compatible. As long as neither party strongly represses emotions or finds it particularly difficult to express feelings, this should be a strong partnership between two like-minded people.

One unsociable or introvert partner with one extrovert or sociable partner

Such a relationship will be difficult and will require much compromise on the side of both partners, as each of you gets your energy in different ways. The unsociable partner is likely to feel swamped and crowded by the sociable partner's desire to be around others. The sociable partner may well feel cramped by the unsociable partner's lack of desire to go out and be with people.

For the success of this relationship, both partners need to have their own space. The unsociable partner needs to be alone at regular intervals and the sociable partner needs to go out and be with people. Long-term willingness to compromise, and a constant understanding of the innate differences of both partners, is the only way this relationship will survive.

Selection of Friends

How many friends do you have? A very wide circle of perhaps two hundred close friends and thousands of good friends? Or five or six people to whom you are very close?

How do you choose your friends? Do you have friends from all walks of life, whom you welcome with open arms, or do you prefer to have friends with similar interests and backgrounds to yourself?

The number and type of friends you have provide an insight into your deeper personality and are useful to know for the purpose of developing relationships – both personal and business.

❦ Alice had got herself stuck in a rut of misery. All her friends were married or in close relationships, but she hadn't had a boyfriend for three years. Deep down she knew there wasn't anything wrong with her. She had a good job but she never met any new people through it. And therein lay her problem. Although she went out at least two nights a week, Alice always met up with her old group of friends – never coming across anyone new.

One evening over a drink with her friend Diana, Alice told her how lonely she was, so Diana invited her to the local sports club disco the following week.

The beginning of the evening passed in a whirl until she was introduced to Hugh. Average to nice-looking, he certainly wasn't what Alice would have defined as 'her sort'. But he seemed very confident. Lots of girls came up to him, gave him a hug or a peck on the cheek, winked and flirted for a couple of seconds and then disappeared with someone else. Hugh was obviously popular and Alice was became increasingly flattered that he was spending so much time chatting to her.

Hugh dragged Alice onto the dance floor for every slow dance. He held her close. When he kissed her, her mind went blank and her body felt like liquid. She felt ecstatically happy and incredibly excited. In the early hours of the morning, she cast away all doubts and agreed to go to Hugh's flat for a late-night cup of coffee.

The coffee was never made. Hugh led Alice into his bedroom and they made love. But he fell asleep immediately afterwards, leaving Alice feeling alone and miserable. She lay awake for a long time with conflicting thoughts running round her mind. She felt guilty and a little ashamed that she had slept with Hugh so soon, but on the other hand she felt happy that someone had wanted her.

When Alice woke up, Hugh was already in the shower humming tunelessly away to himself.

He asked Alice to join him at a party he was going to that night. Not wanting to seem boring, Alice agreed, even though she felt exhausted and would have to cancel a drink with a girlfriend.

Alice felt alone and slightly nervous most of the evening. She knew no one at the party besides Hugh, and none of his friends seemed to have anything in common with Alice or her friends. Alice felt as if she had nothing to say to anyone. These were not the type of people she felt comfortable with and, if it weren't for Hugh, she would have left hours earlier.

That night Hugh once again led Alice back to his flat. They made love. But once again Alice was uncomfortable, although the next morning she woke to feel happy that she had a boyfriend. The pattern continued for a week. Every evening they went out, every night they returned to his flat.

A week to the day after they had met, Alice agreed to meet Hugh at a bar. She arrived slightly late, to find Hugh talking animatedly to a tall, red-headed girl wearing a bra-like top, skin-tight leather trousers and high, high-heeled red stilettos. Alice hung back near the door out of view of Hugh, not knowing quite what to do. To her dismay he flung his arms around the girl and clenched her in a passionate embrace.

Coming up for air, Hugh caught sight of Alice. He shouted across the room, 'Darling Alice, meet Shirley. She and I are long-lost lovers and were just doing a bit of catching up. Don't worry, I'm not dumping you quite yet! I just like to have lots of friends and not be too selective.' He laughed a hard, cold laugh.

Alice looked at Hugh in horror. She paced over to him, slapped him hard on his cheek and stormed out of the bar with tears pouring down her face. Devastated, she stayed at home every night for a week before she had the courage to pick up the phone to call Diana.

'I am so sorry, Alice, I did hear that Hugh was a bit of a cad, but then I thought he might have grown up by now. It's probably for the best. He knows so many people but I don't think he really cares about anyone except himself,' Diana said.

After a while Alice was able to look back on the episode and smile wryly. She had learned a lot. First of all, she is not the outgoing sociable sort like Hugh. Alice likes a small group of friends, with similar interests and outlooks to herself, people whom she can trust, and with whom she can feel comfortable and relaxed. She also realized that she had been desperate for a boyfriend and it had been a grave mistake to jump into bed with someone on the first night.

Nowadays Alice has gone back to her discriminating ways. She has met a couple of nice men at friends' dinner parties and hopes to meet more through the graphology classes that she has recently joined at the local adult education centre. **9**

6 Jon is much more unsociable than Alice. He cares very little about developing relationships. His few friends could be mirror-images of himself. He would not even consider befriending someone who didn't share his religious and political viewpoints or someone who wasn't fit and active. The trouble is that Jon is losing out. He rarely bothers to spend long enough with anyone to discover whether they have similar attitudes to himself.

He recently decided to quit work and cycle across America alone for six months. To him, the perfect holiday will be seeing and talking to no one. **9**

There are many reasons why some people like to have lots of friends from different walks of life, and other people prefer a few close friends.

Sometimes when a person is conservative in outlook, they prefer just to have friends who conform to certain standards – such as class, education, religion, etc. On the other hand, a person who is very busy may have to learn to be selective about who he or she befriends, simply because he or she cannot give of their time indiscriminately.

6 Suzannah had masses of friends when she was at college. However, when she completed her nursing exams and took up work full time, she found that there weren't enough hours each week to see everybody. So she decided just to stay in touch with the people she really liked and drastically cut the number of her friends. This has shown up in her writing, for her lower loops have become much tighter over the last couple of years. **9**

Other people may not want to have lots of friends because they are fearful they will be criticized by them. People who are shy or timid only choose friends with whom they feel safe. Of course there are also people who are so unpopular, mean or horrible that only a very few friends will put up with them!

What to look for?
Look at the lower loops in your writing and decide which of the following categories it falls into.

Long and wide lower loops
This indicates a desire for a wide variety of friends. Such a person likes many different kinds of people. He or she is likely to have a broad social life. The wider the loops, the greater the capacity for new experiences and friendships.

Narrow and long, or narrow and short, lower loops
This indicates a lesser interest in people generally. Such a person will be choosy in their friendships and will normally select friends based upon his or her own personal interests, standards, nationality, education, occupation or other grouping.

Loops completed below the baseline
The further away these loops are from the baseline, the more the writer doesn't care about companionship and friends. He or she may seem to have friends, but personal relationships are mostly superficial; few people, if any, are admitted to his or her confidence. Such a person is fearful of intimacy, wanting to keep those friends he or she does have all to him or herself. Such a person tends to shun outsiders and is loyal to a chosen few. People like this are often talented but loners.

No lower loops, just a lower stick line
This indicates that the writer is happy to spend time alone. He or she prefers to be independent and often does not need many friends or a range of activities. This may be for a variety of reasons, such as lack of self-confidence, sensitivity to criticism, lack of social experience or simply a fear of being hurt through intimacy. To find out the reason why the person likes to be alone it is necessary to look at the other characteristics in his or her writing, as outlined in Chapter 4 of this book.

Some loops and some sticks
Often these writers are naturally friendly types. However, such writing shows that these people also want time and space for themselves, away from others, where they can think their own thoughts.

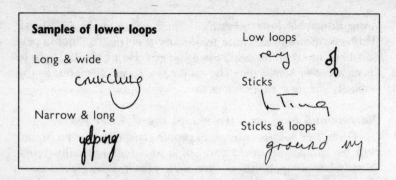

Samples of lower loops

Long & wide

cruclung

Narrow & long

yelping

Low loops

rey   *of*

Sticks

Ting

Sticks & loops

ground my

How are the choice and number of friends likely to affect compatibility in a relationship?

As discussed above in the section on sociability, your relationship and attitude to friendship will play a significant role in your personal relationships. People who like to be alone will find it hard to bond with people who like lots of friends.

Many a cause of a relationship breakdown has been when one partner doesn't like or approve of the friends of the other partner. If one partner has certain conscious or unconscious criteria by which they select their friends, and the other partner has friends that do not meet these criteria, then the selective person may well be unhappy with his or her partner's friends. In reverse, the partner with a wide choice of friends may find his or her partner's friends uninteresting and uninspired. A great deal of compromise would be necessary in such a relationship, with perhaps the best solution being that the two partners see their own friends by themselves, not with their partner tagging along.

Talkativeness/Reticence

Are you a chatter-box, nattering away, expressing every little thought that crosses your mind? Or are you the type of person who doesn't say much, talking just when it's really necessary to do so? Probably you are somewhere in between these two extremes!

It is quite normal to want to express what you think. But extremely talkative people feel compelled to say out loud everything they are thinking – often ideas that are not yet properly formulated. Quite frequently they talk for the sake of talking, whether or not anyone wants to listen. The danger for talkative people is that they may talk without thinking about the implications of what they are saying. Nevertheless, talkative people will find it easy to make friends.

If a talkative person also has imagination evident in their writing, the chances are that he or she will be a teller of larger-than-life stories – the sort of person who embellishes upon tales to make them just that little bit more exciting. If the writer also has other traits such as narrow-mindedness or the tendency not to think too deeply about matters, then he or she is likely to be a gossip.

At the opposite extreme is the person who rarely talks. In graphology we call this person reticent. Such a person does not necessarily want to hide anything, but feels the need to talk only when he or she has something important to say. They like to protect their own privacy. Often the reticent person expresses him- or herself in just a few words.

Other people are more likely to confide in a reticent person than in a talkative one, as a reticent person, who only talks when there is something important to say, is more likely to keep confidences and inspire trust in others. However, these reserved people normally find it harder than most to make friends, as they do not easily open up. Nevertheless the friendships they do make tend to be close and long-lasting.

More often than not you will notice a mixture of reticence and talkativeness in a person's writing. It is quite normal for someone to be quiet and uncommunicative about some subjects but very open and willing to talk about others. No doubt you know somebody who is happy to talk for hours about their work, but when you ask them about their private life they clam up and quickly change the subject.

❛ Julian was the second youngest of a family of nine. He learned to speak very quickly and from the age of three quite simply never shut up! He was the teachers' nightmare. If he didn't have his hand up in the air yelling 'Please, ma'am' he was whispering to his friends in the classroom. From the second he woke up in the morning until the moment he drifted off to sleep at night he was chattering non-stop!

When Julian left school he joined the local newspaper and progressed to become a junior reporter. After a few months he was called in to see the boss.

'Look, Julian, there are a couple of things we need to sort out. I've had complaints from a number of your colleagues that all you do is babble on about anything that crosses your mind, disturbing other people when they're trying to concentrate. I've also noticed that you tend to embellish your stories rather too much. You can be liberal with the truth, but I really think your imagination is going a bit wild. I've decided to move you to the short stories column. Use your imagination to real advantage and write some great stories for us.'

Julian had mixed feelings. On the one hand, he knew that the new position would stretch him, on the other hand, he missed the opportunity to chatter away with other people. Fortunately, things soon picked up. A few weeks later a new girl joined the division. Her name was Marlene and she had beautiful almond-shaped eyes, perfectly smooth coffee-coloured skin and a cute smile. Julian was love-struck.

Back at home it was 'Marlene this' and 'Marlene that'. 'So,' his ma said to him, 'when are we going to meet this Marlene girl?'

Embarrassed, Julian admitted to his mother that he hadn't even taken her out yet. 'Good heavens, boy, what are you waiting for?' retorted his astonished mother.

The next day Julian plucked up the courage to ask Marlene out for a drink after work. 'Sure,' she said quietly, looking up at him coyly. They went out together a few times, Julios babbled away as usual and Marlene said little more than yes or no.

A few days later his mother sat Julian down, handed him a cup of cocoa and said, 'Now tell us about this Marlene girl!'

Julian swirled the cocoa around in his cup, hesitated for a moment, and said, 'Well, the thing is, Ma, she's pretty quiet, I haven't found out much about her.' It was at that moment that Julian realized that he'd done all the talking and she hadn't been able to get a word in edge-ways.

The next time they met Julian insisted that Marlene talk about herself. 'I can't just talk about me, Julian,' she said, 'you have to ask me questions. Don't expect me to talk in the way you do.'

Marlene is the sort of girl who expresses herself in few words. She doesn't feel the need to talk in the way that Julian does. She doesn't mean to be secretive, she simply needs to have a reason if she is going to say something.

Marlene and Julian developed a good relationship. They understood that they were both different: Julian liked to talk all the time; Marlene didn't, but she was happy to listen. Not feeling the need to chatter, she was able to think more carefully. There were a number of times over the coming years that Marlene stopped Julian from getting into trouble.

Martha is a lot more reticent than Marlene, and although she doesn't see it as a problem, it really is. She hardly ever talks. At work she recently didn't receive the promotion she thought she deserved. This was because she never communicated to her colleagues; she didn't tell anyone of her plans and then was upset when no one helped her carry them out. Socially Martha finds it hard to make friends. She generally has to know people for a long time before she starts talking to them. ❯

Most of us are not consistently talkative or reticent. You may find that you are very close-mouthed on some issues and yet talk freely about other things, given the slightest opportunity.

So long as the reticent party isn't hiding anything from his or her partner, more often than not it isn't a problem in a relationship if one partner talks a lot and the other is fairly quiet. But of course in some cases it can be the cause of a relationship's breakdown. We all know that communication is vital for the success of any relationship.

❨ Donna and Tommy married young, following a whirlwind romance. Every evening after work Donna would come home and tell Tommy about her day. He would smile at her and not make any comments. When she asked him how his day had gone he would generally answer, 'Normal', 'Good' or 'Okay'. He never elaborated, even when Donna pressed him.

In bed Donna liked to express her feelings, telling Tommy how she loved him. Tommy was always silent. He never discussed his likes or dislikes in the bedroom, or anywhere else for that matter.

After a year Donna was desperate. 'He never talks to me,' she cried to her best friend. 'I just don't know what he is thinking. Here I was believing that by marrying I'd never be lonely again and I am the most lonely I have ever been in the whole of my life.' Whereas Tommy felt no need to talk or discuss his feelings, Donna had an overwhelming need to express hers. She felt that because Tommy didn't open up to her verbally, he didn't trust or love her any more. In the end Donna and Tommy split up because they felt they couldn't reconcile their fundamental differences. ❩

What to look for?

In graphology, anything to do with communication lies in the middle zone of the letters, and more specifically in the circle letters, such as a,b,d,g and o.

Look at all the letters a,b,d,g and o in your writing and decide if the circles are closed or open at the top.

An easy way to remember this is by imagining that the circle letters are like a mouth. When the mouth is shut, the person is reticent and doesn't talk much; when the mouth is open, the person is talkative.

Majority of circles closed
The person is reticent and doesn't talk unless they have something of importance to say.

Majority of circles open
The person is talkative and likes talking for the sake of doing so.

Mixture of open and closed
The person is talkative about some issues but quiet about others.

The gossip
Check for the following:
- circle letters that are open, indicating talkativeness
- circle letters that are pinched and narrow-looking, indicating narrow-mindedness
- middle-zone letters that look flat and ill-formed, indicating lack of deep thought

If all three of these traits are present in the writing, then the writer may well be a gossip.

The tall story-teller
Check for the following:
- circle letters that are open, indicating talkativeness
- tall and wide loops in the upper letters (b, d, l, t) and or long and wide loops in the lower letters (g, f, p, y), indicating strong imagination

If both of these traits are present in the writing, then the writer may exaggerate stories and embellish facts.

Samples of circle letters

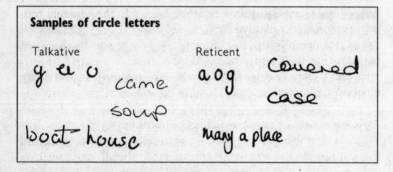

How do talkativeness and reticence affect compatibility in a relationship?
How many successful relationships do you know where one partner seems to do all the talking and the other is relatively quiet? Probably quite a few. The chances are that the quiet partner doesn't talk much among other people but does open up to

his or her partner when they are together privately. It is certainly not necessary for both partners to be talkative, or both to be reticent, in order to get on in harmony. In this case the partners complement each other.

However, if either or both partners are extremely reticent or extremely talkative then this could pose problems.

Talkative partner with a reticent partner

If both partners have their own traits in moderation then this relationship should work well. Frequently the reticent person is quite relieved that his or her partner is doing all the talking, as this means that he or she is released from having to say too much. They say that opposites attract, and in this case they often do. This is because each partner is compensating the other with what they themselves lack.

However, if one or both partners are talkative or reticent in the extreme, then this is bound to cause problems. The reticent individual will quite simply be driven mad by the constant babbling of his or her partner, and may also feel that his or her talkative partner is betraying their relationship and trust by speaking too much about personal things to friends or acquaintances. The talkative person will find it very difficult to get close to or in the long term maintain a relationship with, the severely reticent person. The talkative partner will feel that the reticent partner is not opening up, not sharing his or her feelings and not contributing sufficiently to the relationship. Communication is vital and if each partner feels the need to communicate to vastly different extents, then the relationship will struggle to last.

Talkative partner with a talkative partner

No one else will be able to get a word in edge-ways when around this couple! On the whole, this partnership should work well, as both partners want to communicate. The main trouble this relationship is likely to face is that both partners are talking but neither is listening. They may both go off at completely different tangents and never realize it! Sometimes there is simply not enough space in a relationship for two chatter-boxes.

If either, or both, partners are gossips or tall-story-tellers, beware! Any distortion of facts is unhealthy for a relationship!

Reticent partner with a reticent partner

These partners will understand each other and accept that communication is not of importance to them. They may well develop their relationship in such a way that they understand each other even though few words are exchanged. The danger is that if other troubles arise in the relationship, neither will feel the urge to discuss them, and these troubles could then fester and grow so that ultimately the relationship falls apart.

Sense of Humour

When asked to describe their perfect mate, the majority of people will include a sense of humour in their list of 'must have's. Laughing is one of the best ways to relax, and if we can be with someone who makes us laugh, the chances are we will feel happy and at ease.

It's funny, isn't it, how we always think that if someone has a well-developed sense of humour, that is a positive thing. Perhaps it is because humorous people normally demonstrate sympathy, tolerance and kindness. People with a sense of humour are generally able to see and appreciate the absurdities of life. Often they can laugh at themselves. A sense of humour enables them to maintain a healthy outlook on life, putting their problems in perspective.

A good sense of humour is a major asset when considering sociability. People are drawn to those people with a good sense of humour, like pins to a magnet.

❝ Joe has a great sense of humour. He is a plant specialist working at a garden centre on the south coast of England. He said that he only applied for the job because the centre was called the Square Pebble Garden Centre. 'Crazy name, must be a crazy place!' he joked. When he saw the centre for the first time he knew he had made a good choice.

People come from miles around just to have the opportunity to ask Joe for some advice. Not only is he knowledgeable about his subject, but he makes them laugh. Even the most irate of customers come away feeling good after Joe has dealt with them.

Joe was never a particularly attractive young man. Nevertheless he had more girlfriends than all his chums. Groups of them would gather around him to listen to his self-deprecating wit. The day he married, the female population (bar two – his mother and new bride) went into mourning!

In the early years of his life, Joe's parents lost all their money when his father made a poor business investment. Neither Joe nor his brother Oliver had any of the trendy teenage possessions that other young boys had. Oliver took this really badly. To this day he is resentful towards his parents that he was hard done by. But Joe, with his sense of humour, took it in his stride. Instead of being embarrassed at having to wear outdated flared trousers, he wore them flagrantly as if trying to set a new fashion. His humour let him put his family problems into perspective. His attitude was 'Things can only get better', while Oliver became shy and self-conscious, and snappy towards his friends. **9**

There are of course other types of humour that are not so positive and healthy. Dry humour or wit can become sarcastic – humour that is antagonistic. Sometimes this is simply malicious fun-poking, but at other times it can be biting or facetious. There is a big difference between seeing the bright side of life and taking the mickey out of someone in a spiteful way. Where a writer's humour stroke has become over-embellished and some of the letters have lost their form, it shows a desire for attention combined with superficiality. This person is likely to use their humour in a nasty way – beware!

6 Eddie has a sick sense of humour. When younger, he left dead birds and mice around the house for his siblings to find. He coloured his arm dark purple and blue, so that it look as if he had the most terrible bruise. He showed it to his mother, who panicked and picked up the phone to call the doctor, fearing that he had a haemorrhage. Another time, when at the local swimming pool with his father, Eddie decided to see how long he could stay underwater. His father jumped in fully clothed to rescue what he thought was his drowning son. Eddie thought it was very funny. His father was furious.

Eddie didn't lose his facetious and mean sense of humour when he grew up into his late teens. His mates thought he was a cool lad, but sometimes he just went too far. One of the shop assistants in the supermarket where Eddie worked had a crush on him. Pat was a plain, very overweight and rather shy girl. Many of the staff called her 'fat Pat porky pie' behind her back, because she oversaw the packaged meat section of the store. Of course it was Eddie who had invented the name.

Unfortunately for Pat, Eddie found out about her crush on him. One evening as they were shutting the store, Eddie went up to Pat and asked her to join him and a few of the lads for a drink that evening. Totally gobsmacked and filled with terror, Pat became very flustered and said that she couldn't possibly make it that evening.

In an abnormally gentle and compassionate manner, Eddie said to her, 'I realize that you probably don't want to be around all the lads. To be honest, I just want to be alone with you anyway. How about if you meet me at the store room tomorrow at 5.30 p.m?'

Stunned, Pat hastily agreed and rushed away home.

The next evening, with her heart pounding, Pat made her way to the store room to find Eddie already waiting for her. He took her hand

and asked her to sit on a crate next to him. To her surprise Eddie asked her if she had ever been kissed. Blushing profusely and extremely ashamed, Pat admitted that she hadn't. 'Can I be the first one?' Eddie asked. Pat nodded.

He kissed her, holding her head with one of his hands and running the other up and down and around her back. After a few seconds Eddie sat up and, to Pat's surprise and disappointment said, 'Look, I've got to go now. I'll see you tomorrow, okay?'

A few minutes later Pat came out of the store room and left the shop via the staff entrance at the back. A handful of her colleagues were hanging around on the pavement. They started laughing and cheering when they saw her. Bursting into tears, she ran all the way home.

Her misery and humiliation were made even worse that night when she took off her uniform to find the words 'Eddie woz here' inscribed in chalk on her back.

As you can imagine, it took Pat years to overcome the trauma of Eddie's vile behaviour.

Eddie has a mean and warped sense of humour that is meant to hurt other people. He himself has a strong desire to be the centre of attention, and the way he achieves this is through malicious and often biting fun-poking at other people. Such sick humour is fortunately much rarer than the normal kind-natured, good sense of humour found in the majority of people. **9**

What to look for?

Good sense of humour

The humour stroke is most frequently found – and easiest to check – in the letter m. It looks like a flourish at the beginning of the letter. It should be a smooth and gentle stroke (as seen in the examples below) and there should be no sharp angles where it joins the main m letter.

Sometimes this humour flourish is found at the beginning of other letters – most frequently on capital letters or at the beginning of words.

Sick sense of humour

When the humour stroke seems out of proportion and very large, then the writer may have an exaggerated sense of humour. If many of the strokes in the writing seem poorly formed, as if the letters have been written quickly without care, this also indicates that the person doesn't think deeply. These traits combined together indicate that the person could have a sick sense of humour.

The humour stroke

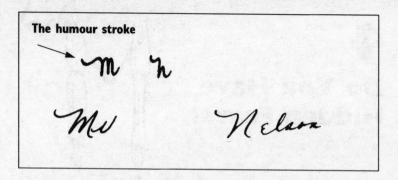

How does humour affect compatibility in a relationship?

A good sense of humour is a wonderful tonic to the well-being of any relationship. When one or both partners can laugh at themselves and see the funny side to life, any problems encountered by either partner will be made light of and the path forward made considerably smoother. If either you or your partner has a good sense of humour, relish it – for it is a true treasure and should help oil the wheels of your relationship.

Do remember that it is relatively rare to find strong humour strokes in writing. If you have writing that doesn't have any humour strokes, this does not necessarily mean that you lack a sense of humour. It simply means that humour is not a prominent characteristic in your personality.

4

Do You Have Hidden Fears?

- *Do you feel insecure or unsure of yourself? Are you often frightened, but not exactly sure what you are frightened of?*
- *Are you the jealous type? Do you like yourself?*
- *How well do you really know your partner? Do you know what your partner's secret worries are? Or how your partner's past affects his or her present?*

6 When he was six years old, John's parents split up. The divorce was acrimonious. He was shunted between his mother and father and eventually, at the age of ten, was dumped with his unloving grandparents. He lived with them until he was sixteen and then escaped into the big, wide world. John has suffered from all the neuroses you can imagine. Although he managed to get a good education, he has been unable to hold down a job for very long and has never had a proper relationship. Sometimes he feels on top of the world, at other times he plunges into black depressions. Twice he has had nervous breakdowns and ended up in hospital. John's life is built on fear. Deprived of love and affection as a child, he cannot give or receive love as an adult. He is deeply insecure.

Heather has similar fears and insecurities, but for different reasons. She comes from a loving, close-knit family but one with old-fashioned attitudes. Sex was a taboo topic in her home and when she brought up the subject she was severely reprimanded and told that 'Sex is dirty and not something young girls should think about.'

Throughout her adolescence, Heather built up in her mind the idea that sex was bad, something to be ashamed of and not something to enjoy. She had a few boyfriends but would never let them touch her, so they left.

She developed a very poor image of herself. She thought she was ugly and that the only way she could possibly attract love was by becoming thin and beautiful. As a consequence she developed anorexia nervosa, the eating disorder. Heather became so painfully thin and so terribly ill that she collapsed and was rushed to hospital. It has taken her five years of counselling and medical help to get back to what she describes as normal. 9

Sometimes it is a good thing that we become afraid. Imagine you are walking along a street at night. It is pitch-black, there are no cars passing and nobody in sight. Suddenly you hear footsteps behind you. They are getting louder and closer. Your heart starts thumping. You cross the road and the footsteps follow you. You start walking faster, and the person behind you walks faster too. Convinced that you are about to be attacked, you break into a run. Your adrenalin is pumping hard, your heartbeat going berserk. You run so fast that in no time you have reached the main road and run into a petrol station, with its lights glowing and plenty of people milling around. You look behind you and your pursuer has gone. You cannot believe how quickly you just ran – after all, you haven't run properly for years – probably since you left school!

When we are afraid, the adrenalin in our bodies builds up, empowering us to run faster. That is a good thing!

Many fears are vital to us, to keep ourselves out of danger. It is good to be afraid of driving too fast, because it reduces the chance of an accident. It can even be beneficial to be afraid of jumping into a relationship too quickly for fear of being hurt. Fear can protect us. But if that fear takes control of our lives it can suffocate us, controlling our minds and stopping us from leading a normal existence.

Some people have fears that are buried at the back of their minds, or insecurities that have developed as a result of being unloved when they were children. Such fears can inhibit or even destroy any chance of success and well-being in adult life. These fears and insecurities are bound to have an impact upon adult relationships – and normally that impact will be negative.

Most people do not admit to their fears or insecurities but try very hard to hide them from friends and acquaintances, and often even from their closest partners. Quite frequently insecure people even hide the true extent of their fears from themselves.

If you really want to get to know someone, or even gain a true understanding of yourself, it is vital that you understand their, or your own, fears and insecurities. Not only do fears impinge upon many other aspects of the personality, but they can severely hinder a person's chance of personal and professional success. Shyness or jealousy may end an otherwise promising relationship. A very low opinion of oneself will surely hinder career success, or even the creation of a loyal group of friends.

Once you become aware of your own insecurities you may feel empowered to face them head-on and take steps to overcome them. Knowing about somebody else's fears will enable you to alter your behaviour towards them, perhaps becoming more tolerant, giving more praise, or doing whatever is necessary to help them combat their fears.

Graphology is a very powerful tool, because it enables you to discover the fears and insecurities of the person whose handwriting you are analysing. Short of dragging your partner into psychoanalysis (which of course is unlikely to work unless he or she wants it to), you are unlikely to find out so much about the inner workings of his or her mind by any other method.

What impact do fears and insecurities have on a relationship?

A very severe impact! Of course it depends on the nature of the relationship, whether one or both partners have fears, what those fears are and how strong they are. But let's face it! If you know what the fears are, you stand a much better chance of overcoming them or making allowances for them, and as a consequence a much better chance of making your relationship work.

In this chapter we will not be comparing the effects of how two people – either or both with fear traits – get along together. The reason for this is that any fear or insecurity, by its very nature, could have a damaging effect on a relationship if that fear is strong. If both partners have fears – even if they are different ones – problems are bound to arise unless they are identified and worked out. Of course, how a fear materializes in one person may be very different from how it materializes in another, and it is dangerous to generalize. All the same, relationships comprising one or both partners with fears are likely to face more difficulties than those that are fear-free.

Jealousy

Jealousy is the fear of being unloved. It shows itself through a peculiar combination of fear and anger. If we are predisposed to jealousy, we become afraid that love and approval will be withdrawn, be this by a parent, partner, colleague or friend. We then become angry towards the person who is threatening to replace us, whether this is a new brother or sister, a step-parent, a sexual rival, acquaintance or colleague.

Jealous people are insecure and feel unable to cope with a situation that others are coping with well. They normally pretend that they are strong – sometimes through loss of temper, underhand behaviour or simply moodiness. But in fact jealousy has its roots in weakness. People become jealous because they feel inadequate and emotionally or physically inferior.

Jealous people often cling tightly to the people on whom they are emotionally dependent because they are terrified of losing the affection of that person. In the workplace jealous people hang on to their position in any way they can, for they are scared of no longer being important, or worried about being replaced by someone else. As we all know, the jealous person more often that not *does* end up losing the partner or position he or she is so scared of losing. This is because they have suffocated the object of their affection to such an extent that he or she has to escape in order to survive.

Jealousy in a sexual or platonic relationship will result in stress and difficulties. If it is caught in the bud, it can be halted or redirected, but if it is misunderstood or allowed to grow and fester, jealousy is bound to cause considerable heartache and misery. A jealous person will be watchful and suspicious of others and will hang on to objects or people in any way he or she can.

Jealousy can be the cause of much unpleasant behaviour. When one person is jealous of another, they may tease relentlessly. Sulking or nagging is often commonplace, as is under-hand manipulation or devious behaviour. Sometimes a jealous person may resort to aggression, trying to overcome his or her rival through force. Alternatively, he may use aggression to stop his rival having what he cannot have. The most frightening example of this is when the loved one is killed in a love-triangle murder case.

A jealous person will rarely admit to being jealous, but

actions speak louder than words! Graphology can help you discover if jealousy is apparent, before jealous actions take place.

❝ Simon and Rufus are brothers. A couple of months ago Rufus started going out with Julie, a beautiful, tall student doctor – the type of girl all other girls would love to hate because of her brains and beauty, but just can't hate, because of her charm! Simon quite naturally is envious of his brother.

'Lucky devil,' he moaned to his best friend. 'Don't know what she sees in Rufus. I'm a much nicer guy!'

Simon's envious feelings are quite normal. After all, his brother has got something that Simon wants! But Simon reacts kindly towards his brother and Julie; he is happy that they are happy, at the same time as wishing Julie, or somebody like Julie, would go out with him.

Unbeknown to Julie, Rufus is a very jealous person. When he sees other men eyeing Julie he feels anger welling up inside him. His smile freezes and his eyes ice over, he feels sick in his stomach. He tries to pretend nothing is wrong, but invariably he grabs hold of Julie and ensures that he is the focus of her attention.

Rufus has become so obsessed with 'keeping' Julie that he is slowly engulfing her. He encourages her to stay over at his flat most nights, so that she doesn't have time to see any of her other friends. He 'forgets' to pass on messages from male friends. He even talked her out of taking up a part-time modelling contract, because he couldn't bear the thought of her being accessible to other men. Deep down, Rufus feels out of Julie's league. He is even jealous of the success she recently had in her medical exams. 'Jobs are for women, careers for men,' he told Simon.

It is quite obvious that Julie will wake up to Rufus' jealousy very soon and no doubt will leave him. The event that Rufus is trying to stop happening is just bound to occur, forced on by his very own actions. ❞

❝ When Leah joined Philipson Global Incorporated – a small recruitment company with a big name – she was overwhelmed by the charm of her boss, Sonia, and the coy confidence of Nicholas, the young Managing Director.

Sonia simply oozed charm. On the telephone she gushed to her clients about how absolutely marvellous it was to speak to them and what an honour it was to do business with them. She explained to Leah in minute detail the steps she had taken during her career to arrive at her current pinnacle of success. 'I am so delighted to have another girl on the team, Leah,' she told her, 'it's time we showed those men how much better women can be.' Sonia jet-setted around Europe and promised Leah that she would shortly be joining her.

Nicholas was full of promises as well. Bolstering Leah's confidence, he told her how wonderful her prospects were and that if she met her targets ('Easy to fulfil,' he promised) she would soon be earning a massive salary. Leah was excited and happy, and eager to meet her challenges.

But by her third month, Leah was beginning to have doubts. She had won two new clients and successfully completed three assignments for Philipson Global Incorporated, exceeding her targets two-fold. Bursting with enthusiasm and expecting a similar response from Sonia, she was immensely disappointed when all Sonia mumbled was, 'You could have done better. I'll be re-evaluating your bonus.'

Sonia seemed to change her attitude dramatically. She was still quite charming to her clients, but to Leah she was cold, distant and relentlessly bossy. It seemed to Leah that she was consumed with jealousy and as a consequence had become dominant and aggressive. Quite why, Leah didn't know.

Things came to a head over the silliest of issues! Leah is one of those sickeningly lucky girls who maintains a consistent weight – well under the average! While she ate chocolate biscuits and jacket potatoes at work, Sonia nibbled at little salads for lunch, frequently declaring to everyone in the office that she was very health-conscious and liked to look good.

One day Sonia turned to Leah and, in a low, icy voice, stated that unless she stopped munching biscuits all day and generally did all the things that Sonia told her to do – unquestioningly she wouldn't have a pay rise or see any of her bonus.

Feeling angry and scared at the same time, Leah decided that her only course of action was to reveal the truth of Sonia's bullying to Nicholas. The second she walked into the room Nicholas started talking in an animated but cold voice. 'I am delighted you are getting on so well with Sonia. She is the best I've got, and I am happy to see that you are being moulded in her caste, although I am disappointed in your results. Sonia has gained three new clients this last month and you haven't got any. You'd, better get moving, we don't carry free-loaders. Off you go now and get on with earning some money.' He opened the door and shovelled her out before she had a chance to say a word.

That afternoon Leah walked out of Philipson Global Incorporated and never went back. Working now in the human resources department of a pharmaceutical company, she simply pulls a scornful face when anyone mentions her ex-employers. 'I feel sorry for them,' she says, 'they won't last long in business treating their employees in that manner.'

Having studied handwriting analysis in her spare time, Leah recently qualified as a graphologist. She decided to dig out some old handwritten memos by Sonia and Nicholas.

Sonia's writing shows strong traits of a domineering nature combined with jealousy. It is easy to recognize that she felt jealous, and threatened by, Leah's success. To combat this jealousy she became dominant and bossy, trying to exert control in the only way she knew how. Nicholas' writing showed him to be a weak character; someone who found it hard to make decisions but who was also domineering. Both of them also demonstrated signs of diplomacy. They certainly knew how to turn on the charm when necessary. Leah understood why the two of them worked well together. They recognized each other's weaknesses and strengths in themselves. They were two of a kind! 9

What to look for?

The best places to look for jealousy in writing are in capital letters, especially the personal pronoun I (e.g. I am going away; I love you) or at the beginning of the letters m and n. Jealousy is shown by a small, flattened loop at the beginning of a letter. These loops always start at the bottom of the circle and are drawn clockwise, up and around, continuing down into the main body of the letter. The loops must be small in comparison to the letter in order to indicate jealousy.

Study the diagram below to gain a clear understanding of what the loop looks like.

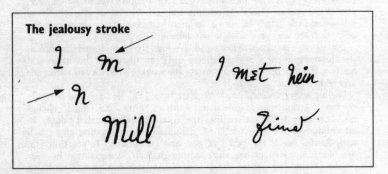

The jealousy stroke

How does jealousy affect compatibility in a relationship?

You can see from the stories above how jealousy can have devastating effects, not only on those who are the victims of jealousy but also on the jealous people themselves. Ultimately they can destroy themselves and their relationships.

If you see jealousy in your own writing, or if you know you are a jealous person, try to control it. Redirect your jealousy into ambition or try talking about it and working out why you are so scared of losing a loved one, a position or something material.

If you see jealousy in your partner's writing, take steps to reassure him or her with your feelings of love. Provide them with a sense of security and attempt to talk about the things that make them feel possessive. Jealous people normally do not recognize the fact that they are jealous, so you will have to be subtle when bringing up the subject. Good luck!

Self-consciousness

People are self-conscious when they are unduly worried about what other people think of them. Generally, self-conscious people have a poor self-image and fear that they may be ridiculed by others. They tend to become ill at ease when around other people, or feel uncomfortably aware that they are being looked at or studied by others. Whether justified or not, these feelings undermine our confidence and lessen our own perception of ourselves.

There are numerous things that may trigger self-consciousness. Stage fright, physical abnormalities, lack of education, different accents, obesity, skinniness or even just wearing the wrong sort of outfit – anything that makes a person conspicuous, and subject to comment or ridicule by others, will make that person self-conscious.

> ❦ Rick was involved in an accident as a small child and as a result has a scarred hand. He suffered enormously from this at school, and even now as an adult dreads meeting new people in case they notice his hand.
>
> Rick's wife Annie is perhaps even more self-conscious than her husband. The daughter of hippie, nomadic but wealthy parents, Annie was sent to boarding school in rural England. Unlike her contemporaries, who wore straight little skirts and neatly pressed shirts, Annie had only tasselled skirts and flared trousers. At parents' day, her parents turned up in caravans or dilapidated trucks, whereas her schoolmates' parents arrived in sleek German or Japanese cars. She was teased mercilessly and had no real friends. Annie dreamed of social acceptance. Even when she was accepted by her contemporaries at university, she still didn't feel as if she fitted in. Terrified of being seen as different, she only mixed with a small 'safe' group of friends.
>
> Rick and Annie give each other enormous comfort and support, as they both understand the handicap of being self-conscious. Overly protective of each other, they rarely go out but keep themselves to themselves. ❧

We all feel self-conscious occasionally. Sometimes we feel perfectly comfortable around our friends or in a social situation, but feel self-conscious or unacceptable in a business environment. Some people feel self-conscious but manage to hide this from anyone else.

What to look for?

Self-consciousness is visible particularly in the letters m and n. Where the final section or hump of an m or n extends above the rest of the letter, self-consciousness is evident. It can also be seen in double t's or l's, where the second t or l is taller than the first. The higher the second bump or letter, and the more often this trait occurs, the more self-conscious the writer is.

The self-conscious stroke

How does self-consciousness in one partner affect a relationship?

Such a relationship can work successfully, so long as the partner unaffected by self-consciousness actively helps his or her partner overcome their fear. If the unaffected partner is not aware of the self-consciousness, or actively takes advantage of his or her partner's self-consciousness then the relationship will quickly fall apart. The self-conscious partner will feel ridiculed even by the person he or she loves most. All self-confidence will be eroded and he or she will become more withdrawn and unhappy. But there is no reason for this to happen if the self-conscious partner is given support and confidence-boosters.

Sensitivity to Criticism

Everybody's greatest need is to be loved, liked and valued. If we do not gain approval from others – especially parents or the people to whom we are closest – we will build up a poor image of ourselves. Eventually we will develop the habit of imagining that people are criticizing or thinking poorly of us, even when they are not.

People become sensitive to criticism as a result of what has happened to them; it is not a trait they are born with or an inherent part of their personality.

❝ Raymond was the eldest child in a large family. Throughout his life he never received any real attention or approval from his mother. Whatever he did wasn't good enough for her. Her joking but scornful manner tore deep wounds in her little son. When he came top of the class she complained that they wouldn't have enough money to send him to university, so he shouldn't aspire too high. When he was chosen to join the basketball team she laughed at him, commenting how amazed she was that they would select a puny little boy like her son. When he tried to help her in the kitchen she told him to get out from under her feet. When he didn't help he was scolded for being lazy. Raymond was a sad and lonely little boy, who grew up into an overly sensitive young man.

He consciously put himself in a position where he did not excel. His girlfriend Justine, who recognizes his talents, compares his sensitivity to criticism to an injury. 'It's like when I broke my arm last year, the slightest little touch was absolute agony. In fact, even the thought of being touched caused me to cringe. That's just like Raymond – it's the fear of being criticized as opposed to actually being criticized that really gets to him.' **〉**

One can imagine that people who are sensitive to criticism put their hands over their ears to avoid hearing words of disapproval. Unfortunately that means that they can't hear words of praise either. Many people successfully hide the fact that they are sensitive to criticism.

〈 Jason and Beverley had been living together for three years when Beverley met a graphologist at a party. Jason was a senior, successful and popular manager at a local engineering factory. People often commented that Jason and Beverley were an unlikely match. Wanting to quell any malicious gossip about their incompatibility, Beverley decided to send in both her own and Jason's writing for a compatibility analysis.

She was stunned when she received the compatibility report back from the graphologist. It arrived in the morning post, after Jason had left for work. She didn't concentrate all morning, she was so surprised by what the report had said. Beverley went out for lunch with her colleague Mary and couldn't stop herself from blurting out some of the things in the report.

'It is so accurate, it's almost freaky,' she told Mary. 'But you know, there's one thing they've got totally wrong. They say that Jason is really sensitive to criticism – you know, really screwed up about what others think about him. That isn't my Jason, Mary. He's pretty laid back, it doesn't fit. I bet he'll have a good laugh when I read that bit out to him.' Beverley sniggered.

'Hold on a second, Bev,' retorted Mary. 'You know, just because he doesn't show he's sensitive to you, or anyone else for that matter, doesn't mean he isn't. If he tells you he gets really upset when you criticize him, the way you tease, he knows you'll criticize him even more. If I were you, I'd be real careful about that bit. In fact, I'd let him read the report himself.'

Beverley sat quietly for a moment. 'Blimey, I'd never even thought about it that way. Just goes to show you can live with someone for years and still not really know them. I'll let you know what his reaction is.'

Beverley took her friend Mary's advice and gave the report to Jason for him to read himself. His only comment was, 'It's spot on!'

Jason cared intensely about what other people thought about him. In his first job he had been torn to pieces by his boss, criticized for everything he did and held up as an example to his colleagues of 'a real loser'. Being proud, Jason did all he could to hide his hurt. Although terrified that other people would think badly of him as well, he knew that to show his lack of confidence would hinder his success greatly.

In fact, because he knows what it is like to suffer from criticism, he takes unusual steps to avoid injuring the feelings of others. Such an empathy makes him a very good and popular manager of people. 〉

What to look for?

Sensitivity to criticism is seen in looped t- and d- stems. The wider and taller the looped d- or t- stem is in relation to the rest of the writing, the more sensitive to criticism the writer will be.

The loop shows imagination, so the greater the imagination, the more the writer imagines criticism and the more sensitive he or she becomes.

It does not matter how tall the t- or d- stems are, or where the t- bar crosses the t- stems. It is just the loop or lack of loop that you are looking for.

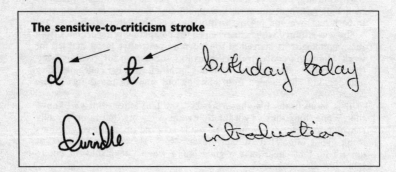

The sensitive-to-criticism stroke

How does sensitivity to criticism in one partner affect compatibility in a relationship?

If one partner is constantly hurt by real or imaginary criticism, he or she will become increasingly fearful of it and will withdraw from others emotionally. Consequently it will be hard for the partner of a self-conscious person to get close to him or her, and the relationship may become very one-sided. On the other hand, the sensitive partner may constantly be requiring reassurance from his or her partner – reassurance that he or she is loved, and good at what he or she does.

Whether the sensitivity to criticism is evident or hidden by either or both partners, the best way to ensure that it does not become a problem in a relationship is to be aware of its existence, to discuss it and not hide it away, and constantly to bolster the sensitive partner's confidence. Unless the sensitivity to criticism is overwhelmingly severe, there is no reason why this trait should undermine a happy relationship, so long as both partners are aware of its existence.

Suppression and Repression

When we have very unpleasant memories, we have the ability to dismiss them from our consciousness and to hide them deep inside ourselves in our unconscious minds. We do not want to recall these memories, because of their unpleasant nature and the resulting bad feelings of danger, anxiety or guilt that remembering them may cause. Although we do not recall these negative memories, they nevertheless have an influence on our behaviour. The hiding away of such thoughts or memories is called repression.

Normally repression begins with the more positive trait of suppression. Suppression takes place when a person consciously stops himself or herself from thinking about an idea, expressing an emotion or acting on an impulse or desire. We all do this frequently in order to conform to the rules of society.

Think of occasions when you have found a stranger very physically attractive and have wanted to touch them. Of course you wouldn't, because you don't know them. So what do you do? You try and dismiss the thought from your mind. Another example is when you are trying to concentrate, perhaps in an important meeting at work. Suddenly images of food come into your mind and you start thinking about what you are going to cook for supper. Quickly you have to banish thoughts of delicious cuisine and concentrate on the meeting. Someone has asked you a question and you didn't listen to what was said!

This conscious mechanism of putting something out of your mind to deal with the issue later is a healthy form of self-discipline. Repression, however, develops when the hiding of thoughts or feelings has become an unconscious habit, so that the person no longer remembers the event or emotion that is being held in check. Repression is something that people do without realizing it.

❥ Maggie runs a self-help therapy group in a small basement room in the heart of the New York Bronx. She invited Mick, a qualified graphologist, to sit in on one of her sessions where the group were acting out past grievances on each other. Mick was asked to look at their handwriting to back up Maggie's analyses.

'Three of my group have extreme problems with repression. Either they can't afford to go to a therapist or they are afraid that a therapist will uncover some repressed emotion they don't yet feel strong enough to deal with. Anyway, they seem to be doing fine here,' said Maggie.

Maggie pointed to a tall man with a long orange beard and warm brown eyes. 'That's Josh. He is running away from something, but we haven't yet worked out what it is. He's highly emotional – feels everything with incredible intensity. He's been taught all his life to hide his strong feelings, so sometimes he simply bursts. He went to prison a couple of years ago for beating up a guy. I reckon that the guy hit on something that Josh was repressing in his subconscious, and those few seemingly inconsequential words just unleashed all his pent-up anger.'

Josh's writing slanted dramatically to the right and was very heavy in weight. The letters were crowded tightly together, making it hard to read. Particularly tight in the middle zone of the writing (the letters a and tops of the letter g, etc.), it showed that Josh was repressing thoughts and feelings that involved day-to-day social situations. It was immediately obvious that he was a highly emotional person and, by repressing these emotions and thoughts, he could build up to a massive outburst – evidenced at least by a huge temper tantrum and at worst by physically hurting himself or someone else.

The young girl Josh was sitting next to was beautiful, petite and Chinese. She sat still and didn't seem to say much.

'Yeah, Moe's the second one with repression problems,' said Maggie, obviously catching Mick glancing at the young girl. 'Moe was abandoned as a child. She has literally frozen all her emotions. She has repressed her feelings for so long that she just can't get in touch with them any more. As you can imagine, people are attracted to Moe by her stunning looks. But no one can get near her. She told me that she's never had a boyfriend – too scared of what they'll do to her.'

Moe's writing slanted backwards. It looked as if she was trying to stop herself from moving forwards into the future. The writing was particularly repressed and squeezed in appearance in the lower loops. This suggests unfulfilled physical and sexual needs and desires.

'Cassie worries me the least of the three. She's the blonde, slightly plump girl walking towards the door. Cassie's parents are extremely rich and possessive. She was taught that certain acts were bad and was punished for doing anything that her parents thought was unacceptable. Unfortunately, Cassie, being the independent spirit that she is, was punished for just about everything! She started coming here a couple of months ago, because she began to get these feelings of overwhelming hatred towards her parents. When they called her and made some criticism, as they always seemed to do, she said that she felt herself going mad. Totally uncontrollable and probably very frightening feelings of destruction.'

'You see why I am not so worried about Cassie?' Maggie went on. 'Cassie is not really repressing her emotions – more like suppression – because she wouldn't have these conscious feelings. Really repressed people are incapable of self-analysis or introspection. No, Cassie just has to distance herself from her parents and perhaps pluck up the courage to tell them what she really thinks about them.'

Based on Cassie's handwriting, Maggie was correct in her analysis. Cassie's writing was not squeezed to nearly the same extent as Josh's or Moe's. Where it was squeezed was in the upper zones, indicating how Cassie had had to accept beliefs on blind faith as opposed to really believing in them. Sensitive to criticism, warm and generous by nature, she obviously did not want to hurt her parents in the way that they had hurt her. 〉

What to look for?

Suppression
Suppression is revealed by occasionally retraced letters in the middle zone.

Repression
Repression is indicated by frequently retraced letters – particularly noticeable in the letters m and n. Retracing occurs when downstrokes of letters, coming down towards the baseline, are retraced by the upstrokes that follow. The overall look of the writing is squeezed.

It is not normally possible to tell where in a person's life the repression or suppression occurs. However, if the writing is particularly retraced in the upper zone, this relates to spiritual or ethical areas; the middle zone relates to everyday, social areas; and the lower zone relates to physical and sexual activities or thoughts.

The suppression and repression strokes

m η r t   concerning

reminding   environment

term   major me

How does suppression or repression affect compatibility in a relationship?

Suppression is unlikely to have any adverse effects on either party in a relationship, even if both partners are practising it regularly. After all, the banishing of thoughts is something that everyone does regularly. It is a conscious mechanism, and anything conscious can be controlled.

Where repression occurs, this can have a debilitating effect on a relationship. Strong repression can result in irrational outburst, which can have devastating consequences. Where people's emotions have been so repressed that they have become frozen, this will also have a negative effect, as they will find it hard – if not impossible – to develop close relationships. Emotionally barren, they will be unable to give or receive love and affection.

Very occasionally, if a person represses their emotions intensely but at the same time is the type of person who feels very strongly, a volcano of emotion literally builds up inside them. Some event may cause this volcano to erupt and the person could get totally out of control. In the most extreme of these cases, suicide is occasionally the result.

A non-repressed person will find it almost impossible to get emotionally close to a repressed partner, who in turn does not feel the need to give or take emotionally. It is rare to find writing that shows intensely strong repression, but those people who do display it generally need to get professional help.

Self-underestimation – the Fear of Failure

Self-esteem is our own personal 'feel-good factor'. Self-esteem is how we value ourselves. A strong self-esteem, or a good feeling of self-worth, is vital to help us achieve in life. Without self-esteem we would have no confidence, and our fear of failure would outweigh our desires to achieve.

A lack of self-esteem – or a poor image of ourselves – is known as self-underestimation. We under-value what we can do; we don't really believe in ourselves; we think that we can't achieve and so we have little or no self-confidence. We feel inferior and incompetent.

People who underestimate their own worth normally deal quite well with everyday affairs but refuse to take on any challenges or look towards the future. They deal with today and let tomorrow worry about itself.

❛ Florence and Paul married straight out of college. Although Florence gained better qualifications than Paul, she quickly fell into the pattern of housewife, bringing up three children and looking after the home. Paul started work at a junior managerial level for a leading supermarket chain. Over the years he followed the normal ladder of career progression.

Paul was not the confident sort. Socially Florence did all the arranging and all the talking. She didn't mind, it gave her a good feeling to take control of the home. What Florence did not realize for many years was that Paul had the same attitude at work. Shy and retiring, he never pushed forwards his ideas and was happy to take a back seat while many of his contemporaries moved jobs, were promoted to work abroad, earned a lot more money and became high-flyers.

One day Florence ran into the wife of an ex-colleague of Paul's. Over a cup of coffee she learned that Paul had pretty much been left behind; he was the black sheep of the bunch. Upset and angry, she decided she would have to push Paul. She felt cheated that her husband wasn't doing as well, that they didn't have enough money to send their kids to private school like their friends. Paul would just have to 'get his butt into gear'.

Day after day, month after month, she started nagging at Paul. Go for that promotion. Apply for a new job. We need the money. When he didn't get the promotion or he failed to get an interview, Florence started sulking and wounding Paul with sarcastic remarks about his failings.

A year of so later, Paul came home one evening and told Florence that he wanted a serious discussion with her. They sent the kids up to their rooms and sat down. Paul told his wife that he had been made redundant and he didn't think it would be easy for him to get another job. But for Florence the real blow came when he said that he wanted a divorce. 'You constantly get at me. I feel bad enough about myself without putting up with the battering from you. I am sorry I didn't meet your expectations. I am not worthy of you or the children, and I have come to the decision that you should be free to find someone who is.' Paul stood up, went upstairs to pack a small suitcase and left the house within minutes. Florence was, quite simply, stunned.

The next day Florence went to Paul's ex-employers and demanded to see the Personnel Manager. A kindly gentleman, he agreed to see Florence against his better judgement.

Florence insisted on being told why Paul had been made redundant and why he had never been promoted in line with his colleagues over the years. The Personnel Manager, Mr Gummer, gently explained to Florence that her husband seemed to be suffering from an extreme lack of confidence. Time after time they had offered him new jobs, or at least the opportunity to take on new challenges, and time after time he had turned them down. Florence was amazed; she knew none of this.

'It seems to me,' said Mr Gummer, 'that your husband has the most overwhelming lack of faith in his own abilities and is obsessed by the fear of failure. We would have made him redundant two years ago, if it had not been that we thought we would compound his personal problems of self-underestimation by taking action that would confirm his poor image of himself. If you don't mind me saying so, madam, I think that your husband needs a great deal of encouragement. He really is a very capable man and I still believe that he could achieve so much more than he lets himself.'

Florence thanked Mr Gummer for his time and left the office. She realized that all she had been doing over the past few years was compounding Paul's problem. Instead of making things better, she had made them considerably worse. ❾

People who underestimate themselves have often been belittled as children. They may have been made to feel inferior by unfavourable comparisons to more successful or competent siblings or classmates. Perhaps the child may have been denied activities that were enjoyed by adults or older siblings, because he was too small or not old enough to participate. Talk and action like this hurt the ego and build the belief in a person that he or she is incompetent.

Even as an adult, if someone is constantly made to feel inferior by others, he or she will ultimately come to believe that that is the reality.

❻ Betty suffers acutely from self-underestimation. She has an unhappy marriage and works all hours of the day to help make ends meet. During the daytime she makes parts of garments in a sewing factory; at night she cleans offices. Her parents divorced when she was young, and neither of them seemed to have time for her when they remarried and then remarried again. Her husband spends little time at home, and when he's not on the road he is in the local pub.

Betty pushes away her feelings of inferiority by dreaming. She imagines herself as boss of the factory, married to some wonderfully kind, wealthy Italian count. So long as she is in her dream world she is happy and feels confident. When reality seeps back in she plummets down to earth, feeling useless and sad. ❾

What to look for?

Self-underestimation is revealed in writing by t-bars that are placed low down on the stem, level or even below the top of the middle-zone letters. The lower the t-bar is placed, the easier the goals are for the person to achieve, and the less they have to challenge themselves in order to achieve their aims. People with low t-bars tend to feel that they are beneath others and unworthy of personal success. They constantly anticipate failure, preferring to stick with what they know and are familiar with.

If the t-bars are low but the rest of the writing is even, well spaced and easy to read, the writer could fear success rather than failure. They may be worried that success brings too many responsibilities or could plunge them into a limelight that they would rather avoid.

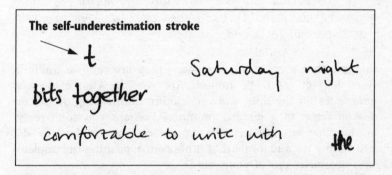

The self-underestimation stroke

How does self-underestimation affect compatibility in a relationship?

People who underestimate themselves can erode existing or potentially successful relationships. The self-underestimating partner may believe that he or she is not worthy of his or her partner, and may not want to plan for the future, making things very difficult for the other partner. If the secure partner becomes successful, the underestimating partner may feel that he or she cannot keep up.

Self-underestimation, like any fear, needs to be recognized and then it can be dealt with. If the trait is allowed to grow it will eventually cause problems of guilt, insecurity and emotional imbalance in a relationship.

5

Do You React in the Same Way?

- *How do you react when you get upset? Do you scream and shout in anger or do you take a deep breath and shrug it off? Or perhaps you retort with sarcastic words?*
- *Do you know if your partner is the violent type? And how does your partner react under stress?*

Imagine that someone upsets you – they are rude or unkind. How do you react? Be honest! Are you the kind of person who 'goes off the deep end', screaming or shouting abuse, or do you retort in a sarcastic manner? Perhaps you don't reply at the time but are irritable for the rest of the day? Or do you simply try and forget that it happened, pushing the unpleasant memories out of your mind?

Rarely do two people have exactly the same reaction to an experience. In fact, many partners find that they respond in very different ways.

❛ Nadia and her boyfriend Patrick had spent weeks organizing a group of their friends to go on a skiing trip to France. Co-ordinating dates, confirming prices, advising on what to wear and what to bring had consumed all their spare time. A fortnight beforehand everyone, with the exception of Murray, had paid their deposits. Murray assured Nadia that he would bring his cheque with him when they met to catch their train at Victoria Station.

At long last the first day of their holiday arrived. At five o'clock in the morning nine of them huddled in the cold, waiting to get on the train that was to take them across Europe. They found their compartments, stored away the luggage and made themselves comfortable. It was Patrick who first realized that Murray wasn't with them. He rushed out of the train onto the platform, in the hope of finding him.

'Excuse me, sir,' bellowed a guard, 'but you need to get back on the train immediately if you wish to travel on it. We are leaving in ten seconds.' Patrick hopped back on, the whistle was blown, and the train chugged out of the station.

Patrick wandered back to his friends and sat down dejectedly. 'Great, he missed the train. What are we going to do?'

Louise, one of Nadia's friends, replied, 'Perhaps he is on the train. He could have got into another carriage and not have found us yet.'

'That's a good point,' Nadia said. 'Patrick, why don't you go and look for him.'

But fifteen minutes later Patrick returned alone.

When they reached their ski resort, Louise, ever the optimist, expected to find Murray already there. 'You know what he's like,' Louise told the others during the journey. 'Murray's such a lazybones he probably just hopped on an aeroplane and couldn't be bothered to sit on the train for so many hours.'

Of course Murray wasn't there. He didn't turn up at all during the holiday, and when they tried to phone him at home, the only voice that answered was that of his answer machine.

Nadia was furious. On several occasions when they discussed him she lost her temper, taking out her anger on Patrick. 'I'm going to murder him when we get home,' she screamed. 'How could he let us down like that. And now we all have to pay so much extra to cover his selfish behaviour.' Nadia ranted and raved for hours.

Patrick didn't respond much. He told everyone to forget about Murray. He intended to deal with him when they got home. But on their return Patrick did nothing. 'I'll call him tomorrow,' he told Nadia every day of the week. But he never did.

Patrick is a nice guy – everyone likes him – but he tends to put off doing the things he isn't too keen on having to do. He is a typical procrastinator. In the end it was Nadia who called Murray.

Louise had been secretly in love with Murray for months. She adored his jet-black hair and piercing green eyes and was hugely disappointed that he hadn't turned up. The first few days of the holiday she spent planning the passionate affair that would develop between them when Murray did turn up. Midway through the holiday she began to despair and became convinced that something awful had happened to Murray – hence the reason that he hadn't arrived. She decided that she would have to return home to rescue him. It was her friend Sarah who stopped Louise from acting on her daydreams.

Sarah herself was relishing the moment when she would see Murray. Her reaction to disappointments and people upsetting her was to retort with a sarcastic tongue. Few people liked to cross Sarah, a successful journalist. She could easily turn people to mincemeat, crushing them with her wounding words. Sarah knew exactly what she was going to say to Murray – biting words that would hurt.

Not too long before the holiday, Dean had nearly been arrested for trying to beat up a stranger at the local pub. Normally docile, when he gets into an argument and has had a couple of beers, Dean can get violent. The other eight were really quite glad that Murray didn't turn up halfway through the holiday, because the chances were that Dean would try to punch him in the face.

Tasha, Dean's girlfriend, generally just pretends that everything's okay.

She doesn't do this by forgetting, but rather by adopting a bravado atti-tude. She told the others that she'd be giving Murray 'a really good piece of my mind, when I next see him. And then that's the end of our friend-ship.' But no one believed Tasha. She was always saying big, brave things but never actually carrying them out when it came to the crunch.

Her friends were forgiving of her, because Tasha had a good sense of humour and was kind in her quirky little way. Besides, a number of her friends were rather concerned that she could end up getting hurt by Dean. Predictably, when they got home, Tasha never said a thing to Murray.

Each of these friends had the same reason to be upset – they would have to pay extra for their holiday to cover Murray's not showing up. They had every reason to feel let down and upset. Although they were all faced with the same annoying circumstance, each of them reacted to the problem in a different way. **❥**

Some reactions have few consequences on our relationships, but there are others that may cause problems. It is these reac-tions that we will be considering in this chapter. After all, it is very useful to be able to predict how someone is going to react. Read on and see what I mean!

Argumentativeness

A person is argumentative if they argue for the sake of doing so. Argumentative people defend their opinions at all costs, for to back down would be like losing face. Such people find a reason to debate any issue.

Argumentativeness is frequently seen as tantamount to anger. Unless it is kept under control, it is generally not consid-ered to be a positive trait.

❦ 'Where did you get that shirt from?' Sheila snapped at her husband Billy. 'That must have cost a fortune and you know we don't have the money!'

'I didn't spend lots of money on it,' retorted Billy.

'Oh don't give me those lies, I can spot a moneywaster when I see one. Frankly, I think you should take it back and get a refund.'

'That's deceitful,' said Billy, getting worked up. 'Besides which, I didn't buy it!'

'So you stole it then, did you?' screamed Sheila. 'I'm married to a bloody thief! WHY can't you do anything properly?'

And so the argument would have gone on and on, but Billy just agreed to take the shirt back. In fact, he hadn't bought it but had been given it by his brother. Sheila, in her typically argumentative fashion, just hadn't given him a moment to explain the real story. **❥**

❝ Kirk is a barrister. Tall, dark and gorgeous, especially in his wig, he is the most popular single man on the London dinner party circuit. When Kirk is around the conversation is always animated and exciting. He antagonizes people but can turn on the charm the second he becomes a little too forceful. To Kirk, arguing is an extension of his job, and he enjoys it purely as an intellectual exercise. If someone can prove through clear, logical thought that he or she is right and Kirk is wrong, Kirk will, – albeit sometimes grudgingly – accept it.

Jody and Grahame live on the other side of the world from Kirk, but sometimes their neighbours imagine that their arguments must be able to be heard throughout Europe. Every night they can hear Jody's voice screaming at Grahame. Jody is basically an insecure lady; she constantly feels that she has to defend and justify her ideas and actions. Grahame, being rather good-natured, thinks Jody's screaming fits are rather a laugh. Most people would be driven mad. ❞

There are many different types of argumentative people. Some people exaggerate and distort realities in support of their argument. Others just stick vigorously to the facts. Some people are able to combine tact with argumentativeness and they make pleasant opponents. Undoubtedly the worst kind of argumentative person is the type who uses violence to back up his or her verbal attack.

What to look for?
Argumentativeness is seen in the small letter p. It is only evident when the p is made with an initial stroke that is higher than the circle part of the letter. The taller and larger the stroke, the stronger the trait of argumentativeness in the writer.

The shape of this initial stroke gives some indication of the type of argument in which the writer indulges.

1. When the initial stroke is made in the form of a loop, this means that the person will bring imagination into his or her arguing and may well distort the facts.
2. When the initial stroke is a sharp point, the person will be able to argue about abstract concepts but in a factual and unimaginative way.
3. When the p-stem (the stroke that goes down below the baseline) is also made of a loop, this means that the writer likes physical activity. The chances are that their argumentativeness could lead to violence. At best he or she likes to argue with force, even if this is not physical force.

Samples of the argumentative 'p'

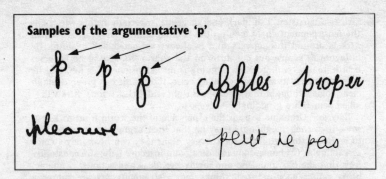

How does argumentativeness affect compatibility in a relationship?

Some people like to argue and others don't. So it is important that you are compatible on this issue.

An argumentative partner with a non-argumentative partner

If you end up in a relationship with someone who thrives on arguments and this is something that you dread, you will quickly become exhausted, upset and want to get out of the relationship. Argumentative people are often insecure and force their way in order to bolster their own self-image. The argumentative partner may well be driven to fury if his or her partner does not join in the argument. Such a relationship will be difficult.

Two argumentative partners together

Two argumentative people will have an incredibly feisty relationship! But sometimes there will simply not be enough space in a relationship for two big egos, both wanting to prove themselves right. If there is sufficient space for both, although they may be happy together, it is unlikely that they will have lots of friends as a couple. People quickly tire of hearing others banter or argue.

Violence

Aggressive, violent behaviour involves actions that are intended to harm or injure another person.

❛ Laura was head over heels in love. She had met Ted two weeks before and their relationship had developed like a dream. Handsome Ted had taken her out for dinner, to the theatre, cooked for her at his place and swept her off to a country cottage for the weekend. He sent her roses at work and charmed her with witty poems. Sex was fantastic and Laura just couldn't concentrate on anything except Ted. She felt as if she were floating.

That night she was cooking at her apartment and he was invited for seven o'clock. Half-past seven slipped by, eight o'clock came and went and still there was no sign of Ted. At a quarter to nine, when the burned food was cooling off in the oven, Ted rang the doorbell. He came in looking dishevelled and pushed Laura away when she tried to embrace him.

'Darling, what's happened?' Laura asked, concerned.

'Oh . . . just leave me alone, will you. You're lucky I made it at all.'

Scared and upset that she might have done something to provoke him, Laura proceeded to serve him dinner.

'I'm sorry it's a bit burned,' said Laura, 'but then I was expecting you at seven.'

'I know you bloody were and I'm not going to eat this rubbish.' Ted picked up his plate, hurled it at the wall and walked straight out of the front door.

Stunned and horrified, Laura cried her eyes out all night. The next day she called work to say that she was sick. She felt unable to face anyone. During the afternoon the doorbell rang and one hundred red roses were delivered by a florist. 'I am so sorry. Please forgive me. I really love you. Yours, Ted,' read the letter. An hour later he was on the phone begging forgiveness, explaining that he had had a terrible day at work the day before, and would she come out to dinner with him that night?

For the next few weeks Laura never caught a glimpse of the raging Ted that she had seen that night.

When Ted asked her to go on holiday with him, she agreed eagerly. The first few days were idyllic. Lying on the soft white sand, basking in the intense heat of the tropical sun and cooling off in the gentle blue sea, Laura glowed as the other girls stared enviously at her as she hung on the arm of her gorgeous Ted.

Then one evening no water came out of the shower in their hotel room. Ted looked annoyed. He rang the hotel reception to be told that the whole hotel had a problem and that they would resolve it as quickly as possible. Ten minutes later the electricity cut out. Ted began pacing furiously up and down the room.

'I'm hungry. I'm going to order room service,' he said. After a brief chat on the phone, Ted threw it on the floor and swore loudly.

'What's up?' Laura asked gently. 'Why don't we go out for supper?'

Laura was horrified by Ted's reaction. He grabbed hold of her and shook her hard before storming out of the room.

Terrified, and in shock, she threw her belongings into her suitcase and took a taxi to the airport, where she booked herself on the next plane home. For two hours she hid in the ladies' toilets, coming out just in time to walk straight onto the plane.

Ted is quite typical of many violent people. They can be the nicest of individuals at times, then suddenly lose all self-control and explode, taking out their anger and tension on their loved ones or even total strangers. As a child he was consistently beaten by his father. At school he became a bully, and when he grew up he beat up his lovers whenever he became stressed or frustrated. 🍣

What to look for?

There are a number of different signs to look for when assessing violence. Unless you find all or the majority of these signs in a sample of writing, then the person is not fundamentally violent.

Variations in slant, letter size and spacing

The writing looks as if it is being pulled in different directions. Check this by measuring the emotional slant angles, as described in Chapter 1. Variations in letter height and spacing between letters and words can normally be seen simply by looking at the writing.

Heavy pressure that in places becomes muddy and smeary

Again, refer back to Chapter 1 if necessary. Heavy pressure means that the writer uses a lot of force when writing. Touch the back of the page to see if you can feel where the writing has pressed through. Often the lines of the writing will be thick. If the lines are very thick in places, or the writing looks messy and smeared, this is one of the indications of violence.

Very heavy angular writing with slashing strokes and sharp angles

This contains lots of sharp lines and points, with lines drawn through letters where not strictly necessary.

Argumentative p's with the initial stroke higher than the circle, and looped p-stems

These two together show argumentativeness combined with physical needs. Often this means violent behaviour.

Larger letters in the middle of other letters

Where some letters are written much larger than other letters within words, this is one of the signs to look for when assessing possible violence.

Samples of violent writing

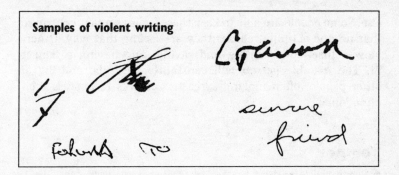

How does violence affect compatibility in a relationship?

Needless to say, violence and relationships do not mix. There are too many unfortunate people who are the victims of violent partners, whose lives are simply ruined. If you even suspect your partner of being violent, get out of the relationship if you possibly can, or get professional help.

Aggressive and violent people are more likely to elicit reciprocal aggressive responses from the people with whom they mix. Often aggressive individuals select other aggressive people to associate with. On the other hand, if the aggressive person is also a bully – the type of person who goes out of his or her way to be unfair and takes advantage of people whenever they are in a weaker position – then that person may knowingly select a weaker person as his or her partner, with whom he can act out his violent, bullying ways.

Violent people tend to breed violent people. To a certain extent, aggression is known to be part of one's genes, but if children are victims or a witness to violent behaviour during childhood, they stand a higher chance of becoming violent offenders themselves when they grow up.

Temper and Irritability

All of us feel angry or irritated on occasion. Normally this feeling is triggered if something hasn't gone the way we wanted it to. We may be angry with ourselves or with somebody else. Some people are able to keep these feelings under control so that no one actually realizes they are feeling that way. Others blow a fuse, start ranting and raving, and having a temper fit. The irritable person will constantly nag, jibe and dig at other people, often making sarcastic remarks to express their annoyance.

Temper

❢ Gareth and Serena met for the first time when she walked into the estate agents where Gareth works, requesting to be put on their register to rent a flat. Particularly impressed by her dark auburn hair and her short skirt revealing long, long legs, Gareth decided personally to show Serena every apartment on their books. Drinks and dinner frequently followed the viewing of properties and two weeks later they were formally dating.

One evening Serena popped into the estate agents and got chatting to Damien, a colleague of Gareth's.

'Has Gareth shown you his red-hot temper yet?' Damien enquired, laughing.

'Absolutely not,' retorted Serena. 'He's been nothing but a gentleman.'

'Well, just remember to duck when he gets angry, and I'm always here if you need a shoulder to cry on. I'm pretty used to it by now.'

Before Serena could ask what he meant, Gareth came bounding into the office.

'Right, Serena, let's go. There's another flat I need to show you!' He winked and held open the door.

'Well, actually, Damien and I were having a rather important chat. Perhaps Damien could show me the flat and I'll see you later?'

'What!' Gareth looked at her in horror, picked up his briefcase and marched out of the office, slamming the door so that the walls trembled around them.

'Welcome to the real Gareth!' sighed Damien. 'Serena, I've got to work with Gareth every day of my life. I don't think it's a good idea if I show you this flat. Why don't you run along after Gareth and I'll go home as I planned to do all along.'

Serena managed to catch up with Gareth just as he was about to get on the bus home. Ignoring her out-of-breath pleas for him to wait for her, he climbed on the bus and sat down next to an elderly lady, so that Serena had to sit in the furthest possible seat away from him at the back of the bus.

As they got off the bus, Gareth turned round to Serena and started shouting at her. Passers-by stopped and listened. Ranting and raving, stamping his feet, he screamed at her. Finally he wrenched open the door of his house and hurled himself inside.

Stunned, Serena sat on his steps and burst into tears. So much for the promise of a great relationship – he had just told her he never wanted to see her again.

Five minutes later, just as she was about to compose herself and wander off to catch the first bus home, Gareth appeared from the side of his house carrying a small bunch of flowers clearly just picked from his neighbour's garden.

'I'm so sorry, darling. Please forgive me, I just went loopy for a while there. Let me make it up to you.'

Gareth's temper quickly became a regular in their relationship. Serena worked out that as soon as something didn't quite go the way that Gareth had planned it, he felt out of control and his temper unleashed an astonishingly strong fury.

Many of her girlfriends were amazed that she put up with Gareth. 'He's never violent,' she explained, 'and his temper fits pass so quickly. It's not like he sulks for ages on end, and he's not the irritable sort. Once he has had a temper fit it really clears the air. It's just part of Gareth and something that I am prepared to accept, because I love him.' **9**

People with hot tempers generally do not have lots of friends, as few people are prepared to put up with them on a regular basis. Rather than being caught in the crossfire, they keep out of the way.

6 Bess had been feeling low for nearly three years. Her unhappiness was compounded by frequent bouts of minor sickness. To begin with she had blamed her depression on the fact that her husband had left her. But that was over two years ago now and she was starting out on a new relationship.

All the same, she still felt such anger towards her ex-husband. Whenever anyone mentioned his name she felt a silent, mad rage boiling up inside her. She buried the anger, for Bess didn't like to show her feelings in front of the children.

It was her boyfriend who finally discovered why Bess was constantly feeling miserable. He realized that she has a temper – an extraordinarily destructive temper. But, unable to express that temper most of the time, she represses it and it makes her ill. Although he never said anything directly to Bess, he guessed that her temper was partly to blame for the breakdown of her marriage. After several unpleasant tantrums, followed by periods of silence and a particularly bad stomach pain, Bess agreed to go to a counsellor to talk through her anger.

Looking back, Bess realizes the extent to which her boyfriend has helped her. Not only did her health improve, but she was able to carry on a relationship without destroying it with her temper. **9**

People lose their temper for numerous different reasons – but normally when their ego is assaulted in some way. They may feel out of control, in fear of something, or threatened. If you have ever lost your temper (and be honest with yourself!), think about what triggered you to lose control, what made you so angry? If you are aware of the triggers, then you may be able to stop yourself from losing your temper in the future.

What to look for?

When a person's temper is strong or easily triggered it will show in his or her handwriting. If the person has writing of an upright or backward slant, or he or she is a very proud person, then other people – even those closest to them – may not be aware that they have a temper. The individual may feel the temper but not let it show to others. So if you are surprised to see temper strokes in the writing of someone who rarely, if ever, loses his or her temper, do not dismiss it as being wrong. It could just mean that the person represses this emotion.

Temper is indicated in writing when you see a short, straight line occurring at the beginning of a word or portion of a word. This line is known as a tick, as it has the appearance of being made with a quick, jabbing motion.

Other signs indicating temper in writing include sharp, pointed, angular lines in general as well as a t-bar that flies off to the right of a t-stem.

Samples of the temper tick

Irritability

Irritable people get annoyed by everyday occurrences. Their feelings are not usually as intense as the strong feelings felt by people with a temper. Irritable emotions are normally milder and shorter-lived, and aggravated by insignificant issues.

People who are irritable become snappy and difficult. They express restlessness, dislikes and impatience with themselves or with other people. Irritable people tend to be dissatisfied – either temporarily or all the time. It is difficult to get on with people who are constantly irritable. They are short with others, and seem perpetually discontented and frustrated.

❝ When her husband died, Martha's son and daughter-in-law suggested that she came to live with them and their children in their large house in the countryside. Reluctantly Martha agreed, but stipulated that the arrangement was to be on a six-month trial basis.

Those months were the worst in the family's memory. 'Do this. Do that,' nagged Martha at her grandchildren. She made constant jibes at her daughter-in-law, implying that she didn't run the house efficiently and that by going out to work she was neglecting her husband and children. She never had a kind word to say to her son. She locked the dog out of the house whenever she had the opportunity, complaining that the animal was dirty.

Martha made her family's life a misery with her constant irritability. Nothing was ever right. Sadly, after four months she agreed that the best place for her was an old people's home.

It was obvious to her son that Martha's new-found irritability was largely due to her feelings of inadequacy. She was annoyed with herself that she was no longer physically able to live alone and as a consequence had to live with her family. No doubt she felt guilty that she was getting in their way. But, whatever the reason, such irritability was enough to make them all go mad. ❞

If someone is consistently irritable, this is likely to have more of an adverse effect on their relationships and their job than someone who occasionally loses their temper and clears the air. Bitterness and nagging are intolerable even to the most patient of people.

Some people are only irritable when they are tired, stressed or nervous. But whatever the reason, it is hard to be close and affectionate with an irritable person.

What to look for?

Irritability can be seen in writing where the letter i or the j dot is jabbed or distorted. The dot looks as if it has become elongated flying across the page. If there are other small flying strokes above the baseline, for instance punctuation or simply marks on the page, this supports the likelihood of irritability in the writer.

Samples of irritability

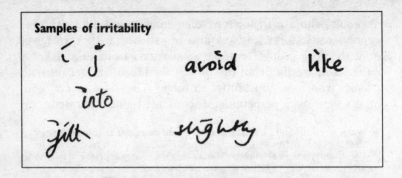

How are temper and irritability likely to affect compatibility in a relationship?

Both temper and irritability are likely to have adverse effects on a relationship. If temper or irritability is very strong in the handwriting, then the chances are that that person will be hard to live with, and few partners are likely to have the necessary patience and loving care to put up with them in the long term.

Both partners with a temper
This is likely to be an explosive relationship. Could be lots of fun – so long as the neighbours don't complain too much!

One partner with a temper, one without
If the person without a temper can tolerate his or her partner's outbursts there is no reason why this relationship should not work. Of course, if the temper gets out of hand or the partner becomes violent then the relationship is likely to break down.

One partner with a temper, the other with irritability
The irritable partner is likely to propel the temper partner into having a temper fit. Conversely, the temper partner could propel the irritable partner into having full-blown temper fits as well. This could be an explosive and difficult relationship.

Both partners with irritability
Although such a relationship could work for the partners involved, they will find it hard to maintain friends, who will be put off by their constant bickering.

One partner with irritability, the other without

Constant irritability is likely to have an eroding effect on a relationship. The person without irritability needs great patience and understanding.

Procrastination

How many people do you know who say they are going to do something and then don't do it? Unfortunately it seems a phenomenon of our times that more people let you down than do what they say they are going to do. Such actions leave other people disillusioned, frustrated and annoyed. Often people don't do something because they simply forget or run out of time. Sometimes it is because they don't want to do it and would rather put it off until tomorrow because there is something better to do today.

People who procrastinate often have good intentions but keep putting them off, seldom getting beyond wishful thinking. Procrastination can, however, halt someone's success on the work front and can also have a negative effect on relationships.

❝ Maria and Andrew had been going out together for five years. Out of all their friends they seemed to be the only couple who hadn't got married.

Maria was beginning to get panicky. At thirty-four she desperately wanted to settle down and have children. Although she and Andrew lived together most of the time, she did not want her family to know about this. They were religious and would have been devastated to know that their daughter was having an affair without being married. So the idea of her having children outside wedlock was not a possibility.

It was difficult for her to discuss marriage with Andrew. Whenever the subject arose he clammed up, changed the topic of conversation or said, 'There's plenty of time for that yet.' He had been telling his mates for years that he was going to marry Maria. Many of their friends had even forgotten that they weren't married – they were such an item! The trouble was he just never got around to doing it.

One day he went home and Maria had removed all her belongings. A little note propped up on the kitchen table explained why.

Darling Andy,

I love you but I can't wait any longer. For five years you have been telling me that we will be getting married next year. But that year never came. Whenever I brought up the subject you didn't want to talk about it. I want to start a family within a marriage. So I am going to find someone who wants to do it with me. This is the most painful decision of my life. I think I shall always love you, but I am fed up with constantly being disappointed. I wish you everything. Please do not try to contact me.

Yours forever, Maria

With a broken heart, Maria went back to live with her parents. A couple of weeks later she received an overseas telephone call, a lady with a strong foreign accent. It was Andrew's mother. During their long chat she told Maria a few stories about Andrew.

Eventually she said, 'Andrew adopts a mañana, mañana attitude. Ever since he was a child he has been a bit of a dreamer. For the last six years he has been telling me every year that he will come home to visit us. He never has. His brother told me that he has had a bad time at work because he is lazy. I am very sad about my son, but I think by leaving him you have done the best thing, Maria. Now there is someone I want you to talk to. Do not put down the phone.'

Surprised, Maria waited on the telephone. Soon there was Andrew's familiar voice.

'Maria, please will you marry me?' Incredulous, she didn't say a word. 'Please say yes,' he continued. 'Tomorrow morning you will be receiving an aeroplane ticket for a flight to visit me and my family here. I will be waiting for you at the airport. I love you and I can't live without you.'

Andrew and Maria had a beautiful wedding. Of course it wasn't the end of their problems, as Andrew continued to put things off throughout his life. He procrastinated about issues of great importance and anything he was unsure about. Maria had physically to stand over him and force him to write out his CV before he would apply for a new job. It was the pattern of their life. He was the dreamer and she the doer. But they love each other so the relationship works. ❯

Procrastinators avoid certain types of activity or decision, but they may do well under pressure. Sometimes procrastination is evident in a person's writing because they are putting off what they would really like to do with their lives. That is the case with Jilly.

❮ Jilly knows that she is procrastinating and is the first to admit it. 'All I really want to do is travel around the world for two years,' she told me. 'Unfortunately I just don't have the money, so I am putting it off until I do. The trouble is I like spending money and I'm finding it very hard saving enough. I've decided to look for a rich husband instead!' Jilly is procrastinating for a specific reason. ❯

What to look for?
Procrastination is evidenced in writing by two things:

1. T-bars that fly to the left of the t-stem
2. Letter i and j dots flying to the left of the i- or j-stem. It doesn't matter what shape these i dots are.

The further to the left of the stems, the stronger the trait of procrastination. Left t-bars indicate that the writer puts off actions, and i or j dots indicate that the writer puts off details.

Samples of procrastination

How does procrastination affect compatibility in a relationship?

Procrastination cannot have a positive effect on relationships because one partner is constantly letting either him- or herself down and not achieving to full capacity, or is letting his or her partner down by promising something but never fulfilling that promise.

Procrastination often results in unreliability. Within short-term relationships this uncertainty may cause a certain excitement and a *frisson* of unpredictability. In the long term there are few non-procrastinating partners who will have the love and patience to put up with a procrastinator. The procrastinator will lose out eventually.

Bluff

People who bluff tend to be all talk and no action! They pretend that they are particularly good at something, or strong or important, when in fact all they are doing is boasting and bragging about something that is not true.

Bluffers bluff in different ways!

❝ During her life, Liza has known three bluffers. One was a girl friend, the second she had an affair with and the third she married! Liza reckons she is an expert bluffer-spotter and hires out her services to any friends who think they may have stumbled across one! She explained what to look for.

'Grace was a friend I made at secretarial college. For months she told everyone that she had got into Oxford University to study law, but she just couldn't be bothered with such a long study and simply wasn't ambitious. All she wanted to do was the odd bit of secretarial work until at twenty-one she had access to her substantial trust fund and could retire in luxury! Grace always wanted to be the centre of attention. She danced most nights away but never drank alcohol. At the time I couldn't figure out why. Now I realize that she didn't want to lose control in case she let her mask fall.

'I, like all our other friends, lost touch with Grace after college. But imagine my surprise when I ran into her at a temping agency five years later. At twenty-five her trust fund should have been in full swing. We went out for a cup of coffee and I realized that she was a different person. Totally down-to-earth, a really nice girl.

'She admitted to me that all her talk had been bluff. Throughout her childhood she had struggled to meet the expectations of her parents. When she failed her A-levels and went to secretarial college it was the ultimate humiliation and failure as far as her parents were concerned. Because Grace had such a poor image of herself she decided to start afresh and make out to her new friends that she was something she wasn't. "I hated all that pretence," she said. "As soon as I left college I could become myself again. That's why I dropped all my friends. I couldn't let them see that I had been lying!"

'Grace taught me a lot about bluffers because she could admit to having been one. Unfortunately by then I was already involved with the second bluffer in my life – Anthony. He gave a marvellous show of bravado. He claimed to be a champion skier and a fabulous rugby player. As he was in the army at the time, he was sent out to the former Yugoslavia to assist in peace-keeping. I sent him letters and food and book parcels most days. He wrote me long airmail letters giving detailed descriptions about his bravery. "Can't tell you too much you realize," he wrote, "I am bound to secrecy!"

'When he came back I gave him a real hero's welcome. Unfortunately it wasn't long before I realized it had all been bluff. I met a friend of his who told me the real story: how Anthony had been terrified; he ran in the wrong direction, fell over and sprained his ankle so that he couldn't stay with his platoon.

'Of course I soon learned that he was a novice at skiing and had never made the rugby team. Poor Anthony blew up his own achievements and flaunted them at others to hide the truth – that he was really rather inadequate!

'I married Oliver a year ago. He is a lovely man, and his form of bluffing is rather different from most others.' He bluffs to hide his real emotions. Very scarred by a disastrous relationship a few years ago, Oliver makes out that he is confident and strong. He loves attention and pretends to be in control all of the time. The truth is he is deeply cautious and finds it very hard to let anyone get close to him emotionally. I am pregnant now and expecting twins! Oliver and I are looking forward to bringing up our little bluffers!' 〉

As a rule, bluffing damages a person's integrity – because if they are bluffing they are generally lying. Anyone who 'pulls the wool over someone else's eyes' is not to be trusted. Socially, a bluffer is unlikely to have many close friends. People quickly tire of their outrageous claims and the bluffer will find him – or herself discredited and alone.

Bluff is a front used to conceal weakness or fears. These could be fear of failure, disapproval, inability, ridicule or rivalry. Whatever the fear, bluff is used as a shield of armour under which the fear can hide. Because a person feels inadequate, he or she will add a showy touch to their behaviour by pretending that everything is under control.

Of course some bluffers – especially those where the trait is not so well developed – are harder to expose. Being able to check for bluff in handwriting is very useful, especially if you are just embarking on a relationship with someone and they are claiming great things about themselves! Remember that bluff may just be a reaction to help a person get through a difficult situation without losing face. Bluff may not be a permanent feature of that person's personality.

What to look for?

Bluff is seen in writing when there are exceedingly heavy, often long, blunt strokes below the baseline that look entirely out of proportion to the rest of the writing. Often these downstrokes get larger and heavier, the longer they become.

Samples of bluff

How does bluff affect compatibility in a relationship?

Bluff can be damaging because it means that one partner is trying to conceal something from the other. Obviously any form of deceit is dangerous in a relationship. If the real reasons for the bluffing are exposed, then it may be possible for the person to overcome his or her fears, to confront them and dispel them.

Using graphology to check out bluffing is invaluable. But then you must decide in which areas of their life the bluffer is bluffing! It will be necessary to tread carefully with bluffers, as you are dealing with their insecurity. Sometimes, when the bluffer learns to trust you and feels secure in the relationship, he or she will gradually learn to drop their cover of pretence and bluffing may become a thing of the past.

Stubbornness

Stubborn people like to be difficult! They decide on a course of action or a standpoint and refuse to be swayed from it, even when it is obvious to themselves and others that they are wrong. Stubborn people simply refuse to accept other people's viewpoints.

6 Ruth is stubborn. Adopting such an attitude is a defence for her; she cannot accept the possibility of losing face. What she doesn't realize is that her friends laugh at her and don't take her seriously. 'She can't honestly believe that,' they say, 'she's just being difficult for the sake of being so.'

As a child, Ruth was described by her mother as 'stubborn as a mule'. One day in particular stands out in her mother's memory. It began at breakfast time when Ruth started pushing her food around on her plate, refused to eat the crusts of her bread and slouched in her chair. When her mother told her to sit up she slouched even more. She simply refused to take in what she was told to do. Halfway through the day, Ruth's mother received a telephone call from the school apologizing for disturbing her but asking if she could come to see the headmistress when she picked Ruth up from school that afternoon.

In the late afternoon she was ushered into the stark, brown-panelled room of the headmistress.

'We have a problem with Ruth. This morning she was in a biology lesson. As you may be aware, Ruth and her class are currently studying reproduction. I understand that they have learned about the reproduction of tadpoles and mice, and today they were shown a non-explicit, rather clinical film on human reproduction. Halfway through this film

Ruth and a classmate got into an argument, whereupon Ruth insisted that the film was a joke and that she had not been conceived sexually but delivered by some kind of a bird, to you, her parents.

'The biology teacher, Mrs Mates, switched off the film and tried to explain gently to Ruth and a few other members of the class the true facts of life. Unfortunately Ruth just would not accept what she was saying. Your daughter stood up, started shouting and behaved really rather appallingly. Mrs Mates quite correctly dismissed Ruth from the classroom.

'It seems to me that on the one hand it is rather sweet that Ruth can be so innocent in this day and age. On the other hand, this behaviour is indicative of her normal behaviour. She is such a stubborn young lady, she will never listen to anyone else's point of view, an attitude that is very disruptive in the classroom. So I was wondering if there were any problems at home?'

In the car on the way home Ruth refused to talk to her mother. She rushed up to her room and stayed there all evening. Sobs could be heard through her bedroom door. Of course Ruth realized she was in the wrong but she just couldn't admit it to anyone.

As Ruth grew older and emerged the other side of adolescence she did mellow to a certain extent. But she does find it hard to maintain relationships – even though she now appreciates the true facts of life! A couple of weeks ago she wrote to the problem page of a famous women's magazine asking for advice on why it was that she couldn't keep a steady boyfriend. Two to three weeks into a relationship and they finished with her. She hasn't got an answer yet, but no doubt it will tell her that she has to be more flexible, more understanding and forgiving of other people, and more prepared to accept graciously that she is, on occasions, in the wrong. Most importantly, like all stubborn people, she should learn to be more self-confident and to start laughing at herself. **)**

What to look for?

The stroke to look for in handwriting in order to check for stubbornness is a straight, rigid downstroke following an upstroke. The downstroke must slant backwards. This formation looks like a large inverted v, as in the samples below.

Samples of the stubbornness stroke

How does stubbornness affect compatibility in a relationship?

Stubbornness is the blind refusal to change an opinion or decision, even though logic and reason dictate that you should. So if one partner is stubborn, or especially if both partners are stubborn, it could be the cause of severe difficulties in a relationship. If both parties refuse to see reason and give way over a matter of controversy, then the most enormous row could break out with neither party prepared to give in.

Stubbornness is quite frequently the cause of a relationship breakdown when both partners (or neither) in their heart of hearts really want the relationship to end. However both (or one of the parties) are simply too stubborn to give way or do not want to lose face by asking for a reconciliation.

Sarcasm

Sarcasm is deadly!

'Sticks and stones may break my bones but words will never hurt me!' That may be true, but sarcastic words are designed to hurt. People who are sarcastic tend to have a bitter spirit and they want to punish, ridicule or belittle an adversary using words. Even when combined with humour, sarcasm can hurt.

'Stan is a cartoonist with a wicked sense of humour. He can capture every expression and expose the weakest side of his subjects. Famous people – especially politicians – open their morning papers with dread, in the fear that they may be the subject of Stan's sarcastic wit. Funny as the picture and slogan may be, there is always a hidden dart, ridiculing or belittling the subject.'

Sarcastic people often lack the ability or drive to cope with their own problems. As a result they develop guilt or self-reproach. They have a hidden desire to punish – and normally take that punishment out on other people who are more secure than they are. The sarcastic sting is a form of self-protection. Subconsciously the sarcastic person thinks, 'I want to bring other people down to my own level. I shall use sarcasm to make myself look stronger and other people look weaker.'

❝ Linda moved into Brad's apartment last year. At the time Brad was convinced that Linda – bright, attractive with excellent career prospects – was the girl he was going to marry. He couldn't believe his luck that she should fall for him. Now he wasn't so sure.

Every morning he awoke with a heavy grey lump in his chest. He had taken to pretending that he was asleep when Linda left for work. The thought of waking up to her sneering remarks was just too awful to contemplate. But he knew that he would only have a couple of hours of peace until Linda rang him up at work with the first jibe of the day.

That Wednesday he was sitting at his desk trying to resolve a complicated financial problem when his secretary put through what she described as an urgent call from Linda. Before he could say hello, Linda was off on a verbal attack.

'Too important to answer your own phone, are you? I used to think you'd make it to the top. Now I know differently. People who need so much sleep can never be truly successful, or are you just lazy? Since you're obviously too busy or forgetful to call me, I just thought I'd call to say good morning and to remind you that we are invited to that beautiful, sweet sister of yours for dinner tonight.'

Brad took a deep breath and said very quietly, 'No, Linda, you are wrong. I am going to my sister's tonight. You are not invited. In fact you will never be invited again. And by the time I get home after seeing her I expect you to have removed your belongings from my apartment and to have got out of my life. Now if you could kindly excuse me, I have rather important work to do.' He carefully put down the receiver and placed his head in his hands.

When he got home that night Linda was lying on the bed crying her eyes out. They had a long discussion, with Brad explaining that he just couldn't tolerate her sarcastic remarks day in, day out any longer. He still cared for her, but she was bringing him down.

Although she was successful in her own right, Linda always felt that other people were superior to her. The only way she knew how to combat her inferiority complex was by wounding others with her sharp tongue. She had been aware that she was being increasingly sarcastic towards Brad, but it was almost as if she had a perverse desire to see how far she could push him before he would respond. Since he hated any sort of argument or verbal banter, Brad would never have been a suitable adversary for Linda. The sarcasm would have come between them sooner or later.

Linda recently met Donald, who is equally sarcastic, if not more so. Being on the receiving end, she is now beginning to realize how debilitating sarcasm can be. She misses Brad dreadfully and six months later still nurtures a hope that she will get him back. ❞

What to look for?

Sarcasm is shown in needle-like points, normally in the t-bars and i and j dots. Look for lines or jabs that taper at the end into a sharp, narrow line or point.

Samples of sarcastic writing

How does sarcasm affect compatibility in a relationship?

However much one partner may claim they love the other one, if they are being sarcastic they are consciously or unconsciously looking to hurt. Mild sarcasm can of course simply be caustic wit, but strong sarcasm is bound to hurt one or both parties eventually. If someone is constantly being ridiculed or put down, they will eventually be so debilitated, or pushed so far, that they will react against it, in the way that Brad did. Two sarcastic people stand a better chance of understanding each other, although they could also end up pushing each other too far so that the relationship breaks down.

6

Do You Want the Same Things in Life?

- Are you fired up with ambition, determined to make a success of your life? Or are you quite happy to swim with the tide, content with whatever comes your way?
- How does your partner feel — the same way or differently?
- What about the way you run your life? Are you both highly organized, armed with long lists, knowing where everything is? Or are you the disorganized types, leading a life of confusion?

Most people have a hidden agenda in their life: a short, or sometimes, long, list of things that they want to do or achieve. A section of this list may relate to the type of partner they are seeking and could be worded along the lines of a Lonely Hearts advert. 'Tall, dark and handsome. Intelligent, caring, sense of humour. Non-smoking. Eager to wine and dine and shower me with kindness.'

Other parts of the list may relate to work . . . Some people are motivated by money or power and have a compelling urge to reach the top of their chosen field. Others are quite content to live a quieter, less stressful life. They have no burning ambitions and do not relentlessly push themselves.

The way we live our lives and what we want to achieve during our lives have an impact upon our personal relationships. If our mate's way of life or philosophy does not fit with our own hidden agenda, then major compromise has to be made by one or both partners.

Quite often we do not discuss our hidden agendas. For many people their 'wish list' is not comprised of conscious thoughts, just ideas or desires stashed away at the back of their minds. However, if a potential partner does not fit in with our hidden agenda, it is unlikely that we will want to continue with the relationship.

In this chapter we are going to look at how our ability and desire to achieve will affect our relationships. We will be considering:

- *Ambition and desire for responsibility*
- *Determination and enthusiasm*
- *Will power*
- *Materialism*
- *The organized life versus the confused life*
- *A varied versus a conservative lifestyle*

Do You and Your Partner Have What It Takes to Succeed?

❜ Night after night John used to set out his plans for success. 'Give me five years and I will be running that company!' he would boast to his girlfriend. Certainly John worked long hours and appeared to be consumed with the desire for success, but for some inexplicable reason his girlfriend had a niggling doubt. 'I just don't think he's got what it takes,' she admitted. 'And to be honest, I'm not sure I want to hang around long enough to find out.' ❜

Within every person's handwriting are signs that indicate the likelihood of that person reaching his or her goals. We are able to assess how ambitious someone is and how successful they are likely to be. There are a number of different elements that we have to study, and bringing these together as a whole allows us to evaluate the likelihood of success.

In order to be successful you need to know what you want, you must have sufficient strength of mind and energy to go after it, you need enthusiasm to keep you going, and force and determination to carry on in spite of obstacles. If you possess all these, the chances are you will achieve everything you set out to accomplish.

Goals

Goals are the things that we decide to do, the course of action we decide to take, the plans we make for the future. Sometimes these goals are short term and easy to achieve – for instance, you decide to go shopping in the local town for a new pair of shoes. And sometimes these goals are long term and highly challenging – for instance, you decide you want to get a new job by the end of the year.

Handwriting analysis *cannot* tell you what the goals are that the writer sets him- or herself, but it can tell you how difficult those goals are likely to be and how far into the future the writer is comfortable in planning. Normally the harder the goal, the further into the future the writer will plan.

Levels of goals are divided up as follows:

- *Very low goals*
- *Low goals*
- *Average goals*
- *High goals*
- *Visionary goals*

Very low goals

❝ Deidre sets herself very low goals. She suffers miserably from lack of self-confidence. She is so shy that she dreads walking out of her front door for fear of what the neighbours may think about her. Deidre is only comfortable with the present. She hates to think about what the future may hold in store for her.

For years she has worked in the local packaging factory. Time and time again she has shunned the chance for promotion, refusing to take on any further responsibilities over and above those that she already has. She rarely talks to colleagues. Most people have learned to leave her alone, fed up with getting so little response from their efforts to befriend her.

When Derek became her manager, he decided to go out of his way to help Deidre. He encouraged her to talk to him and, after months of cajoling and encouragement, he began to realize that she shunned any challenges in her life because she was so convinced that she would fail. Her attitude was 'better not to try because it's bound to go wrong anyway'.

Deidre is typical of very low-goaled writers. She rarely plans beyond a day at a time and will only undertake things that she is positive she can do. She has a complete lack of self-worth and massively underestimates her potential. ❞

What to look for?

The t-bar crosses are placed so low on the t-stem that they are practically touching the bottom of the stem. Very low-goaled writers always place their t-bars well below the top of the middle-zone letters.

Samples of very low goals

t t *together*

tonight

the transaction

Low goals

People who set themselves low goals make goals that are day-to-day and familiar. They shy away from challenges and from long-term planning, preferring to plan things only when they are positive that they can achieve them. Unlike very low-goaled writers, they are not necessarily fearful of failure but they certainly underestimate their own abilities. Low-goaled writers rarely fulfil their potential.

❛ Arthur has changed. Last year he married for the first time at the age of sixty. He also took early retirement. As far as he is concerned, he has achieved pretty much everything he has ever wanted to, so there is no reason to set challenges for himself. His writing now shows that he sets himself low goals.

His stepson Denis also has low-goaled writing. Denis' self-confidence took a major battering a couple of years ago when his wife filed for divorce and he lost his job, all within a couple of months. An attractive man, he should be able to find a new girlfriend. Certainly plenty of beautiful and intelligent local women are chasing him. However, Denis steers clear of them, convinced that they are way too good for him. He sets himself low goals and so he is not obtaining the happiness he deserves. ❜

What to look for?

Low goals are indicated when the t-bar crosses the t-stem at, or just below, the level of the top of the middle-zone letters.

Samples of low goals

Average goals

People who have average goals are able to plan for the future but work towards practical goals. Their aims are fulfillable and not wildly ambitious. Such people are considered to have an average self-confidence and are normally secure in themselves, knowing and appreciating their own abilities and limitations.

❢ Caroline was urged by her friends to pursue a handsome young Italian boy over on a student exchange. 'Yes, he is gorgeous, but he's hardly going to be interested in me! I'm not putting myself down,' she insisted, 'just being realistic. I don't even speak a word of Italian!'

When it came to choosing whether to continue with higher education Caroline decided to quit school and look for a job. She tried to explain to her disappointed parents why she had chosen that course of action.

'I am an average student. It's hard work for me to learn things, I'm more of a practical person. I'll look for a job that gives me scope for improvement and promotion, but I'm never going to be a high-flyer. I've accepted that and you have to accept that too,' she told them.

Caroline isn't putting herself down, she is being totally realistic. There is little point in her sweating away over studies that she would never excel in, so she chose an alternative course of action. ❢

What to look for?

Average goals are shown in writing when the t-stem crosses the t-bar at approximately two-thirds of the way up the stem of the letter. This is normally just above the top of the middle-zone letters.

Samples of average goals

t ←————   *entertained*

traits   *something*

High goals

People who set high goals for themselves reach out to the future and have the ability to plan far ahead. Such writers tend to be self-confident and ready to take on challenges.

❛ Gillian is highly ambitious and willing to take on challenges that most people would shun. She is not scared of failure but always sets out convinced that she will succeed. From a young age Gillian knew she wanted to run her own company, and when the opportunity arose to acquire a restaurant premises, she grabbed it. She wrote out a complex five-year plan demonstrating how she would make the business a success, and she convinced her bank manager to lend her a considerable sum of money. Gillian loves planning for the future and intends to open another three restaurants in local towns over the coming year.

Many suitors are put off Gillian, for she is a strong, fearless young lady. She expects commitment from boyfriends and likes to plan far ahead. 'I need an older man,' Gillian jokes. 'Men my own age can't seem to cope! I ask them which days they would like to meet up next week and they go pale and stutter, "We'll see." If I mention that a holiday would be nice three months ahead they tend to have apoplexy! Never mind, Mr Right will come along sooner or later!' ❜

What to look for?

Writers with high goals cross their t-stems high up. The t-bars are either placed right at the top of the stem, or within the top third of the stem.

Samples of high goals

Visionary goals

There are two types of people with visionary goals: those who
have other very strong abilities to achieve and those who do
not. If a person has visionary goals and also has strong will
power, enthusiasm and dynamic determination, then that person will be able to envisage the future and make all of his or
her dreams come true. Such a person is convinced that he or
she is needed at the top. They want to be famous or achieve
something extraordinary and it is very likely that they will
make these dreams come true.

Those people who have visionary goals but do not have strong
will power, determination or enthusiasm are normally armchair
planners – the type of person who dreams about the wonderful
things that they are going to achieve, but never quite gets
round to making it happen. The goals they set themselves
are frequently so difficult and distant that they are simply unat-
tainable. Quite often these people have suffered failure and,
rather than losing confidence, they over-compensate by reaching for an unrealistic future, escaping from reality.

What to look for?

Visionary writers place their t-bars above the top of the t-stems,
so it appears that the t-bar is floating in the air above the stem.
The greater the gap between the top of the t-stem and where the
t-bar is placed, the more distant are the writer's goals.

Samples of visionary goals

T

Thanking

Leadership

How do goals affect compatibility in a relationship?

The setting of goals is unlikely to make or break a relationship. If both partners have widely different goals – in extreme cases, one partner sets very low goals and the other sets very high goals – this is not necessarily an indication of incompatibility. It may in fact be of benefit to the partnership, as one partner will compensate for the lack of forward planning of the other partner. We need to look at all the other factors comprising achievement before we can evaluate compatibility.

Will Power

Will power is a sense of purpose. If you have strong will power you have the ability to choose a course of action for yourself, the ability to direct yourself. You will expend a great deal of energy in ensuring that you achieve your goal.

When a person has strong will power they devote considerable energy to achieving their goals. Of course this is not always a good thing. It is necessary to look at the goals themselves. A thief may spend much time and energy planning his crime and seeing it through. If someone has excessively strong will power they will spend all their energy pursuing one course of action to the exclusion of any other possible courses, routes that may perhaps be better or easier to fulfil.

People with weak will power lack a sense of self-direction. They usually need other people to help them set their course so that they can achieve their goals. Such people make better employees than managers. If a person is unable to set his or her own path of direction, then he or she will be unable to assist others in pursuing their goals.

Individuals lacking strong will power are not necessarily condemned to a life of failure! They may well reach the goals they set themselves, but they will need to have enthusiasm and determination to compensate for weak will power. Of course the more difficult the goals they set themselves, the more will power they will require for success. So it is vital to consider the two factors hand in hand. People lacking will power find it difficult to overcome obstacles and do not have the energy to keep on persevering.

The higher a person sets his or her goals, or the further into the future he sets them, the more will power he will need to achieve those goals. If someone sets herself low, easily achievable goals, rarely planning beyond tomorrow, it is not necessary to devote lots of energy and self-direction to achieve those goals. However, if the goals are distant and challenging, vast amounts of energy and commitment will be required. If the will power is not available, the distant goals will not be achieved.

❛ Duncan sets himself high goals and has strong will power. He is self-motivated and doesn't require encouragement or direction from other people. If he decides to do something, he will make every effort to ensure that he achieves it. He recently returned from a hiking trip around the world. In India he met Jarita. They fell madly in love and had a wild, passionate relationship. 'Spend the next two months travelling with me,' Duncan begged her.

Eventually Jarita agreed, but it took a lot of persuasion on Duncan's behalf. Jarita sets herself low, easily achievable goals. She had never travelled outside her country and could not envisage herself coping. It was an adventure she would never have dreamed of, had Duncan not encouraged her. With Duncan undertaking all the planning and expending all the energy to make sure they had a great time, the trip was highly successful. All the same, Duncan returned home alone, leaving Jarita in India.

'I have asked her to marry me and live with me here in Toronto,' Duncan explained. 'But I don't think she'll come. It breaks my heart, but to be honest I don't think she's got sufficient will power to undertake such a massive challenge. I do understand, but it makes me sad. I can't go to her as I'm not sufficiently qualified to get work out there. Life is very difficult. I am going to spend all my energy in getting more qualifications and looking for work in India.'

When they are together, Duncan propels Jarita along with sufficient energy and will power for the two of them. When apart, Jarita's will power is not strong enough to carry her towards the great challenges that lie ahead. ❜

What to look for?

Will power is evidenced again in the t-bar. However this time you need to look at the weight of the t-bar. A t-bar that is written with a lot of pressure, and looks and feels heavy on the page, indicates strong will power. A t-bar that is written with light pressure, particularly in contrast to the rest of the writing, indicates weak will power.

Samples of will power

Strong will power   Weak will power

Enthusiasm

Enthusiasm adds zest to the desire to achieve. When someone is enthusiastic they are emotionally involved in what they are doing. They are driven to achieve, putting in more energy than is necessary just to get the job done. As they go along they become excited about their goal, and as enthusiasm is infectious they often stir up excitement in others as well.

Enthusiasm adds to the chance of success. It is certainly a positive attribute to own as it inspires and attracts other people. However, if enthusiasm does not exist in a person's writing this is not in itself a negative attribute. Enthusiasm is not necessary if the person has low or average goals, or if he or she has plenty of will power. It is only needed if the writer has high goals. If enthusiasm is strong but will power is weak, then the energy is not directed and will be dissipated. It shows inclination but it is unlikely that the writer has the force to make his or her aim become a reality.

❝ Penny is full of energy and enthusiasm. She seems to go overboard about everything she does, gushing excitedly about new projects or the wonderful things that she is going to do. Penny is not lucky in love. Boys do not find her attractive. This has nothing to do with her physical appearance, for she is a striking girl with big blue eyes and a curvaceous figure. Her over-enthusiastic demeanour repels potential suitors. The boys think that she is trying too hard to make a good impression.

Penny has the enthusiasm, but she does not have the will power to go with it. She becomes excited about new things, but quickly loses interest. As a result people consider her to be somewhat fickle. She talks big, but nothing seems to happen.

For most people, enthusiasm is a great advantage. It attracts them friends and success. Penny is the exception to the rule! **❜**

What to look for?

Enthusiasm can be seen in the length of the t-bar. The longer the t-bar, the more enthusiasm the writer has. Enthusiasm is normally evident if the t-bar is at least the width of two middle-zone letters. However, it is also important to look at the pressure of the t-bar, relating back to will power.

If the pressure gets lighter towards the end of the bar, or if it tapers out altogether, this indicates that the writer loses enthusiasm as he goes along. He may start off on a project full of excitement, but this soon dissipates over time.

If the pressure starts off quite light but gets heavier towards the end of the t-bar, this indicates that the writer starts out with limited enthusiasm, but the further she gets involved in the project, the more enthusiastic she becomes. This writer is most likely to fulfil her goals.

Samples of enthusiasm

Determination

There is one more element to add to the equation of success, and that is determination.

Determination is staying power. It is the ability to stick with a project, overcoming any obstacles along the way, carrying on until the project is completed.

There are two parts to determination – the length and the strength. The stronger the determination, the more zest and energy the person puts into a project. However, this really needs to go hand in hand with length of determination. If the length is short, this means that the person will rapidly lose interest, so unless the project is short in timescale, that person will quickly become distracted and may move on to the next project before completing the first one. If determination lasts a long time, then that person is likely to have the staying power to continue until the project is completed.

❝ Craig is a very successful business executive, but at first glance his writing indicates the opposite. There is no evidence of will power, and it seems as if he lacks any sense of self-direction. However, his determination is strong. Craig works for a large multinational, running a leading division. Self-direction is not something that is needed in his job. His directions come from the board, his role is simply to fulfil these directions as quickly and cost-effectively as possible. Determination is what is needed, not will power *per se*. ❞

What to look for?
Determination is shown in long, heavy strokes descending straight down from the baseline. The longer the length and heavier the weight of the lower stems of the letters g, j and y, the more determination is shown.

Samples of determination

How does the ability to succeed affect compatibility in a relationship?

Have a look at all the success indicators in your own and your partner's writing. Work out the level of your goals as well as how much will power, enthusiasm and determination you both have. Evaluate your chances of success by looking through the following summary.

Summary

High goal needs strong will power, strong enthusiasm and strong determination to succeed.

- *If strong will power is lacking, success may be achieved if direction is given by someone else.*
- *If enthusiasm is lacking, success may be achieved but the extra zest to add excitement to the project is missing.*
- *If determination is lacking, success may be achieved so long as there are not too many obstacles along the way.*
- *If two or more of will power, enthusiasm and determination are not strong, then it is unlikely that the person will achieve his or her high-flying goals.*

Low and average goals will be achieved if the will power, enthusiasm and determination are average or strong.

How does the ability to achieve affect compatibility in a relationship?

The ability to achieve is of particular relevance in the workplace. However, it also plays an important role in relationships. If you have high expectations of yourself and of your partner, you will feel let down and disillusioned if your partner does not or cannot reach his or her goals. It is important for both partners to be aware of each other's desire for, and ability to achieve, success. It is not necessary for you both to want the same things out of life (although a shared sense of purpose will add strength to the relationship) but it is necessary for you to understand each other's dreams and desires and the likelihood of fulfilling them.

Two highly ambitious partners together

This relationship should work well so long as the couple are not competing against each other for success. Quite often there will not be enough space for two ambitious people in a relationship.

Two non-ambitious partners together

This couple will not be going anywhere! However, they will certainly sympathize with and understand each other. They have similar goals in life and have every chance of being happy together.

An ambitious partner with a non-ambitious partner

Quite often one partner takes on the nurturing, supportive role, while the other partner thrusts him- or herself into success or even fame. In this case complementary traits work well. Of course it is vital that both partners appreciate their differences in this respect, otherwise disappointment may mar the relationship on the part of the ambitious partner, and unwanted pressure and a sense of failure may mar the relationship for the non-ambitious partner.

Self-confidence

Self-confidence is a key personality trait, one that affects many, many other characteristics. If you are lacking in self-confidence you underestimate your own abilities (see Chapter 4) and this may hinder success in every aspect of your life.

The self-confident person has an innate belief in his or her ability to succeed and a feeling of self-worth. This does not mean that such an individual is pompous; he or she is quite willing to ask for assistance when needed or to admit he or she is wrong, if that is the case. Self-confident people are not afraid of tackling new or difficult projects. They tend to take a positive approach and have a healthy belief in themselves.

Self-confidence is of considerable benefit to individuals and in turn can help in the success of relationships. Without self-confidence a person would be fearful of taking on anything new. They would fail both in the workplace and socially, fearful of going out and making new friends. Self-confident people inspire trust in others. They make strong leaders and stable friends. They are often socially minded.

❛ Tracey and Miles had been going out together for just over a year. They were studying the same catering course at the same college and were just about to sit their final exam. Miles was in a complete state.

'I know I'm going to fail. It's not worth my even sitting this exam.' He pulled his hair and buried his face in his arm. He then started pacing up and down the corridor. 'Why didn't I start studying earlier. And why the . . . are you grinning at me?' Miles shouted angrily at Tracey.

'Oh calm down, Miles, you'll do just fine.'

This was fairly typical of the pair. Tracey was full of confidence. She wasn't sure that she would pass with flying colours, but she knew she was simply doing her best. She was pretty sure she'd make the grade and looked forward to the challenge of the job that was being offered to her on the basis of her exam results. She was scared, and the adrenalin was rushing, but she was nevertheless composed.

Miles was a wreck. He suffers from a lack of self-confidence, always sure that he can't succeed, when normally he does. Tracey has been a great help to him, preparing him for the exams, trying to make him look on the positive side. When he finally gets in the exam room, he will waste the first vital fifteen minutes thinking: I can't do it, I don't understand the questions, until eventually he will be calm enough to read the questions and realize that he does know the answers. ❜

What to look for?

There are a number of signs to look for when evaluating self-confidence:

1. The t-bars should be strong and placed high up on the t-stem. This indicates high goals and strong will power, which in itself suggests self-confidence.
2. Signatures that have an underscoring below them. This is an additional support to self-confidence, but if it does not exist it does not mean that self-confidence is lacking.
3. Large-sized capitals. If capitals are very over-inflated and huge, this indicates ostentation and not self-confidence, so evaluate carefully.

How does self-confidence affect compatibility in a relationship?

Self-confidence is a bonus in any relationship. If one or both partners feel self-confident in themselves they will project this positive feeling onto the relationship. There will be little or no fear, they will feel confident that they are doing the right thing and will hold themselves in high esteem. If one partner lacks self-confidence, he or she will be assisted by the self-confident partner, whose self-esteem will inevitably rub off. Self-confidence is positive. A lack of confidence is negative and a hindrance. No evidence of either will neither hinder nor assist a relationship.

Samples of self-confidence in writing

Materialism

Materialistic people want tangible things. They tend to live for today and let tomorrow worry about itself. They like worldly comforts and aspire to own smart homes and fast cars. Often such people are the sociable type.

The non-materialistic person has no such concern about worldly goods. Such people pay little attention to their physical surroundings, not worrying about where they live or what clothes to wear. More often than not they are concerned with concepts and philosophical ideas. They tend to be great thinkers, perfectly happy wrapped up in their thoughts, and equally content alone or in company.

❝ Stephen is a university professor lecturing in philosophy. He is the stereotype of a non-materialistic person.

Unlike many of his colleagues, Stephen started his career in industry. He hungrily pursued the materialistic path, accumulating large sums of money. Rich, successful and charismatic, he married Vanessa when he was just twenty-three.

Three years older than her husband, Vanessa was already an up-and-coming young banker. When she met Stephen, their combined salaries made them one of the wealthiest, most jet-setting couples she knew. Vanessa felt as if she had arrived. And it felt good.

After five years of life in the fast lane, Stephen began to have increasing bouts of self-doubt. Deep rifts were appearing in a once-happy marriage.

He began to wonder why he was slogging himself to death. He was no longer so impressed by all the money. It certainly wasn't buying him happiness. Besides, he didn't want to die young from an over-stressful life.

One fateful day he returned home to Vanessa and announced that he had handed in his notice and was returning to school to take a doctorate in philosophy.

His wife was horrified and furious. How could he take such an irresponsible action when they had a mortgage and were planning to start a family! How could he have taken such a life-shattering move without consulting her first! What was going to become of them in the future! Vanessa was simply devastated.

Eventually she decided that she didn't want to share such a future with him. Stephen left his wife in the family house, bought an apartment for himself and within a couple of years the divorce became final.

Upon completing his doctorate, Stephen got a job lecturing at a leading university on the other side of the country. He sold his apartment, his car and many of his belongings. Packing just a few clothes, his stereo and computer, he caught a bus to his new life.

Stephen felt as if he had shed a heavy load. He felt light, carefree and truly happy for the first time since he could remember. He finally understood that the trappings of a materialistic life were not for him. He didn't need a car or a telephone. He didn't need the responsibilities of the fast lane. He was perfectly content with his books and records. Philosophical thought was all that mattered to him. He laughed at his young students dreaming of piles of money and high-powered jobs. He spent contented hours contemplating the 'what ifs?'. What if he had been married to his ever-ageing, ever-nagging wife for the rest of his life? What if he had never known what it was like to luxuriate in the young, nubile bodies of admiring female students? Yes, he was definitely happier without materialistic trappings.

Vanessa was shocked by her ex-husband's new life. She just could not understand how someone would want to jack it all in. She would have understood had Stephen wanted to sell up and live a simple life on a desert island. But to leave the good life to become a poor professor living in a shabby studio flat on a dull red-brick university campus was utterly alien to her.

Vanessa is a kind person. She has lots of friends and in her spare time sits on a number of charity fund-raising committees. Her father was a doctor and her mother a housewife. They never had enough money for the nice things in life because they wanted to save to give their children the best education that money could buy. Vanessa went to a private school where all her friends wore designer clothes and practised their signatures in order to fill in their cheque books. In the eyes of her friends she was poor, so she was different.

She was determined to succeed, making enough money so that she and her family would never want for anything ever again, so that she and her family would never be ashamed by their lack of wealth. Vanessa appreciated good food and wine, was thrilled by fast cars and delighted in the finest clothes.

To share in Stephen's new life was anathema to her. So when he decided to throw it all away, she simply could not understand him. As far as she is concerned, people judge you on your outward appearance, not on the quality of your mind. For Vanessa, money is inextricably tied up with success.

Vanessa recently remarried a banker. She is happy once again and expecting their first child. The nanny is lined up, but until the baby is born she is unsure whether or not she will return to work.

Just because Vanessa is a materialistic person does not mean that she is a bad person. Far from it! It is just that she has different ideals in life from someone who cares little for material things. **❯**

What to look for?

Materialism is shown by the size of the middle-zone in letters. Look at the letters a, c, e, o, etc. If these are much larger proportionately than the upper and lower extensions, then the writer is predominantly a material person, living for today and appreciating everyday objects.

If, however, the middle parts of the letters are small, squashed or insignificant in comparison to the upper or lower loops, then the person is not materialistic. If the upper loops are very long or big, and the middle-zone letters very small, then the writer will prefer a non-materialistic way of life, choosing theories and concepts as opposed to more mundane everyday comforts.

Samples of materialistic and non-materialistic writing

Materialistic   Non-materialistic

experience

birthday

thank you

happened

How are materialistic and non-materialistic partners likely to get on with each other?

Opposites often attract. There are no reasons why materialistic and non-materialistic people will not get on together. But on the other hand they may have little in common when it comes to discussion of life's aspirations. It is vital that they understand their differences in attitude. If these differences can be accepted, then a happy medium may be able to be reached. Where a materialistic person is in a relationship with a non-materialistic partner, good communication and broad-mindedness should be present in both for this relationship to thrive.

Organizational Abilities

How organized are you?

Some people like to be organized. They know what they are going to do from day to day. Their belongings are put away in tidy piles and their life fits neatly into segments. But just because they want everything to be orderly does not necessarily mean that they have true organizational ability. A person with real organizational ability can dream up plans and put together new arrangements as well as actually making them happen. They can originate plans in their minds and put them into practice. Organized people are able to create a logical order, simplifying matters for efficacy.

❮ Anthea is a highly organized person. Her house is constantly immaculate. She never loses anything and she is always on time for meetings. At work, Anthea is the anchor of her department. If someone leaves something lying around, she will put it away. She rewrote the department's filing system, she helps everyone plan their days and still has time to complete all her own tasks. Colleagues and friends are constantly amazed by how she does it.

Anthea's first real love was the complete opposite to herself. His life was always in a shambles. He lost things and was often confused. His flat was constantly in the most terrible mess and he never held down a job for more than a month or two because he quickly lost interest. He was for ever forgetting to turn up to meet Anthea and she had to spend most of her time apologizing to friends on his behalf for forgotten appointments. He was hopelessly unreliable and Anthea was continuously disappointed by his behaviour. But whenever they met she was charmed by his sweet nature and good looks, and time after time she forgave him. It wasn't until he asked her to move in with him that Anthea realized how fundamentally incompatible they were and that she had to end the relationship. 'I could not have lived such a shambolic existence!' she explained.

Having been hurt by a disorganized partner, Anthea promised herself that she would never get involved with such a type again. When she met Angus she thought that he was the answer to all her dreams. Perfectly turned out, Angus always did what he said he was going to do. Anthea couldn't help smiling to herself when she saw his home. All his suits were hung up so that they were perfectly aligned in his wardrobe. Ties were arranged by colour and his shirts were immaculately ironed. Angus was considerate and seemingly well organized. But, unlike her first lover, Angus kept Anthea at a distance. He rarely saw her during the week, never gave her his work number, explaining that he couldn't take calls at work, and never invited her to socialize with his friends or colleagues. Anthea was in his spell and the more distance he maintained, the more infatuated she became with him.

'Two peas in a pod, we are!' Anthea explained to her friends. 'I just need to give him plenty of space and time. I think he must have been hurt by a previous relationship, so I'm not pushing to get too close. But watch this space. I really think I've met the man for me!'

One Saturday evening Angus did not appear at 7.30 p.m. on the dot as he normally did. After ten minutes Anthea began to get nervous, knowing that he was never late. After half an hour she rang his apartment. A male voice answered the phone, but it was not Angus. 'Who am I speaking to?' he asked Anthea. She explained and asked who he was. 'I think I need to come and see you,' the man replied, and before Anthea could ask any further questions he put the phone down.

Ten minutes later her doorbell rang and in the porch stood two policemen. 'Can we come in, luv?' they asked.

Anthea suffered the most terrible shock as they explained to her that her beloved boyfriend was in fact a highly wanted criminal, suspected for a string of crimes including fraud and theft. The police were on his trail following an enormous burglary the night before. But Angus had vanished without a trace.

Angus plans his crimes and getaways with such precision and care that he is completely confident that he will not be found out. His organizational skills are as much an asset to him as they are to anyone that possesses them. Unfortunately Angus puts these skills to appalling use. 〉

To be well organized is normally of great advantage, assisting both social and business relationships. People like well-organized individuals, who are clear in their own mind where they are going and who are able to communicate their ideas, successfully directing others. Individuals who have the ability to plan find it a lot easier to overcome life's everyday problems.

What to look for?

Organizational ability is seen in the small letter f. If organizational ability is evident the letter f will look perfectly balanced. The loops both above and below the baseline will be similar in height and width, and the letter will look as if it has been drawn with care.

There are a number of different ways that we can draw the letter f. Here are some of them:

f (no loops)

This writer has balance, but has no imagination. He or she can organize but is not flexible and lacks the ability to rearrange if anything goes wrong.

f (upper loop)
This writer can envisage a plan and can work out what needs to be done, but does not have sufficient imagination to make the plan a reality.

f (lower loop)
This writer finds it difficult to come up with a plan in the first instance but has the ability to make it happen, putting it into place.

f (balanced loops)
When the upper and lower loops are balanced and of similar proportion, the writer has the ability to come up with new arrangements and actually make them happen.

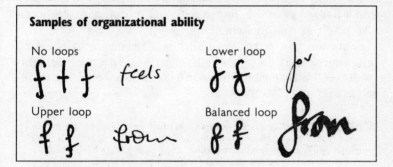

Samples of organizational ability

No loops

Lower loop

Upper loop

Balanced loop

How does organizational ability affect compatibility in a relationship?

Organizational ability is an asset in any relationship, but it does not have as great an impact on the relationship as confusion (which is the next trait we will be considering in this chapter). It is certainly a benefit, as both partners know where they stand with each other. They are able to plan their relationship, and unless terror of commitment is so strong as to override organizational ability, the couple will be able to look to the future.

Confusion

Confused people have too many irons in the fire. They tend to take on too many commitments or develop so many interests that they are unable to pay attention to any one in particular, and as a result all of them suffer. Confused people are disorganized. They spend a great deal of time doing all sorts of things but achieving very little.

Confusion also affects people's thoughts and feelings. Confused individuals find themselves awash with conflicting emotions. They do not know which impulse to act upon and often end up behaving irrationally and irresponsibly. In extreme cases, such people have difficulty in following social etiquette and behave badly, simply because they do not know which way to turn.

People become confused for many different reasons. They may quite simply be interested in lots of different things so that they find it hard to prioritize. Immaturity and subconscious fears can also result in confused emotions.

Confusion can wreck relationships. If someone is confused and disorganized he or she will forget to turn up for appointments, will miss opportunities and constantly be letting themselves and other people down.

❻ Rupert is hopelessly scatter-brained. On their first date, he sat for an hour in the wrong pub, waiting for Sally to turn up. Meanwhile, two roads away in the Hound and Hare, Sally was joined by a group of mutual friends. Amazed that Rupert hadn't turned up, for they knew how infatuated he was with Sally, they set up a search party to trawl the pubs of the small town in search of the lost lover. After a number of other setbacks, Sally and Rupert started going out together. Sally was forgiving of Rupert's forgetfulness and confusion.

Rupert is extremely kind-natured. Whenever somebody asks for a hand, whatever that may be – from weeding the garden to driving halfway across the country to pick up an ailing grandmother – Rupert is the first to offer to help. People take advantage of him, knowing that he won't say no. And the trouble for Rupert is that this kindness compounds his scatter-brained behaviour. He quickly says yes to one person, forgetting that he has agreed to do something else for someone else half an hour before.

At the beginning of their marriage, Sally was proud of her husband's kindness, happy that he was able to help others. But after she had had their first child, she began to get fed up. Rupert was never at home. When she did see him he was completely preoccupied with other things. The crunch came shortly afterwards.

Sally went home for a day to visit her parents and left Rupert with the baby. When she returned in the evening she was met by a distraught Rupert. The baby was nowhere to be seen. Sally started screaming, 'What have you done with my baby!'

Rupert had gone shopping in the afternoon and somehow had lost their child! He had parked the pram somewhere, but couldn't recall where.

Fortunately for them, their neighbour, Mrs Carver, had been in town that afternoon and had found the little baby wailing in its pram outside the baker's shop. She took the child home, and only came knocking on Rupert and Sally's door when she saw that Sally's car was back in the driveway.

Sally couldn't put up with Rupert's irresponsible behaviour any more and she moved out. She visited her lawyer to initiate divorce proceedings, and explained to him why their marriage had irretrievably broken down. 'He is so busy with so many different things, and those things never seem to include me. You know, I can't think of anything Rupert actually achieves. He is for ever losing his job and we depend on my meagre salary to live on. I can't even trust him to look after the baby! Our marriage definitely has no future. I can't go on living with such a messed-up person.'

As Sally found out, a confused person is very difficult to live with. A disorganized person expends lots of energy on very little. They are often tired and emotionally worn out for no apparent reason. In fact it is because they are not channelling their energy, but dissipating it on many futile activities.

What to look for?

Confusion is easy to spot in handwriting. When the writing looks very messy and the loops of one line are tangled up with the loops of the lines above and below, you are looking at the writing of a confused and disorganized person.

Sometimes the loops reach up or down into the line above or below but do not actually overlap and touch each other. In this case the writer is cramping his or her writing but is not actually disorganized.

Samples of confusion

How does confusion affect compatibility in a relationship?

Confusion and disorganization are inevitably going to have a negative impact on a relationship.

One disorganized partner

By his or her very actions, the disorganized partner is going to put a strain upon the relationship. His or her organized partner will feel frustrated and even let down by the confused actions of his or her mate. The organized partner may find him- or herself running around, tidying up and apologizing for the actions of their other half. Such a relationship will be difficult.

Both disorganized partners

This relationship has a better chance of working as both partners will understand each other. Their house will be in a constant state of chaos and the world will view them as unstable and unreliable. As a working relationship this partnership would be a disaster. On an emotional level it could work, although the couple may be shunned by the mainstream of society.

Conservatism

In this section we will consider how you and your partner feel about change. Do you both crave new experiences? Do you love doing new things, visiting new places and meeting new people? Or do you prefer sticking to what you know? Are you more of a traditionalist?

The word 'conservative' is frequently used in a political context. Typically conservative parties follow more traditional policies and on the whole favour gradual change. Whether or not they agree with and support the policies of their conservative party, conservative-type people adopt a similar attitude to life.

Conservative people tend to live their life within the guidelines that society considers to be normal. In a Western culture such people have a traditional outlook – they adhere to middle-of-the-road beliefs, wear clothes that are of a style that blends in with the norm and dislike 'rocking the boat' in any manner.

Natalie and Nathan are a conservative couple. A modest person, Natalie dreads any occasion that may throw her into the limelight. Most people think that she is shy, for she never volunteers her opinion or speaks without being spoken to. In fact she is rather conservative, preferring to go along with the majority view, rather than risk disapproval from friends and colleagues. If given the choice, Natalie prefers to steer away from change. She is happiest visiting the same resort every year for her holidays, and found it emotionally upsetting and disorientating when they recently moved house.

Nathan is not quite as conservative as his wife, but he is certainly most comfortable when leading an 'ordinary' life. A dependable person, he is well liked and respected for his strong values. There is only one person with whom Nathan has a particularly strained relationship, and that is his mother-in-law. Unfortunately, this in itself is putting pressure on Natalie and Nathan's marriage.

Maeve is obsessively conservative. Natalie is often embarrassed to be seen out with her mother. She wears clothes that are ridiculously outdated. When Natalie has suggested that she goes shopping, her mother retorts, 'My clothes are perfectly good enough, thank you! They are smart and well made, not flimsily put together with the cheap fabrics that are common these days. I am comfortable with my clothes and shall wear them until they fall apart.'

The problem for the young couple is that Maeve is constantly trying to thrust her old-fashioned ideas onto them. Her favourite phrase is 'In my day . . .', and then she proceeds with her criticism. Maeve's standards are so strict and Victorian in attitude. If Natalie or Nathan steps out of line, then all hell breaks loose.

Every day before breakfast Maeve calls to find out what the couple are doing that day. She checks up on every little detail of their life. 'Did you vacuum the stairs? How are you making that chicken soup? Surely not with a cooked carcass? What are you reading? What, that trash! Why is Nathan spending so much money on something useless like a television? Not a new pair of shoes again!' And so it goes on, and on, every interminable day.

One Sunday lunchtime, Maeve stopped round after she had been to church. She bustled into the kitchen where Natalie was cooking, all agitated and flushed. 'How, just how, can you let Nathan do that?' she exclaimed in a low, gasping voice. She sat down and rubbed her hands over her face. 'What shame! What will the neighbours think?'

'What, mother? What are you talking about?' Natalie asked, an edge of concern creeping into her voice.

'Your husband is spraying the front lawn with a dark green paint! What on earth is he doing? Why isn't he mowing it in nice straight lines? What will the neighbours think?'

Natalie started grinning. 'Oh, we don't like straight lines. We've decided to go for the natural look. The trouble is, the cat pees on the grass and it goes brown in patches. So Nathan got some green spray from the garden centre to cover it up until the grass grows again.'

'How dare you use language like that in front of me! And how could you be so irresponsible? Why can't you two lead a normal quiet life! I have had enough!' Maeve got up and, with her chin in the air and her tweed hat perched on top of her head, walked through the kitchen and out of the house, gripped by a rigid but controlled rage.

Later that day, Nathan gave Natalie an ultimatum. 'I am fed up with your mother interfering in the way we live our life. I intend to run my house and garden the way I want to. She is making you miserable and me angry. Enough is enough. Either you tell her to butt out or I'm out. I love you, Natalie, but I cannot take it any longer.'

For the purposes of graphology, a person such as Maeve is described as ultra-conservative.

Maeve is typical of ultra-conservative people. She is deeply insecure and likes everybody to think well of her. Unfortunately she has got stuck in a rut of standards that were popular thirty years ago. She is quite jealous of Nathan for having taken away her daughter and so is trying to impose her rigid values upon them both, as a means of maintaining control over their lives. Maeve hates change and will take extreme steps to ensure that everything stays the same in her life. **❯**

Conservatism can be a good trait to possess, as it provides a check on impulsive and highly emotional behaviour. On the other hand, conservatism can also inhibit people. A highly talented or creative individual will be severely hampered by conservatism, for he or she will not want to break free of convention to try something new, and as such may waste his or her talents. Conservative types may find themselves in a rut from which they fear to break out.

Ultra-conservatism is rarely a beneficial trait. Certainly it inhibits success and creativity, but it is also normally indicative of a fear within the person – something like jealousy, or fear of criticism or some other insecurity. Ultra-conservative people may be hard to live with, as they will require their partner to live within the same strict guidelines that they set themselves.

What to look for?

Conservatism

The writing looks compressed and cramped widthways. Letters, especially the letters m and n, look as if they have been squeezed inwards, so that the letters are taller than they are wide. The circle letters of a, e and o have narrow circle formations, and all letters have little spacing between them.

Ultra-conservatism

The writing is similar to conservatism but the evidence is even stronger. The writing will look very squeezed together and in extreme cases may be hard to read. The writing looks very narrow but very tall.

Samples of conservative and ultra-conservative writing

never mind it didnt matter anyway

thank you very

Desire for Variety

People who like change and variety loathe monotony and regularity. They have to do different things and go to different places to relieve the boredom and routine that quickly set into their lives. Such people tend to have a wide variety of interests but, unlike people who have a confusion of interests, these folk are organized and can compartmentalize their various pursuits, devoting sufficient energy to each.

❝ When Malcolm left school he began work as a baker's assistant. He loved the bread and the cakes and the dealing with the public, but he could not bear the routine of rising at the crack of dawn, following all the set procedures to bake the bread, taking lunch at the same time every day and locking up shop at six o'clock on the dot each night. The monotony quite simply drove him mad; unusually for him, he found he had little energy and emotionally he felt depressed.

Desperate to find another career that he was more suited to, he visited the local careers office, where he was invited to have his handwriting analysed as part of a battery of tests and interviews. His desire for variety was obvious, and the adviser recommended that Malcolm seek a job that offered him as much scope for change as possible.

To his joy, Malcolm was offered the position of salesman for an office equipment company. He travelled thousands of miles in his car, visiting different offices in different parts of the country. Every day was varied, every day presented new challenges, and he loved his job.

It's impossible to track Malcolm down at the weekends. Sometimes he is hang-gliding, sometimes sailing and sometimes playing football. He travels whenever he can, visiting deep, dense jungles, diving into tropical seas or climbing treacherous mountain peaks.

His love life reflects his desire for change. Malcolm finds it impossible to keep one relationship going for any length of time. He quickly loses interest and moves onto the next. From time to time he juggles three or four girlfriends at once. He has no desire to be unfaithful, but his buzz comes from variety.

A while ago he fell deeply in love with Shelley, an assistant pharmacist.

> Their relationship went from strength to strength over a two-month per-
> iod, until Malcolm decided the regularity of their meetings was getting too
> much. Shelley hated his idea of an open relationship, seeing other people
> as and when they wanted to, and said that if that was the way he wanted
> to live, they could no longer go out together. 〵

A desire for variety can exist in all or just some aspects of our lives. Some people need variety and change in their social life. They relish a large circle of friends, people with different interests and ambitions. Some individuals need variety in their love life; they cannot commit to one partner, for they quickly tire of the regularity or predictability of the relationship. Other people seek variety in their work or interests, liking to be in different surroundings as frequently as possible. Still other people crave variety on an intellectual level, learning about different things, reading and studying varying theories.

What to look for?

Change and a desire for variety are seen in writing that has exceptionally long downstrokes. These lines or loops should be at least two and a half times the length of the middle-zone letters.

When the downstrokes are very long and look like a stick, this indicates that the writer likes change but is only comfortable with familiar environments, situations, places or people.

When the downstrokes are very long and made with a broad loop, this indicates that the writer has a strong need for variety and the more new experiences he or she has, the more he or she wants.

Samples of desire for variety in writing

How do conservatism and a desire for variety affect compatibility in a relationship?

Conservatism is an important factor to consider when assessing compatibility. A person is conservative or ultra-conservative, likes variety and so is the opposite of conservative, or does not show a specific inclination to either attitude. So how do these different types get along together?

One conservative partner

As already shown, a conservative person is a traditionalist. If his or her partner has no strong opinions either way, then a relationship with a conservative partner should be easy and successful. Such a person will not spring surprises on their partner and will be solid and rather predictable in behaviour. The conservative partner is likely to be reliable, albeit rather restrained.

One ultra-conservative partner

An ultra-conservative partner will be hard to live with. He or she will require a partner to live within his or her own extremely traditional guidelines. Pressure could build up on both sides. The ultra-conservative partner could become nagging and clingy, while building up disappointment and resentment over his or her partner's non-traditionalist behaviour. His or her partner will soon feel restricted in thought and behaviour and may not want to live such a 'narrow' life.

One variety-seeking partner

A person who likes variety may be considered restless. Such an individual takes on lots of different things in his or her life and will be most unhappy leading a routine existence. If his partner prevents him from leading a life of variety, tension will build up and the partner seeking variety will need to get out of the relationship. Where a partner is deprived of her need for change, she may find it advantageous to undertake physical activity, so that the built-up energy can be released. Such a person will make an interesting and exciting companion, but must be given the space to pursue his or her varying interests if the relationship is to succeed.

Two conservative partners together

This couple have a similar outlook on life. They will conform to what society considers to be normal and will feel most comfortable with traditional attitudes and minimum change. They should get along well together, assuming that all else in their personalities is compatible.

Two ultra-conservative partners together
This couple also have a similar outlook on life. However, their relationship will not be as easy as that of the conservative couple. Both may be plagued by insecurities and may well repress their emotions. Few people will meet the standards that this couple set themselves and as a consequence they are unlikely to have a wide circle of friends. Communication will be difficult in this relationship and the pressure on each partner to think and act within strict guidelines will be intense. Happiness may be elusive.

Two variety-seeking partners together
This couple will have plenty of fun. With a similar attitude to life, they will constantly be on the move, sometimes seeking change for the sake of it. It would not be surprising for such a couple to have an 'open' relationship, as monogamy may be a difficult concept for either partner to accept.

Conservative partner with ultra-conservative partner
Fundamentally this couple have a similar attitude. All the same, if the ultra-conservative partner is obsessive, the relationship will struggle, as he or she will constantly be looking over his or her shoulder to check whether standards are being maintained.

Conservative partner with variety-seeking partner
Compromise will be required by both partners for this relationship to work. Fundamentally these partners like to live a different type of life. They have opposing attitudes, but this in itself could result in a lively relationship, debating their different viewpoints and agreeing to disagree. Clearly the success of this relationship depends upon the maturity and ability to compromise of both partners.

Ultra-conservative partner with variety-seeking partner
These partners have totally opposing views on life. Such a relationship would have little hope of lasting once the initial attraction has worn off.

7
Do You Have the Same Standards?

- Are you both totally honest?
- Do you set yourself similar rules by which you live your lives?
- Are there some things that are of great importance to you but are trivial or of no importance to your partner?
- Do you have the same values? Or perhaps you haven't yet found out!

Having similar standards and values, or at the very least understanding each other's values, is vital for the success of a relationship. Problems frequently arise because issues such as values and standards do not become apparent until it is too late. By the time fundamental differences are realized, the chances are that either one or both parties in the relationship will already have been hurt.

How do you know whether you can really trust someone? How can you tell if they are scrupulously honest?

The beauty of handwriting analysis is that you can become aware of the similarities and differences in your standards and values without actually going to the lengths of experiencing them. So this puts you in the ultimate of powerful positions – being able to control your own destiny and knowing what might happen before it does! This will become much clearer to you as you read the accounts throughout this chapter.

Honesty – the No. 1 Value!

Whether you are embarking on a personal or professional relationship, honesty has to score highly on the list of 'must haves'. How can you be sure that your partner is as debonair, kind and honest as you think? Normally you can't know until you have put him or her to the test. And then it could be too late.

6 Sandra was working abroad for a year. When she met Marco she was swept off her feet by his good looks and kindness. He offered to help her find an apartment, introduce her to a wide circle of friends and even assist her in building up a list of contacts useful for her job. True to his word, all of this became a reality within a couple of months. He moved into the flat with her. Although she was concerned about the ease with which he seemed to be controlling her life, she was, all the same, really quite happy.

The next month Sandra flew home for a couple of weeks for a holiday and to celebrate a family wedding. She tried calling Marco many times to find out how he was and to tell him that she missed him, but never managed to get hold of him.

Towards the end of the fortnight she received her credit card bill. To her horror she found that over five thousand pounds had been spent on her card over the previous three weeks – including a week when she hadn't even been there! When she arrived back at her apartment it was totally empty. All her valuable possessions had been stolen and, along with them, her confidence and trust in other people.

Sandra had little way of tracing Marco. She knew nothing about his family, and his friends claimed that they had no idea where he had gone. To her surprise the police requested a sample of his handwriting to assist them in their investigations. The writing was analysed by a graphologist, who gave an in-depth report on Marco's personality. Based on this analysis and on analysis by a document evidence specialist (someone who studies handwriting to judge forgeries), the police were eventually able to trace Marco. He is now in jail. But Sandra was devastated. 'If only I had been able to analyse his handwriting I might have foreseen all of this,' she told me.

Is he or she honest?

Perhaps this should be the first question that we ask when analysing someone's writing, for if they are not honest, the chances are that you won't want anything to do with them.

But some people say that there are different levels of honesty. Telling a white lie to protect someone's feelings is not considered dishonest by some people; others consider it deceitful.

Everyone has different standards, but if you and your partner have the same standards, the chances are that you will understand each other better and have an easier relationship.

Normally you don't have the opportunity to test someone's honesty. So this is where handwriting analysis can be so valuable. When we analyse someone's writing for honesty, we recognize that there are different degrees of honesty. But before we can really understand honesty, we need to understand the different levels of dishonesty. These include total dishonesty, known as deceit; self-deceit, where you kid yourself; and secretiveness, where you hide things from others.

It is vital that you check to see whether both your own and your partner's writing displays any of these honesty/dishonesty traits.

What to look for!

For all of these traits you must look at the circle letters – the letters a, d, e, g, o and q. It doesn't matter if the circles of these letters are open or closed. What does matter is the *existence or absence of loops* leading into or from the circles of these letters. All of these examples will be explained in greater detail in this chapter, so read on!

Deceit

Deceit means that a person knowingly lies or is dishonest. He or she is not just making a mistake, but has purposefully planned to deceive.

You must be careful when analysing deceit in someone's writing. It is very rare that a person is all bad! In fact many of us show deceit in our writing from time to time. Remember that there are different levels of dishonesty – from telling a little 'white lie' so as to protect a friend's feelings to committing a major fraud! You will often find that deceit is closely tied up with feelings of insecurity and real or imaginary guilt.

❝ James is a liar and it has a deep-rooted cause. James is not his real name. His family emigrated to England when he was two years old. Although they are kind, honest people, he is really ashamed of his parents, who are uneducated but street-wise, can't speak any English and are rather poor. Over the years James has constructed a story about himself in which he is an orphan of rich parents. James feels inferior and has got into the habit of hiding and covering up things that need not be hidden. Over the last couple of years this has got so out of hand that he has resorted to drug dealing in order to finance his expensive lifestyle.'

'Elspeth was recently jilted by her boyfriend Phil. She was livid and resentful and decided to make Phil's life as miserable as she could. She lied to him and told him that she had lost the key to his house, which he had given her during their relationship.

Knowing he was abroad, she entered the house, tipped all his drawers upside-down, opened the taps in his bath and let the water run. She took his car keys from his desk. She then locked the front door to the house behind her. She got into his car, released the hand-brake, left the keys in the ignition and wound the windows down. Elspeth then walked away.

By the time Phil returned home after his weekend abroad, the whole house was ruined. The place was flooded and the floor in the bathroom had collapsed through the ceiling of the kitchen. It looked as if the most terrible storm had hit the house. Outside, his car had gone.

When Phil rang Elspeth she feigned horror at the disaster that had struck him. And when the police asked her for an interview, she lied eloquently. But a month later she was arrested for criminal damage, trespass and theft. She had been sighted by the milkman!

Elspeth was knowingly deceitful. She planned her actions and consciously lied to Phil and the police. The deceit shown in her writing is similar to that shown in the writing of criminals, thiefs and even murderers. **9**

What to look for?

There are a number of traits to look for when studying deceit in handwriting. But in order for a person to be judged really deceitful their writing must show all of these traits consistently.

As with all the honesty/dishonesty characteristics, you must look at the circle letters – the letters a, d, e, g, o and q.

The main sign to look for when evaluating deceit is *two loops in a circle letter*. There should be an initial loop as you go into the letter and a loop at the closing of the circle formation. The samples below demonstrate this clearly.

There are a number of other things that you should look for, which will confirm whether or not dishonesty exists in the writing. The more of the following you find in the writing, *in addition* to the double loops in circle letters, the more likely it is that the writer is dishonest.

1. The pressure of the writing is very pasty, varying from thin lines to thick, blotchy lines.
2. The writing looks rather rigid, perhaps as if it has been copied out of a school book, and is rather characterless and slow-moving.
3. There is retouching – for instance, if the letters are rewritten but this in itself doesn't improve legibility.

4. The baselines are wavy and erratic.
5. The writing slants strongly to the left.
6. The writing is particularly thready (low-lying and ill-formed) and none of the letters seems to stand up straight.
7. Capital 'I''s (as in the pronoun 'I') are written so that they are hard to read.
8. The capitals are much larger or smaller than the rest of the writing, or generally look out of proportion with the rest of the writing.

It is very unlikely that you will see all of this in a sample of writing. But even if you are convinced that someone's writing shows dishonesty, be careful – you do not want to be sued for libel!

Samples of deceit

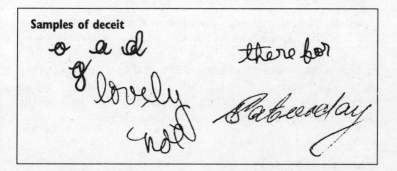

How does deceit affect compatibility in a relationship?

Deceit and relationships are not compatible. If one or both partners are deceiving each other, trust is broken down as soon as the deceit is exposed and it is unlikely that the relationship will continue. If deceit is strongly evident in a person's writing, it would be best to steer clear of that individual.

Self-deceit

Self-deceit is perhaps the most common form of deceit. It is simply an unconscious method of escaping from reality or refusing to face problems by blocking them out.

❮ Kevin has a real problem with self-deceit. His best friend was killed in a car accident five years ago. Kevin never accepted what happened. He didn't allow himself to grieve properly and managed to block all thoughts of his friend and the accident from his mind. To do that he dropped all of their mutual friends and started hanging out with a new crowd – a crowd that was into alcohol and motorbikes. Deep down he knew it was crazy, but he started riding his bike way over the speed limit. It was as if he was trying to tempt fate and punish himself for what had happened to his best friend.

Fortunately Kevin was lucky. The inevitable happened. He was thrown from his bike and ended up in hospital suffering from mild concussion. Luckily, he had a great doctor who insisted that Kevin had counselling. He is now the first to admit that the root of his problems lay in the fact that he was lying to himself. He pretended that he could cope with the loss of his best friend and acted in a way that denied any feelings of loss and fear. Kevin jokes that he must be the only person in the world who was happy when he lost his licence. He said that he feels as if a huge weight has been lifted off his shoulders and he can now face up to reality. ❯

Self-deceit need not be as dramatic as it was in Kevin's case. Think of the times when you have said to a colleague, friend or even just thought to yourself, 'Sure, I'll have that finished by next week' – when you know full well that it just isn't going to happen! That's self-deceit. Or what about the time you ate an extra chocolate biscuit, telling yourself that one more really won't make any difference! That's self-deceit too!

What to look for?

To check out self-deceit in writing you need once again to look at the circle letters – a, d, e, g, o and q. Self-deceit exists if the writer draws an *initial loop inside the circle part of the letter*. The samples below demonstrate this.

Remember that the larger the size of the initial loop and the more frequently it occurs in the writing, the greater the degree of self-deceit in that person's character.

If self-deceit is really prominent in someone's writing this could mean that writer has rather deep-rooted emotional problems that he or she has blocked away and doesn't want to face up to. That person may seem utterly normal and charming on the outside but inside they may be fighting emotional battles; so just be aware!

Samples of self-deceit

How does self-deceit affect compatibility in a relationship?

Self-deceit is likely to have an adverse effect on your relationships. If you are kidding yourself about issues, this is bound to have repercussions on your partner. You may be able to delude yourself, but it will be harder to delude your partner. This may be the basis for arguments or the hurting of feelings.

Secretiveness

New graphologists are often surprised that secretiveness has anything to do with honesty or dishonesty. But it certainly does!

At times we all want to hide facts. That doesn't mean that we want to distort them or change them. We just don't want to reveal them. Similar to self-deceit, secrecy is something that all of us indulge in some of the time. If the hiding of information becomes excessive, then you are dealing with a secretive person; someone who doesn't like to express him- or herself and generally talks round an issue. A secretive person protects his or her secrets without lying about them.

❝ Connie is like that. She sees no reason why she should divulge details about herself to anyone. She is the sort of person with whom you can have a great conversation; she seems really nice. It is not until afterwards that you realize that she managed to get you to tell her everything about yourself, but you learned absolutely nothing about her! It's great for her job, where her boss trusts her with every little secret, knowing she won't let on to anyone, but it's lousy for her relationships. Matt is an ex-boyfriend. He said that Connie is a really straight person, she wouldn't knowingly lie to anyone. But after they had been going out together for six months, he still didn't know a thing about her family and she never let on how she felt about Matt himself. He explained that she was just too quiet and secretive for him. 🥯

What to look for?

Secretiveness in handwriting is visible again in the circle letters of a, d, e, g, o and q. This time you need to see if there are any final loops coming out of the circle formation. In other words, does the letter end with a loop? The larger the loop, the more secretive that person is. Have a look at the specimens below to understand what this means.

Samples of secretiveness

o a d   *as people*

goz   *London*

How does secretiveness affect compatibility in a relationship?

Beware of secretiveness! It can cause numerous problems in relationships. The chances are that a secretive person won't want to get too close emotionally. There is nothing worse than when you are pretty sure that someone has strong feelings for you, but he or she just won't admit it – perhaps for fear of being hurt or for fear of others disapproving. Secretiveness is quite common and can be destructive!

Having now covered all the 'dishonesties', we must look at honesty in handwriting.

Honesty

Honesty is sometimes defined as frankness. If you are honest, you are straightforward and probably reliable as well. Honesty in handwriting is reflected when there is an absence of any of the dishonesty traits.

Honesty is normally seen as a commendable state. Dishonesty is normally frowned upon. Few people would like others to think that they are dishonest. In addition to being trustworthy and reliable, honesty and frankness normally indicate that a person will think clearly and not be biased or prejudiced in his or her thinking.

❻ John is an unusual Member of Parliament: his writing reflects what his constituents think about him – that he is honest and has integrity. This in itself means that people both respect him and have confidence in him. ❾

But do remember that honesty and frankness in themselves may not always be a good thing.

❻ Janet is a highly emotional girl with writing that shows her to be totally honest and frank. The problem is that she tends to blurt out unpleasant truths in such a way as to offend or hurt her friends. Her honesty has got her into all sorts of problems. If she were a little less talkative and a little more diplomatic, Janet would have many more friends than she has. ❾

What to look for?

The main characteristic to look for when checking out honesty is, once again, the formation of the circle letters. They should be plain and simple without any loops inside the circle, or leading to or from the circle. It doesn't matter if the circle is open or closed. The more rounded these circle letters are, the more likely the person is to be honest. Look particularly to see if the letter e has a wide circle at the top. The samples below demonstrate what the circle letters should look like.

Samples of honesty

o a a   room   open
d g

boat   and motoring

How compatible are partners with differing levels of honesty?

Well, the only way to find out is to measure the writing of both parties separately and compare the two.

Once you have discovered which, if any, of the honesty/dishonesty elements are apparent in the writing you are analysing, you will be able to assess how well the two writers are likely to get along together.

The following list is meant to be a guide only. It assumes that the traits are apparent to quite a strong degree in the writing.

An honest partner with a dishonest partner

These two have totally different standards. The honest person is likely to lose out and be betrayed. It is almost impossible for this relationship to work out.

An honest partner with a secretive partner

These two are likely to have problems. The honest person will feel left out and resentment will soon build if the secretive person doesn't open up. The secretive partner may get impatient with the honest partner for revealing too much to other people.

An honest partner with a self-deceitful partner

This relationship could work, but the honest person may become frustrated by the fact that the self-deceitful person is hiding things from him- or herself. Deep-rooted self-deceit will ultimately destroy the relationship, for true emotions will be repressed and communication may break down.

Two honest partners together

This is an ideal relationship.

A dishonest partner with a secretive partner

This is another tricky relationship, particularly dangerous for the secretive partner, who may build up resentment. Awareness of each other's standards may ease major problems.

A dishonest partner with a self-deceitful partner

This is a relationship where one partner is deceiving another partner, who is already deceiving him- or herself! What a mess! The chances are that the self-deceiving partner will kid him- or herself that the other partner is honest. The relationship could work for a while, but don't hold out long-term hope.

Two dishonest partners together
These two people will understand each other, but they never be able to trust each other.

A secretive partner with a self-deceitful partner
This is a relationship where one partner will not open up and the other partner will be hiding things from him- or herself. Communication is likely to be difficult. If the traits are strong, then communication will probably break down at the first hint of trouble.

Two secretive partners together
Neither party will expect the other to open up, so this relationship could work quite well, depending on other traits present in each personality.

Two self-deceitful partners together
With both parties deceiving themselves, this relationship could be an emotional bombshell, depending upon other traits present. If both partners show similar levels of self-deceit, this relationship could work.

Having understood and compared the values of honesty and dishonesty, it is now time to study standards. We all have different standards that we feel we must adhere to. We will concentrate on four standards that can have a profound impact upon a relationship. These: are pride, vanity, dignity and independence.

Pride

Pride is often misunderstood. In graphology we *never* mean self-righteousness or arrogance when we define pride. On the contrary, pride is a positive thing. It sets the standard by which a person lives and is the yardstick for what he or she is and wishes to achieve.

People with pride generally have a desire to be approved of, both by themselves and other people. This gives them self-esteem and the urge to achieve. People who take pride in their work do a better job. People who take pride in their appearance avoid carelessness and slovenliness without even thinking about it. If pride exists in your personality you will set yourself higher standards of conduct than any friends or colleagues without pride. But if you have too much pride, then your pride turns into vanity. And this is not such a good thing!

> ❝ Marcel is proud. He is always well turned out, is intelligent, works hard and is successful in bringing in new business at work. He cares about what he says, what he does, how he dresses, where he goes and with whom he associates himself. It is important to him that other people think well of him.
>
> Justin is also proud but he is a criminal! He is proud of having committed the 'perfect' crime. ❞

So beware! What a person is proud of may be considered unworthy or reprehensible by someone with a different standard of behaviour.

What to look for?

You measure pride in handwriting by looking at the t- and d-stems. As we have already discovered, t- and d-stems have different parts to them. Study the diagram below. For pride you must look at the length of the t-stem. Pride is evident if the stems are twice to two and a half times the height of the middle-zone letters. It doesn't matter if the stems are looped or retraced.

Samples of pride

to do   *cramped*

delighted   *handwriting.*

How does pride affect compatibility in a relationship?

If someone is proud, it means they will not let their standards slip. Pride is a positive asset in a relationship. If one partner possesses it, depending on the strength of their character, he or she will ensure that his or her partner also adheres to the requisite standards. Pride enhances many other positive characteristics, such as thinking, integrity and sociability.

Vanity

Vanity occurs when a person has an excessive love of him or herself that grows and grows. Often it starts developing when a proud person doesn't gain the approval of others and so eventually becomes vain in order to compensate.

❛ Jeremy is vain. Brought up single-handedly by a busy father, he never received real love and praise from anyone. His father gave him a new car when he passed his A levels, but was too busy to spend time with the boy to discuss his future and give him encouragement. Eventually Jeremy started exaggerating his abilities and achievements, and as he began to listen to himself he became more and more vain.

It was a real shock to everyone when Jeremy failed his second-year exams at college. For Jeremy himself it was devastating. The problem was that his vanity had led him to become so narrow in his thinking that *in his opinion* he was above question and saw no need to change himself. This complacency led him to think that he was naturally intelligent and didn't need to study to the same extent as his colleagues. What a mistake! Incidentally it was just what Jeremy needed. Although he will always be prone to vanity, he is a much nicer fellow nowadays!

Mary is also vain, but for the opposite reasons. Her family spoiled her dreadfully. As a little girl, her parents constantly told her and everyone they met how beautiful and clever they thought their little darling was. As she grew up, Mary, the cute doll, looked at herself in the mirror and expected the whole world to pay rapt attention to her every move.

Mary and Jeremy met at a drinks party a couple of years ago. They were attracted to each other immediately – after all, on the surface they had a great deal in common. But the relationship exploded well before it could really develop. There just wasn't enough space for two vain people; they were constantly competing for love and affection, never giving to each other. ❜

What to look for?

Vanity is apparent in very tall t- and d-stems. The height of the stem must be over two and a half times that of the middle-zone area. Again, it doesn't matter if the stem is retraced, looped or even just a simple downstroke. The longer the stems, the greater the vanity present.

Samples of vanity

How does vanity affect compatibility in a relationship?

Vanity is detrimental to a relationship, whether existing in one or both partners. Vain people are self-absorbed and prefer taking to giving. As a result, relationships with such types become one-sided – all take and no give. Vain people find it hard to listen to others and as a result communication becomes difficult.

Dignity

In many ways, dignity is rather similar to pride. When we think of a dignified person, we generally think of someone like the Queen Mother – an individual with poise and integrity, someone who has self-esteem and self-confidence.

A dignified person is someone who has set themselves a number of standards, which he or she uses as a yardstick for living out their life. These standards are usually, although not always, conventional standards, for the dignified person aims to avoid criticism. Even when subjected to criticism, a dignified person will accept it with equanimity. The dignified person adheres closely to the code of conduct that he or she has come to approve of, and also expects others to approve and value such standards, copying his or her exemplary behaviour.

❝ When Melissa first got her own flat, she spent every weekend cleaning, decorating, sewing and fixing, so that her own small space gleamed and sparkled in the best of taste. She bought as many housekeeping magazines as she could lay her hands on, and copied their ideas. Even when she was working long hours and partying hard, Melissa still found time to clean her flat. She would never allow her standards to drop.

Melissa and Terry had been dating for six years. Marriage was rarely discussed and Melissa was beginning to feel uneasy. Surely he would have asked her by now if he was going to. But she could not allow herself to bring up the subject. Conventional in her attitudes, she felt that it was up to the man to propose. In the run-up to their seventh anniversary, Melissa decided she had to lay her cards on the table and told Terry that if he didn't want to marry her, he should come clean and they should split up. Awaiting his answer, her heart was in her mouth and she felt terrified, as if she were sitting opposite some stranger.

'Melissa, you're right,' Terry replied. 'To be honest, I'm a bit scared of the commitment of marriage, but I couldn't bear to live without you. Yes, let's get married!'

It was hardly the proposal that Melissa had dreamed of. She felt disappointed and inexplicably saddened. But before long she was swept up in the wedding plans, choosing her dress, sending out the invitations and selecting the menus. Terry was working hard, but he had time to book a fabulous honeymoon.

The big day came and, looking radiant, Melissa swept into the church on the arm of her father. As she was about to set foot down the aisle, their best man, Freddie, came hurriedly towards them. In an animated whisper he said, 'Melissa, wait! Where's Terry? I thought he'd be with you. He didn't sleep in his hotel bed last night. I haven't seen him since yesterday afternoon. Oh no! I think he's done a runner.'

Melissa and her father waited another fifteen minutes. Their guests were becoming restless and it was apparent that Terry was not going to turn up.

Pale-faced and shaking, Melissa detached herself from the arm of her father, gathered up the train of her dress and strode purposefully down the aisle. There was an unnatural silence, everyone waiting for her to speak.

'Ladies and gentlemen, thank you for waiting. I regret to say that the wedding will not be taking place today. But since my parents have been so kind as to lay on a delicious banquet, I would ask you to return to their house and enjoy yourselves.'

While her own mother was in tears, Terry's mother having mild hysteria and the rest of the guests shocked and saddened, Melissa conducted herself with dignity all day, despite the terrible shock and humiliation of being stood up at the altar. The perfect hostess, she did not allow herself to break down until the very last guest had left their house.

Melissa forgave Terry, who returned a day later. But she declined his next proposal of marriage the following week. Ever dignified, she told him that she would remain friends with him but that their relationship was finished for ever.

Melissa eventually married a charming man, ten years her senior. Their wedding was a small, family affair. And they walked up the aisle together! ❞

What to look for?

In handwriting dignity is recognized in the stems of t and d letters. The stems should be almost or totally retraced. The closer the retracing (so that it looks like one line) and the more frequently this occurs, the stronger the trait of dignity in that writing. Look at the specimens below to see what this means. You will notice that it doesn't matter what the height of the t- or d-stems are, although more often than not dignity and pride go together, so the stems will be quite tall.

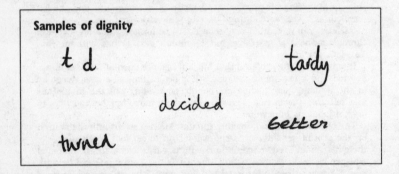

Samples of dignity

How does dignity affect compatibility in a relationship?

Dignity, in either or both partners, is an asset to any relationship. A person with dignity is invariably respected. Rarely losing his or her cool, he or she will help the less dignified partner to maintain their composure. Dignity will reduce the impact of insecurities or problematic personality traits and, by doing so, will ease the path of a relationship.

Independence

A person is an independent type if he or she thinks for him- or herself. In other words, he should come to his own conclusions without following other people or being unduly concerned about what other people think.

Surprisingly enough, an independent type is rarely rebellious or the sort of person who protests against society's norms for the sake of it. Instead, she makes up her own mind and acts accordingly. Sometimes she may conform, at other times she may break rules and go against custom, doing whatever she thinks right at the time.

Unlike a proud or vain person, who needs the approval of others, the independent type simply needs to meet his or her own standards, to gain approval from him- or herself.

❝ Max turned up for his sister's summer wedding in a short-sleeved white tennis shirt, no tie, white cotton slacks and plimsolls. All the other male guests wore suits and ties, some even wore morning dress. The ladies wore flowery, silky little numbers with ornate hats. Max stood out like a sore thumb, and his girlfriend was scarlet with embarrassment all day!

His father pulled him to one side and gave him a severe reprimand for looking such a slob. As far as Max was concerned, he understood that others might not approve of the way he was dressed, but he felt that it was crazy to wear a thick woollen suit on a hot summer's day. He tried to explain to his father that what he was wearing didn't hurt anyone else and he could see nothing wrong in disregarding a dress code. Fortunately Max's sister thought the whole thing hilarious, but it took his father a long time to forgive Max and to this day he really doesn't understand the way Max thinks. ❞

Independent thinking can be a great asset, but if the independent type constantly tries to force his or her ideas on others, this can cause tremendous friction.

Many problems of incompatibility arise when an independent type is in a relationship with a more conventional person.

❝ Lisa and John visited a marriage guidance counsellor early last year. They had been married for eighteen months, but soon after their honeymoon they started falling out. Things got so bad between them that they simply refused to talk to each other. It was Lisa's best friend Doreen who actually persuaded them both to go for marriage guidance counselling. The counsellor used graphology as an additional tool in his interview. It was vital in a case such as this where neither party wanted to talk! The problem was blatantly obvious to the counsellor once he had analysed their handwriting.

John is excessively vain and also very sensitive to criticism. It is really important to him that others like and admire everything he does. Lisa, on the other hand, is a very independent type. She will go her own way and not care what others think about her. She just cannot understand John, and thinks that he is weak and stupid. Of course John is painfully embarrassed by Lisa, and takes undue offence whenever she makes any comment relating to what he says, does or looks like.

Unfortunately for all parties involved, this story has no happy ending. Lisa filed for divorce six months ago. On one thing alone they both agreed! And that was that they would never embark on a serious relationship again without using graphology! ❞

What to look for?

Once again you need to look at the t- and d-stems. These must be short – less than two times the height of the mundane area (middle zone) of all letters in the writing. As with pride and vanity, it does not matter if the stems are retraced or looped, it is simply their height in comparison to the rest of the writing that determines the extent of independent thinking in the writer.

Since the height of the stems is the opposite to that required for vanity or pride, it goes without saying that a person cannot be an independent type and be vain or proud!

Samples of independent-type writing

to do   things

into dark   bit worried

How does independent-type thinking affect compatibility in a relationship?

The independent type does not need to conform. In the days when living together before marriage was considered *risqué*, it was the independent types who broke convention and co-habited. Independent thinkers get on best with like-minded people. They often feel claustrophobic around more conventional types, hemmed in from thinking and acting in the way they feel most comfortable.

How well do people with different standards get on together?

Two proud partners together

This relationship should work well. Both partners will under-stand each other and hopefully respect each other. It could be a powerful partnership. Strong disciplinarians, they will maintain their high standards within the confines of their relationship.

Two vain partners together
It is unlikely that there is sufficient space in a relationship to accommodate two vain people. Both will take and neither will give. It is unlikely that such a relationship could work well.

Two dignified partners together
This relationship should work well, with both parties respecting and understanding each other.

Two independent types together
Neither partner will be too concerned what other people think. So long as one partner is not an independent thinker purely on a philosophical level and the other independent on a material level, this relationship has great potential.

A proud partner with a vain partner
If vanity is excessive, then the proud person may face problems. Otherwise such a relationship could work. It will not be a 'marriage made in Heaven' and at times compromise and communication will be limited!

A proud partner with a dignified partner
This combination provides the basis for a successful relationship.

A proud partner with an independent-type partner
Friction may arise in this relationship as the parties will think along very different lines. The proud partner will be upset by the independent partner's non-conformity; the independent partner will feel constrained by the proud partner's standards and values. If they are both open-minded and have other compatible characteristics, then this relationship could work.

A vain partner with a dignified partner
It is likely that the dignified person will eventually be exacerbated by the vain person. Whenever vanity is apparent it suggests that problems may arise. Such a relationship could work although it will not be easy.

A vain partner with an independent-type partner
As in the case above, this relationship has little chance of success. Both parties are so fundamentally different that it would take great 'give and take' for it to work.

A dignified partner with an independent-type partner
This relationship will work so long as the independent type doesn't expect the dignified person to relinquish any dignity. If dignity is also apparent in the writing of the independent type, then this will be a successful relationship.

Generosity

Generosity is often considered to be of key importance in the success of relationships. Surprisingly, real generosity is quite rare. Real generosity exists without motivation; it is a sincere desire to give to or share with others, without any ulterior motive. Most people are kind or generous because they have a reason to be.

❝ Cara always gives money to charity collectors when they jangle their boxes at her on the high street. She admits that she is motivated to give because she doesn't want other people to think that she is stingy. That's not real generosity as understood by graphologists.'

'Damien is overwhelmingly generous to his girlfriend Emma. He lavishes jewellery and clothes on her, sumptuous dinners at well-known restaurants and wonderful holidays to exotic locations. Recently his father became quite concerned at his son's extravagance, knowing full well that Damien's bank account was overdrawn. A gentle and kind man himself, he gradually coaxed the truth out of his son. It became clear that Damien was being so over-generous because he was terrified of losing Emma. He genuinely thought that if he didn't buy her the best she would leave him for someone else. So even Damien's generosity had a motivation behind it. In fact Damien's writing had almost become extravagant. ❞

Study your own and your partner's writing. To what extent are you being really generous and unselfish, as opposed to bringing yourself some sort of gain from being generous?

Explained another way, generosity – for the purposes of handwriting analysis – is an extension of giving beyond the call of duty. Giving can involve anything of value – time or attention in the form of friendliness or helpfulness, material gifts or money. Generous people even share their thinking and philosophies.

❛ Rachel is a classic example of this. She is a doctor researching cures for a number of serious diseases. She never claims the credit for the discoveries she makes, allowing her colleagues to receive the acclaim and glory. Her attitude is that it doesn't matter who discovers what, so long as a cure is successfully found. ❜

Interestingly enough, generosity is normally evident in the writing of people who are secure and well balanced and have faith in themselves.

What to look for?

Generosity is apparent in handwriting when you find unusually long finals on structures or words, the width being at least that of the preceding letter formation. The generosity stroke may appear not only at the ends of words but also between the letters of a word.

Generous writers tend to leave adequate or more than adequate spaces between lines and in margins. A generous writer will never crowd his or her words onto a page. If the writing also displays the letter e with broad loops and well-rounded circle letters free of deceit or secrecy, this just enforces the degree of generosity in the writing.

When the finals are exaggerated in length, over two and a half times the width of the two preceding letters, or when the margins are so wide and the lines and letters so far apart as to be out of proportion, then you are looking at the writing of someone who is truly extravagant. Not such a good thing!

Samples of generosity

e a → *the Kind*

an end for

difference

How does generosity affect compatibility in a relationship?

If generosity exists in either partner within a relationship, this is equivalent to having a trump card. Generosity eases the path of any relationship. It is a wonderful gift and those who are on the receiving end of it are blessed indeed. A generous partner will be forgiving, patient and kind. Many characteristics that could lead to a relationship breakdown will have their impact reduced by the presence of generosity.

Meanness

The opposite to generosity is of course meanness. Mean people show a grudging reluctance to part with anything belonging to them, whether this be sharing emotions, thoughts or material belongings. This meanness of spirit affects the whole personality and has a negative effect on any relationship.

❝ Fiona is a mean person. She spent the first ten years of her life in an orphanage where she had no toys and little affection. As she grew older she developed an unconscious fear of wanting anything, terrified that once again she would have no material possessions. She never gave to anyone. Unfortunately this affected the rest of her emotions. She dared not express her emotions or be kind to anyone. Fiona is a desperately unhappy person, but she just will not admit this to herself. Once again this is a story without a happy end. She is now over fifty, lives alone and has few friends. Her meanness is so deep-rooted that it is unlikely to ever change. ❞

Really mean people tend to have a lot of fear in themselves, normally because they are afraid of want, or material deprivation. It is rare to come across a very stingy person, but if you do so, be warned – you won't be able to change them!

What to look for?
Just because there is no evidence of generosity in writing does not automatically mean that that person is mean or miserly. Meanness is shown by restrictions throughout the writing. The writing is tight, there are few open circle formations and often the writing will looked cramped and squeezed, with the letters, words and lines close together.

Of course there will not be any long endings to letters or words. It is also helpful to look out for lots of hooks at the beginning and ends of words or letters, as this will mean that the writer craves having things and then wants to hold onto them.

Writing that shows meanness is likely also to indicate that the person is overly conservative, disliking any change.

Samples of meanness

How does meanness affect compatibility in a relationship?
Stinginess spells disaster for a relationship. If one partner is unable to give, then the relationship will become very one-sided. The non-stingy person will soon become fed up of giving all the time and never receiving, in terms of love, affection and material belongings.

Let's see how compatible people are with varying levels of generosity and meanness. As you have done before, evaluate both partners' samples of writing. Remember that if the writing shows generosity, then it can't show meanness, and vice versa.

Do not be concerned if the writing shows neither meanness nor generosity – this is quite normal. If that is the case with both samples of writing, then you have no comparisons to make, so you can skip this section.

A generous partner with a mean partner
Major problems will occur, as one partner will be doing all the taking and draining the other partner emotionally and materially. The generous partner will eventually become emotionally and materially debilitated. Such a combination is unlikely to result in long-term success.

Two generous partners together
This relationship should work well. The partners should be aware that others might take advantage of their combined generosity.

Two mean partners together
If meanness is not in excess, this relationship could work as the partners will understand each other. If meanness is strong or other subconscious fears are apparent, then each partner could find him- or herself in isolation. This will not be a warm, loving relationship – but then again, this may suit some people.

One generous partner
If one person demonstrates generosity, but the other person's writing contains neither generosity nor stinginess, then the chances are that this relationship will work well. So long as the 'non-generous' partner does not take advantage of the generosity of the other partner, there should not be any untoward problems in the relationship.

One mean partner
If one person demonstrates meanness, but the other person's writing contains neither generosity nor stinginess, then the relationship may work. However, any problems will be dependent upon the extent of the one partner's meanness. If it is strong, then the relationship could become one-sided, with one partner doing all the emotional and material taking, and

the other doing all the giving. Use your own judgement to evaluate the impact of these traits.

Loyalty

People often perceive loyalty to be tightly bound up with honesty. Don't accept that! What about those individuals loyal to terrorist causes? They may be loyal but they are certainly not good, honest people. Loyalty to the wrong cause or person can be as dangerous as a complete lack of loyalty. So judge it with caution!

Some graphologists leave out loyalty altogether in the evaluation of writing, for the very reason that it is hard to tell whether it is a positive or negative trait. But for our purposes, in looking at compatibility, it is useful to assess loyalty. Most of us want our partner to be loyal to us, so if one person is loyal or values loyalty highly and the other does not, problems can arise.

People are never loyal for the sake of being so; there is always a reason why we are loyal. Normally, if we are loyal to a person, institution or cause, the loyalty either satisfies a material or emotional need or helps us achieve something.

❜ Peter was promoted last year because in his boss's eyes he was extremely loyal to his company. He worked for a small publishing house that was suffering enormously due to the recession. It looked very likely that the company was about to go into liquidation, so the Managing Director suggested that all the staff seek employment elsewhere. Most of the staff left quickly, but Peter stayed on and insisted on working for a month without pay.

Fortunately the next month the company was bought out by a large multinational. Peter not only kept his job but was promoted. As the Managing Director said, 'Peter acted well beyond the call of duty and we are delighted to recognize his loyalty by giving him promotion and a substantial bonus.' ❜

What to look for?

The easiest way to tell if someone is loyal through their handwriting is to look at the dots above the letters i and j. These should be round (but not drawn as a circle) and neat. There are a number of other characteristics that support this. These are:

1. Honesty – the lack of loops in the circle letters
2. Pride – t- and d-stems two to two and a half times the height of the mundane area
3. Positiveness – a firm downstroke descending straight to the baseline
4. Decisiveness – firm stroke endings
5. Generosity – extra-long word and letter finals

If all of these characteristics are present you will be looking at the writing of a very loyal person.

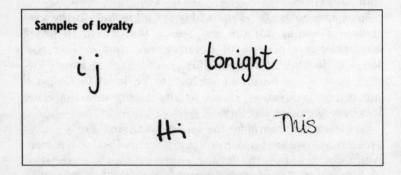

Samples of loyalty

How does loyalty affect compatibility in a relationship?

Generally speaking, loyalty is very important in a relationship. If we are not loyal to our spouse or partner we will break down the trust and sense of security that are essential to a strong relationship. Excessive loyalty to a cause or institution can in itself cause problems in a relationship. Sometimes, this loyalty will be so obsessive that the loyal partner spends more time, energy and commitment on the cause to which they are loyal than on their partner. As with most personality traits, loyalty is good in moderation and harmful in excess.

Trust and Reliability

When asked what are the most important things for a relationship, the majority of people, male and female, say trust. When that trust is broken, relationships often break down. But what is trust?

❝ For Mary it meant doing what you say you are going to do. Because Martin was consistently unreliable and never turned up to take her out when he said he was going to, Mary lost any trust in him. **❞**

❝ John thought that trust was maintaining those unwritten standards that existed, not only between him and his wife, but between himself and his workmates. He would never disclose his workmates' secrets, was utterly scrupulous when dealing with money at work and would never cheat on his wife. To John, it was really important that everyone with whom he came into contact knew where they stood with him and trusted him. **❞**

It would be impossible to trust someone who acted irrationally, was unpredictable and never did what he or she said they were going to do. Everyone wants to feel secure in a relationship. If we can predict how our partner is likely to act, it is probable that we will trust him or her. Of course, if someone is dishonest there is no way we will ever trust them again.

Reliability can be considered a part of trust. The word reliability is normally understood to mean worthy of confidence, trustworthy and dependable. If we want to trust someone, then that person will normally need to be reliable, a person we can depend on, come what may.

❝ David is completely unreliable. Sometimes he is really emotional and extrovert, at other times he withdraws into himself. With such unpredictable emotions, there is no way that you can depend on David.

Helen, on the other hand, is reliable. She always turns up at places on time and feels really bad if she doesn't do something that she promised to do. Not so long ago she was meant to be visiting her aunt in Scotland. The day before she went down with flu. Determined to go anyway, she dragged herself off to the station and forced herself on the train. By the time she got there she was feeling so ill that she ended up spending the next three days in bed – totally defeating the point of spending some fun time with her family! Her nickname is 'the rock' – because she can always be relied upon. **❞**

What to look for?

There isn't any one trait that we can look at in someone's writing to tell whether or not they are trustworthy and reliable, but instead we have to look at a number of different characteristics. When we pull all these characteristics together, then we can make up a picture of trustworthiness. If a piece of writing shows evidence of honesty, loyalty, regularity of emotions and pride, then for sure the writer is reliable. It the writing shows any signs of deceit, confusion, emotional ups and downs, or strong evidence of other fears, it is doubtful that the writer will be reliable and trustworthy.

Samples of trustworthiness and reliability

come in

fault entirely

As we discussed at the beginning of this chapter, some things are really important to one person but of no importance to another. It is up to you to decide how important the values and standards covered here are to you. Honesty may be the 'be all and end all' to you, whereas dignity may be of little importance. But understanding these values and standards, and knowing what to look for in handwriting, is of fundamental importance. With this knowledge you can be sure to understand yourself and your partner better and take the first steps towards building a harmonious relationship.

8

Are You Sexually Compatible?

- *Did the earth move for you? Was it the most mind-blowing experience, the most passionate coupling? Was it romantic, gentle and calm?*
- *Or was it a downright disappointment? Boring and unfulfilling?*
- *Or perhaps you don't yet know? Does the prospect of finding out fill you with tingles and tremors?*

How do you know if that initial attraction is going to result in the most amazing sex you have ever had? Well, until you try it, you don't! Quite often the person we find extraordinarily attractive on first sight turns out to be a real disappointment in bed, and the quirky-looking person who mistakenly touches your hand, sending sparks through your body, ends up being the most fantastic lover you have ever had.

Even if everything is great in bed with your new partner, how do you know that sex is going to continue to be good? What happens when the passion is spent and all that remains is a tiny ember? Unless you can see into a glass ball you won't know how your sex life is going to develop. But, if you compare your writing with that of your partner, you can make a sensible estimate as to how sexually compatible you are now, and consequently how sexually compatible you are likely to remain in the future.

Everyone has a different attitude towards sex. Unfortunately, because sex is still considered to be slightly taboo, most of us find it difficult to talk about our feelings, sexual likes and dislikes. Normally you need to have answers to the questions below from both partners before you can assess how compatible the partners are likely to be on a sexual level.

- *How important is sex in your relationship?*
- *How much physical energy do you have? How often do you want to do it?*
- *What is your attitude towards sex? Do you enjoy it? How passionate are you?*
- *Do you have any sexual hang-ups?*
- *What are your sexual preferences?*
- *What is your sexual orientation?*

The trouble is that if you are just beginning a new relationship, or even if you are an established couple, the chances are that you are not going to want to ask your partner all these questions! The beauty of handwriting analysis is that you can get the answers without asking the questions. And that is what this chapter is all about: gleaning the answers to these questions from both partners' writing and then assessing their sexual compatibility.

Sexual Energy

Do you and your partner have the same appetite for sex? When we are tired or ill the last thing in the world we feel like doing is making love. This is quite simply because we don't have the energy! It is a physically active pursuit and without the correct energy it just isn't going to happen.

For some people sex in a relationship is the 'be all and end all'. As far as they are concerned, if the sex is no good then there may as well be no relationship. For others sex is important but certainly not the make-or-break factor of the relationship. However, problems arise when one partner wants sex frequently but the other partner does not. Quite often this incompatibility is a result of differing levels of sexual energy.

❦ Candy is an air stewardess. She flies on transatlantic flights several times a month. She is beautiful, witty and attentive – quite the perfect hostess. She remembers travellers' names, their food preferences and even makes sure she has their favourite journals on board for them to read.

Candy wears a simple gold wedding band. But she is not married! Candy has had so many proposals and unpleasant advances that she has decided to pretend she is married to ward off unwelcome attention.

Of course this ploy does have its disadvantages. A couple of times over the last year she had noticed a particularly attractive American gentleman. His smile sent shivers through Candy. Every week, she glanced down the passenger list in anticipation – was his name there?

A while ago Candy stayed overnight in a plush hotel in New York.

'Hi, Candy, how are you doing?' yelled Greta, a colleague, from the other side of the lobby. 'Will you join us for dinner?

'So how's life?' Greta enquired. 'I notice you've "lost" your ring! Got your eyes on someone, have you?'

Candy looked down at her hand with a start. 'Oh no, I've really lost it!' she exclaimed. 'I must have dropped it in the gym. Remind me to go and look after dinner.'

As Candy was returning alone to her room, someone tapped her gently on the shoulder.

'Excuse me, but I was wondering if I could buy you a drink?' And standing before her was the very gentleman she had so admired on those transatlantic crossings.

And so began the romance between Candy and her handsome passenger, a man called Brad. For two months they saw each other every time Candy stayed in New York.

One evening Brad asked Candy to marry him. 'I want to spend some real time with you, not the odd night here and there. Let's get engaged. Quit your job. Come and live with me here in New York. I'll look after you.'

Candy's initial reaction was no. How could she leave everything behind and, most importantly, lose her independence? On the other hand, she had fallen in love with Brad.

After a couple of weeks with her mind in confusion Candy applied for a new position with the airline, as a member of the ground staff in New York.

The first night she moved into Brad's place, they made love in front of the fireplace. 'Mmm, I want to do it all over again right now!' murmured Candy.

'You wild woman,' joked Brad. 'Give me half an hour!' But half an hour later he was fast asleep and Candy was wide awake.

Candy found New York exciting. She adored Brad's minimalist apartment and relished being around his friends. She joined a local gym and exercised morning and night. But Brad's energy seemed to have disappeared.

Towards the end of that first week Brad said, 'You tire me out, darling! Tonight I need a night off. Sleep in my arms, but I'm just not up to sex. I need to sleep.' The following night Brad told Candy he was still too tired for sex. And that pretty much set the pattern of their relationship. Candy wanted to make love every night, several times a night. Brad liked hugging and stroking but only wanted to make love occasionally.

To begin with Candy didn't mind too much. She woke up early and went for a run. During the day she was running around the airport, and in the evenings she went to the gym. But after three or four weeks she began to feel that it wasn't enough. She always had plenty of energy after work, but Brad generally flopped out once he returned home. Candy still adored being around him. She liked his humour, and he was kind and loving.

One day as Candy was sorting out her clothes, she tipped upside-down a pair of old tracksuit bottoms that she hadn't worn for a while and out fell the 'lost' gold ring. She sat on the floor, slipped it on her finger and stared at it.

'Am I really doing the right thing here?' she asked herself. 'Yes, I think Brad is gorgeous; yes, he is a great friend and brilliant to be around. But we really are not compatible as lovers. He simply never wants to do it, and I am going mad. I think I'm settling for second best here. It's not what I really want.'

Later that night Candy gently explained to Brad that, as far as she was concerned, things were not working. She wanted to remain friends, but they simply were not compatible as lovers. Their physical energy levels were so different, she honestly didn't see how it could ever work out.

Many tears were shed, but eventually they both agreed to go their separate ways in search of partners with similar sexual needs. **,**

There are many reasons why one partner has lots of energy and the other doesn't. Lack of energy can be to do with illness or weakness, a lack of interest in physical activities or the channelling of energies elsewhere so that there is no energy left for love-making.

What to look for?

Anything to do with physical and sexual energy shows itself in the lower loops of letters – particularly in the letters g and y.

When you are looking at the extent of sexual energy you should look at the lower loops or sticks coming down from letters such as f, g, j, p, q and y. Then evaluate the degree of pressure exerted on the page. Feel the reverse of the page and look at the width of the lines. The heavier the writing and the greater the pressure exerted, the more energy the writer has.

Sexually energetic types

The loops and stems of the g and y in particular will look and feel heavy. Feel the reverse of the page; it should feel heavily indented.

Averagely energetic types
The loops and stems will have about the same pressure and weight as the rest of the letters in the writing.

Unenergetic types
The loops and stems will look lighter in pressure than the rest of the writing. If all of the writing looks very light, and no indents can be felt on the reverse of the page, this indicates that little energy is available for any physical pursuits.

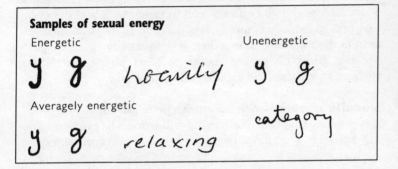

Samples of sexual energy

Energetic   Unenergetic

Averagely energetic

How does sexual energy affect compatibility in a relationship?
Compatibility of energy is vital for a successful relationship.

Sexually energetic people have considerable amounts of energy, enjoy physical pursuits and very probably relish sex. Their sex drive needs to have an outlet. Averagely energetic people, as the description suggests, enjoy being active and enjoy sex, but do not let the activity consume them, dictating the way they live their lives. Unenergetic people have little energy available for sex. Although they may have plenty of energy for other pursuits, it is unlikely that sex will play an important part in these people's lives.

So how do these types get along together?

Two sexually energetic types together
Both of these partners adore sex, have considerable energy and will spend a lot of time together making love. They are the passionate types and should get on very well. Of course if there are

problems in the relationship outside the sphere of sex, the sex in itself may not hold the couple together in the long term. Nevertheless, this combination bodes well.

Sexually energetic with an averagely energetic partner

All too often when partners have differing levels of energy, the more physical partner will seek his or her fulfilment elsewhere if he or she can't get it within a relationship. The less physical partner may well feel pressured against his or her will to meet the sexual demands of the energetic partner. If this difference is not discussed it can quickly lead to resentment and the eventual breakdown of communications. Then there is nothing left to bind the relationship together. If the sexually energetic partner can direct his or her energy to other physical activities, such as sport, then the relationship will work.

Sexually energetic with an unenergetic partner

It is unlikely that this relationship will work. The problems arising between a sexually energetic and an averagely energetic partner will just be compounded in this relationship. The sexually energetic partner will feel unloved and hurt by the unenergetic partner's reluctance to make love, whereas the unenergetic partner will feel upset and angered by the pressure put upon him or her by the energetic partner. In addition, the unenergetic partner is unlikely to enjoy the passionate love-making style of the energetic partner.

Two averagely energetic partners together

This relationship should work well. Both partners will enjoy sex but appreciate that there are many other activities that they can share besides their time in bed. Again, assuming all is well outside the physical realm of their relationship, this pairing should be successful.

Averagely energetic with an unenergetic partner

The lack of compatibility of sexual energy does not help this relationship. The averagely energetic partner will encourage and cajole the unenergetic partner to share in love-making, but one or the other partner will have to compromise. Eventually the averagely energetic partner is likely to become bored by the disinterest of his or her partner.

Two unenergetic partners together

Sex is unimportant in the lives of both of these partners, and they will rarely indulge in it. This does not mean that they are not romantic or sensitive, but physical pursuits are simply not their cup of tea!

Sensuality and Sensuousness

Romantic or practical, indulgent or moderate? How do you both feel? Sensuality and sensuousness are closely linked, but a little different. There are two issues to consider when deciding which is which. First, how important are the senses to the individual? Second, how strongly are these senses indulged? If the senses are important to a person but are not overly indulged, then that individual is defined as sensual. If, on the other hand, the senses are very important to the person and they are heavily indulged, that person is defined as sensuous. Read on to discover what this all means!

Sensual people have healthy appetites for anything regarding the five senses of sight, sound, smell, touch and taste. They relish good food and wine, appreciate beautiful things, love melodic music and adore physical contact. Sensual people are acutely sensitive to unpleasant experiences, often being physically repelled by unpleasant smells or tastes and strongly reacting against ugly sights and sounds. Sensual people are fundamentally tactile beings. Easily aroused themselves, they tend to take enormous pleasure from caressing and touching their lover.

Sensuous individuals constantly give in to their innate desire to be gratified via their senses. Such people seek fulfilment as an end in itself. They eat simply to indulge their strong appetite, caring little if they put on weight or make gluttons of themselves. They often have many lovers, as they give in to their need for constant sexual satisfaction. Overly sensuous people are often described as too indulgent, decadent or greedy. Unfortunately, when people constantly give in to the overwhelming desire to fulfil the senses, it can lead to excess and, ultimately, self-destruction.

Although sensuous people are likely to have a strong preoccupation with sex, sensuousness in itself does not indicate that a strong sex drive is actually expressed. Nevertheless if the writing shows one or more of the strokes set out below, at the very least that person's mind is preoccupied by sex, and the chances are that they will physically indulge in it as well. If the writing is extremely smudgy and dark, this can indicate violence and even a predisposition towards sexual perversion.

❢ At a charity dance the disc jockey announced that to get the party moving everyone had to participate in a game. Loud groans emanated from all the tables.

'Ladies, kindly remove your left shoe and place it in the centre of the room. Gentlemen, you must select a shoe from the pile and then find your Cinderella! Match the shoe with the owner and invite her to dance.'

Barbara removed her red suede sling-back shoe apprehensively. 'Knowing my luck, I'll have to dance with the oldest, fattest, ugliest man with the largest number of ex-wives in the room!' she muttered to her best friend.

When a gentleman broke into their conversation, holding out a red suede shoe and asking them if either of them was the owner, Barbara couldn't conceal the look of relief on her face. Earl was tall, dark, with slicked-back black hair and a gleaming row of white pearly teeth. He wore a brightly coloured waist-jacket made from silk brocade.

Earl began the conversation by admiring Barbara's beautiful dress. 'I adore fine fabrics!' he told his rather bemused partner. After their first dance, during which Earl seemed to be totally absorbed by the music, shutting his eyes and swaying in delight to the gentle, rhythmic sounds, Earl led Barbara to the bar and announced that he was going to select her the most delicious cocktail she had ever drunk. Indeed the multi-coloured drink was in Barbara's words 'quite sublime!'

Later on, in the early hours of the morning, Earl and Barbara were walking away from the dance floor when a voice shouted, 'Barbara! What a surprise!'

Barbara turned round to see an old friend she'd lost touch with a couple of years previously. After a quick hug, Barbara introduced Earl to Amy. 'So, Amy, who are you with this evening?'

Amy glanced over her shoulder towards the bar, and *sotto voce* she replied, 'No one. But the bloke who chose my shoe just won't leave me alone. He'll be back from the bar with my drink any second now. Can you try and help me get away from him?'

Before Barbara could reply, a fat, middle-aged man, wearing a shiny tuxedo over a shirt that was struggling to conceal his large hairy belly, lumbered up to their group and, stroking Amy's arm, handed her a drink.

'Hi, my name's Bert. Who are you?'

Before they could reply, Bert continued, 'Isn't she gorgeous, this doll here!' Amy squirmed and Barbara tried to suppress her grin. 'I chose her 'cos of her gorgeous suede shoes. Show them here, lovey.'

All four of them looked down at Amy's feet and simultaneously all four of them gasped. Amy and Barbara appeared to be wearing the identical pair of red suede sling-back shoes.

'What size are you, Amy?' Barbara asked.

'Oh darling,' murmured Bert, fondling Amy's hair, 'you're just the right size for me.'

Amy pulled away and said, 'A thirty six, and you?'

'I don't believe it, we're wearing the same shoes in the same size! That means I could be dancing with Bert and you could be dancing with Earl! Oh poor you, Amy, you really were unlucky tonight!'

In the following weeks, Earl wined and dined Barbara; he took her to concerts; he invited her for weekends in the country, where they lay in fields and watched the sunset; he gave her beautiful presents. He never forced himself upon Barbara. He waited until she was ready before he made love to her. And when he did so it was with a fiery but gentle passion that she had never known before. He took delight in her pleasure and was never happier than when she was holding his hand or stroking his hair. Six months later Barbara and Earl were married. They are still deeply in love, utterly compatible and content with each other.

Earl is a sensuous person and, to a lesser degree, so is Barbara. He adores indulging his senses but never to excess. He loves life and he loves beautiful things, but he is in control of his senses.

A year or so later Barbara ran into Amy again. Over a cup of coffee they exchanged gossip.

'You know that Bert guy who was chasing me at the dance last year?' Amy said. 'Well, you won't believe it but he was in the papers a couple of weeks ago. He's been declared bankrupt and he's being sued for sexually harassing a famous TV presenter. The article was all about people who live life to excess. Apparently he's quite famous. But he ate and drank and smoked so much that he ran out of money. According to this presenter, he's sex-mad. Has to do it all the time, everywhere, with anyone! Makes me feel good, that does!'

Sure enough, Bert is overly sensuous. He over-indulged in everything, so that his life ran totally out of control. **❩**

Both sensuous and sensual people can be the most passionate, exciting and imaginative love-makers, enjoying life to the full. Of course a sensual person is best matched with another sensual person, for he or she will find it hard to exist without sensory gratification.

A sensuous person is likely, in the long run, to be unattractive to any partner. Such people are often so addicted to sex that they will find it hard to be faithful if their partner is away for any length of time. They are frequently greedy and self-interested types, looking to fulfil their own needs rather than their partner's.

What to look for?

Sensual writing
This is composed of thick lines, perhaps where the writer out of choice writes with thick-nibbed pens. The thicker the width of the strokes of the writing, the more important the senses are to the writer.

Sensuous and overly sensual writing
This is indicated by writing that looks smudgy or bleary, or has lines that look thicker and heavier in some places than in others. It is also indicated by letters that are clogged up with ink. Graphologists often refer to this as the pastiosity of the writing.

Samples of sensual and sensuous writing

Sensual   Sensuous

colder   *Lient gue*

Handwriting   *words*

How do sensuality and sensuousness affect compatibility in a relationship?

Sensual partner with a non-sensual partner
These two are very different, appreciating different things in life. Nevertheless, the non-sensual partner may be able to appreciate the sensual partner's love of food, wine, atmosphere, music, etc. but is unlikely to want to join in. Their sexual desires are different and considerable work would need to be put into this relationship to sustain it.

Sensual partner with a sensuous partner
Although both partners enjoy sensual things, and both should take pleasure in languorous sex sessions, the sensual partner

acts in moderation and the sensuous partner acts in excess. It may be difficult for the sensuous partner to remain faithful as he or she will require constant gratification of the senses in which the non-sensual partner may not want to indulge. The sensuous partner will need to take control of his or her excesses for this relationship to work.

Two sensual partners together
This relationship should work well as both partners adopt a similar attitude to sex and pleasurable pursuits. Unlike their sensuous contemporaries, they will not over-indulge, but simply enjoy themselves within their means. Assuming all else fits together well, this should be a healthy sexual partnership.

Two sensuous partners together
These partners are fundamentally compatible, adopting a similar approach to life. They both enjoy the good life to excess. This couple could end up seeing either their health or their money run out as they over-indulge in anything sensual. Sex is vital to both of them, and sex together should be good. Nevertheless, self-destruction is quite possible with this extravagent duo.

Sensuous partner with a non-sensual partner
These two are generally incompatible. One partner has a strong desire to live life to the full, gratifying his or her senses, while the other partner feels no such desire and probably takes a much more conservative approach to life. On a sexual level there is no compatibility. One partner will want to indulge in frequent, lengthy, arduous sex sessions, the other will have no such interest. The sensuous partner will quickly become bored, seeking fulfilment elsewhere.

Sexual Anxieties

There are many people who have hang-ups about sex. Perhaps they do not enjoy it, or perhaps they are unable to perform. Many of these problems can be discovered by analysing a person's handwriting. In this section we look at some of the most common sexual anxieties.

Sexual Disinterest – Not Tonight, Darling!

Disinterest in sex is rather common. Often it is a temporary disinterest, caused by external pressures such as too much work, illness, inhibition, or even boredom. The way to check whether or not this disinterest is permanent or temporary is to study the person's writing over a period of months or years. If the writing changes to show the disinterest signs, then this indicates that it is temporary. If the writer always seems to have writing in this genre, then it is an indication of a permanent disinterest.

Let's look at the reasons for sexual disinterest in further detail.

‘A couple of years ago Dawn was consumed with worry. Redundancy threatened just over the horizon. Both of her sons had had poor school reports. Her mother was ill and it looked as if she would soon have to be moved into an old people's home. Dawn's ex-husband had stopped paying her child-benefit payments. All of these worries preyed on her mind and made her feel increasingly weary. The relationship with her long-standing boyfriend, Gary, had begun to falter. Dawn never felt like making love and found herself taking every step she could to avoid it. She would pretend that she was asleep or she could hear one of the boys crying. She began to put Gary off from coming to see her, because she knew she didn't want to sleep with him. Naturally Gary was very upset and couldn't understand Dawn's sudden chilliness.

Dawn's friend Sharon, a professional counsellor, was learning graphology at the time. Looking at Dawn's writing, she told her that she could see that she was currently going through a tough patch. She went on to say that the writing showed that Dawn was deeply anxious and this was probably playing havoc with her libido. Dawn promptly burst into tears, gratefully relieved that someone seemed to understand her problems. Sharon helped Dawn tackle each of her problems one by one. Within six months Dawn had a new job, had been to her sons' schools and helped steer them on a course of intensive homework, helped move her mum into a home and lodged proceedings against her ex-husband for non-payment. Soon afterwards Dawn felt like a new person. She rang up Gary and slowly they started to rebuild their relationship.

Patrick had a similar problem, but his was work-related. His high-flying job on Wall Street meant that he had to work eleven hours a day, frequently taking transatlantic flights to meetings in Europe. He was under immense pressure to bring in huge profits. His young wife never saw him and, on the few occasions that they were together, Patrick was too exhausted to do anything but hold his wife in his arms and fall asleep. His work simply sapped all his sexual energy. His wife wanted children. She gave Patrick an ultimatum. Either cut down the work or she would leave him. Patrick couldn't decide. He loved his wife but he also loved his job. He felt that he couldn't do without the addictive excitement and his massive salary, which of course he never had time to spend. Patrick dithered for too long, and his wife walked out of his life for ever.

Another reason for avoidance of sex can be boredom. Beth and John have been married for thirteen years. Their friends all harbour a bit of envy for the couple. Beth doesn't work – she doesn't need to, as her husband earns a lot and she herself has a private income. The couple have two beautiful children, a girl and a boy, perfectly behaved and both doing well at school. Beth entertains frequently. John is constantly giving his wife presents, small and sometimes large tokens of his affection. Three times a year he whisks his family away to some exotic location halfway around the globe. What their friends don't know is that Beth and John stopped having a sexual relationship some years back. Their love-making pattern became monotonous, every Saturday evening, which then became every other Saturday evening, and so on, until it petered out altogether. Quite simply Beth and John, although they love each other dearly, became bored by their sexual encounters and tacitly came to an understanding that they just wouldn't do it any more. Neither of them felt the need.

Chloe's writing also shows signs of disinterest in sex, but for rather different reasons. She is totally preoccupied with herself and her daily life. She doesn't have a boyfriend and hasn't had one for a few years. This is mainly because she is utterly self-centred. From time to time she has a one-night stand. To her, sex is a trade-off for other favours from her partners. An example of this occurred with her last boss. She didn't particularly like him but thought that she would achieve a quick route to promotion if she slept with him. Unfortunately the result was the opposite: she lost her job.

Kevin was her last long-term boyfriend. She used to tell him that she would sleep with him if he did the washing, or she would perform certain sexual favours if he would buy her a new dress or take her out for dinner. Sex was a bargaining tool, a means to an end, not something she enjoyed doing. 🌒

What to look for?

Disinterest in sex is shown by a number of different strokes, but always within the lower loops or sticks of the letters g and y.

Disinterest because of illness or anxiety

Look for uneven pressure, breaks in the loops or stems, and tremors or jerks in the writing. Often the loops of the g and y will be disproportionately large but will have breaks in them.

Disinterest due to pressure of work

The y- and g-stems will often be short sticks. If the sticks or thin loops appear to be pulled towards the right, this indicates stress and overwork.

Disinterest due to boredom

The g and y will either be sticks or average-sized loops, but all lower endings will be short and will consistently look the same, in a rigid, rather monotonous way.

Disinterest due to self-interest
The writing will be totally or almost totally within the middle zone. Loops and sticks, both upwards and downwards, will be almost non-existent.

Samples of sexual disinterest

Due to illness

singing

Due to work pressures

anything

Due to boredom

anything

Due to self-interest

leaving darling

How does disinterest in sex affect compatibility in a relationship?
Naturally disinterest in sex can have a catastrophic effect on a relationship. If neither partner is interested in sex, all well and good. It will simply be a celibate, or near-celibate, relationship. However, if one partner has a healthy sexual appetite and the other partner has a disinterest in sex, then the relationship is on a collision course to failure. The interested partner is unlikely to settle for a celibate life, and will either seek satisfaction elsewhere or will try and compel the disinterested partner to have sex. The disinterested partner will feel threatened and uneasy, simply magnifying the sexual problems he or she has even more. The only solution to such a relationship is to get professional counselling for the disinterested partner if the problem cannot be solved alone.

Impotence – Wants to but Can't . . .

Someone is defined as being impotent if he or she cannot perform the sexual act due to some physical dysfunction. It is interesting to note that psychiatrists and many doctors believe that impotence is more often the result of some emotional problem than having its root in a physical or hormonal disorder.

❝ Many people, both men and women, at some time in their life find that they cannot have sex. The first time Alec and Gemma made love, it was a total disaster. Alec could not perform. He was mortified. It had never happened to him before, and he so desperately wanted to make love to Gemma. Fortunately she was understanding and sympathetic. They put the experience down to nerves, and sure enough a couple of nights later everything was just fine. ❞

However, some people are severely affected by impotence. People who suffer from this often find that they cannot combine feelings of affection with the physical act of sex. Perhaps they can 'perform' with strangers, with whom they can maintain an aloofness, but when it comes to having sex with a loved one, it all falls to pieces.

Of course the inability to have sex is bound to have a negative impact on any relationship, and if the problem is severe the way to solve it is through therapy or medical assistance supported by a loving partner.

Normally the only way that you can find out whether or not your future partner is, or is not, impotent is by actually trying it out! But using graphology allows you to gain an insight into what to expect. Nevertheless it is important to be aware that impotence is often a transient situation. Similar to disinterest, it can be the result of stress, illness or preoccupation with something else.

What to look for?

Impotence is difficult to assess. You should look at the lower loops, particularly the letter g. The writing should show at least two or three of the following signs:

- *The lower loops or stems of the letter g will be lighter in pressure than in the middle zone.*
- *The stem or the whole letter will appear broken or with a variance in pressure.*
- *The lower g will have a wobbly, shaky look.*
- *All of the lower g's will be retraced.*
- *The lower g is so short that it hardly descends from the baseline at all.*

Sexual Guilt and Repression

Some people have been brought up to believe that sex is bad, dirty or even dangerous. As a result these individuals may end up repressing their sexual desires, refusing to make love and in extreme cases pushing sexual thoughts out of their mind altogether. When they do succumb to making love, these people are utterly consumed by guilt, which inhibits their enjoyment of the act. This in itself can hinder performance.

Guilt and repression in relation to sex are all too common. As a society we find it hard to talk about sex, so as a result people are encouraged to internalize their feelings about it. If such feelings are ones of dissatisfaction or confusion, these become trapped inside the person, ultimately having a negative effect not only on the individual's emotional health but also on their physical well-being.

❢ When Poppy was a young child of six or seven she went on holiday with her parents to the south of Spain. The three of them shared a room, with Poppy sleeping on a small divan and her parents in the large double bed. One night the little girl awoke to hear strange sounds in the bedroom. They seemed to be coming from her parents and she was terrified. Rather than saying anything out loud, she placed her pillow over her head and pulled the sheets up over the top of it. Minutes later the sounds stopped but she began wheezing from lack of air. The next thing she could remember were the soothing voice and warm arms of her mother around her.

Poppy's parents were strict and rather Victorian in their attitude. Sex was never discussed at home. Saucy television programmes were switched off. Poppy grew up to be ashamed of her body and very scared of sex. Not only did she believe it to be a bad thing, but she had also repressed the memory of hearing her parents making love. In the recesses of her mind she linked love-making to the terror of not being able to breathe.

Growing up into a beautiful young woman, popular and exceptionally bright, Poppy had numerous admirers. She lost her virginity to her boyfriend when she was twenty-four years old. It was a devastating experience, painful and incredibly disappointing. To compound this, Poppy was consumed with guilt. Imagined images of her mother, furiously condemning her, haunted Poppy for weeks, both when she was awake and in her dreams. She felt dirty and ashamed at what she had done, regretful that she hadn't waited until she was married. She swore that she would never have sex again until her wedding night. Sure enough, her boyfriend soon dumped her, fed up with the prospect of waiting.

Poppy became increasingly nervous and her self-esteem plummeted.

She exercised enormous control over herself and tried not to show her feelings in public. Nevertheless a number of her close friends commented on how strangely aloof she had become.

After a couple of years she met Lucien, a man of high principles and strong religious beliefs. He was pleased that Poppy wished to save herself for their marriage.

Their engagement was short. The wedding itself was beautiful, but that first night was difficult and a taste of what was to come. Ashamed of her own body, Poppy would not let her husband see her in the nude. Over the coming weeks and months they made love, but Poppy refused to talk about her feelings, was only willing to try the missionary position and generally seemed disinterested in sex.

After a long while, constantly trying to be patient and understanding with Poppy, Lucien came to accept that their love life was going to be fraught with problems, primarily because Poppy seemed to repress her feelings and ignore her sexual desires. Initially he had blamed himself, thinking that perhaps he was not a good enough lover for his wife, and then later on he even had doubts about whether she really loved him. Eventually he began to grapple with the truth of the matter, that Poppy seemed to be hiding her feelings both from him and from herself. **9**

People who suffer from guilty feelings about sex or who are unable to get in touch with their feelings are best advised to seek professional help, as both guilt and repression normally have links with the person's childhood, blocks that can often be eased by therapy. Both sexual guilt and repression are bound to have significant ill effects on relationships.

What to look for?

Once again the place to look is in the lower loop of the letter g. Repression is evident if the loop is extremely narrow or if the upstroke of the pen retraces the downstroke.

Guilt is evident when you see felon's claws in the writing. A felon's claw is a formation rather like the letter c fallen flat on its face. Have a look at the samples below to understand this better. Guilt is particularly evident in a person's writing when you find felon's claws in the lower-zone letters, within capital letters or in the personal pronoun 'I' Drooping middle-zone letters may also indicate guilt.

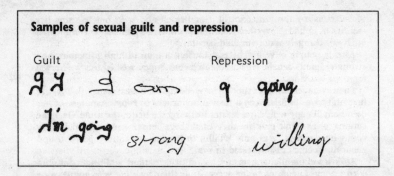

Sexual Orientation

In this section we are looking at unusual sexual preferences, the sort of preferences that you may like to know about before embarking on a relationship!

Promiscuity

Is he a stud? Is she a nymphomaniac?

❛ Kelly's nickname is 'numero uno nymphette'. She knows it is and she doesn't care. Kelly would be quite happy if she could sleep with a different man every night. She doesn't quite achieve that, but she has had hundreds of lovers, many of whom she wouldn't recognize if she ran into them. As is typical of nymphomaniacs, Kelly is on a deep quest to find love. The trouble is that she has plenty of random sex but never develops personal relationships.

Kelly's parents didn't do her any favours. They treated her like an adult from a very young age, rarely displaying any affection for her and preferring to leave her for long hours in the care of community centres and well-meaning friends. Kelly's mother often told her that she really didn't like children and couldn't wait for the day when Kelly grew up. Her father spent little time at home. At the age of fourteen, Kelly discovered that her parents weren't married and that her father was still married to another woman with whom he had three children. Kelly was devastated and this revelation just compounded the problems that had already developed during her childhood. So on her sixteenth birthday she left home, and soon afterwards she started on the sex trail.

For years now Kelly has been feeling depressed and abandoned. She desperately envies those of her friends in long-term relationships, but she just doesn't know how to go about creating such a relationship herself. Kelly sees sexual contact as comforting. It is the closest that she can get to feeling loved and wanted.

A little while ago she stumbled across a girl called Robyn who seemed to be treading the same circuit, in and out of similar men's beds. After an initial period of jealousy the two began to develop a friendship. Unlike Kelly, Robyn is angry with men. Sexually abused as a child, she feels that by sleeping with men, but not building a relationship, she is using them in the same way that she was used and abused in the past. 'I use their bodies and withhold any emotion. Woe betide the bloke who wants to start a relationship. In for a shock, he would be!' she explains.

Neither Kelly nor Robyn stands any chance of developing a normal relationship in their current state of mind. Both of them need to seek professional help to rid themselves of their negative feelings before they can hope to build a normal relationship.

Bob is similar to Kelly. He has numerous lovers but deep down is unconsciously seeking a loving, secure relationship. The problem is that he was emotionally wounded when jolted by his fiancée five years ago, and he has never got over it. He whispers her name when in bed with other lovers; he adorns his room with photos of her; and he still dreams that one day they may get back together again. In the meantime he has become cold and defensive towards other women. He wants them, but he doesn't want them to get too close. **9**

Assuming that you are looking to develop a monogamous relationship, then promiscuity in either partner, male or female, is going to be unacceptable.

The fact that someone beds many different partners is normally an indication of a deeper emotional problem. Such people can be great friends, but it is probably unwise to develop a relationship with them as they will find it difficult, if not impossible, to remain faithful to you.

What to look for?

Promiscuity in writing is evident if you can see either or both of the following:

- *The g-stem looks like an over-inflated balloon shape, which is three and a half times or more the length of the middle zone.*
- *The g-stem looks like an over-inflated balloon shape and many of the letters are clogged with ink so that the lines look smeary and thick, written with heavy pressure.*

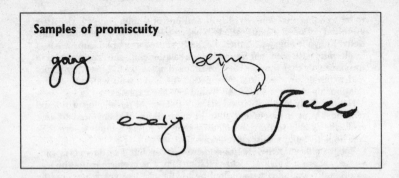

Samples of promiscuity

going

bem

evely

Jully

Sexual Experimenters

What does your partner really like to get up to in bed? Sexual experimenters, often considered to be kinky or weird, frequently boast that there is nothing within the sexual sphere that they haven't tried. People who practise bondage, spanking, hard-core pornography and any other 'unusual' sexual act are defined as sexual experimenters. Others who do not have the same desire to experiment may consider sexual experimenters to be perverted.

❝ Agatha had been widowed at a young age under tragic circumstances. It wasn't until her youngest child left home that she began to think again about relationships. The problem was that she rarely met eligible men. So, unbeknown to her friends or family, she decided to reply to a few Lonely Hearts adverts in the local paper.

She had a couple of mediocre dates with unexciting men. Then she met Gordon. His advert had described him as 'a debonair, middle-aged, divorced gentleman, looking for love and excitement, romance and companionship'. He listed his hobbies as 'cooking, racing cars, woodwork and other more unusual pursuits'.

As far as his looks were concerned, Gordon could have been Agatha's dream man. Sporting a neat moustache, he was similar in build to her late husband, well built but physically trim. On their first meeting he was dressed in a cashmere navy blazer and shining shoes, and at every meeting thereafter he was a smart but seemingly conservative dresser.

Gordon treated Agatha to many wonderful evenings and days out over a period of several weeks. Constantly the perfect gentleman, he never did more than kiss her. One evening he took her hand and asked if she would spend a weekend with him in the Lake District where he had rented a house. Agatha knew what this meant. Making love was very definitely on the cards. Blushing slightly, she agreed to join him.

They had a wonderful weekend, perfectly romantic, and their relationship continued in this vein for a month or so. Although Agatha had been to Gordon's house, whenever they made love it was in her bed in her house. She began to wonder why he never proposed that she come and stay with him.

One day she said, 'Can't I come and stay at your place sometime?'

Gordon went very quiet and still. After a few long seconds he replied, 'Yes, perhaps it is time. Why don't you come round next Saturday night?'

Gordon cooked a sumptuous meal, which they ate in front of a blazing fire, listening to gentle classical music. After the meal he took her by the hand and led her upstairs saying, 'I've got a surprise for you, darling!'

To Agatha's horror Gordon's surprise was an array of equipment and clothes he clearly intended to use in their love making. Frightened and shocked, Agatha ran out of house never to see him again. ❥

Gordon is a gentle, kind person but he has unusual sexual perversions, which horrified Agatha. The problem for him is that the women to whom he is attracted would never, ever want to share those perversions with him.

Sexual experimenters are rarely satisfied with lovers who do not wish to share in their own erotic games. Although they may remain in a normal relationship, experimenters will invariably feel compelled to seek erotic satisfaction elsewhere. As a result, such people may develop deceit, as they do not want others to know about their strange perversions.

If you are in, or wish to develop, a relationship with a sexual experimenter, it is necessary for you also to share your partner's unusual interests, otherwise there is little hope that such a partnership can develop on a physical basis.

What to look for?
Sexual experimenters generally have unusual g-stems. These can be any of the following:

- *Reversed direction in the lower endings*
- *Distorted-looking letters, stems or loops*
- *Downward-pointing lower stems or loops*
- *A felon's claw-type loop in the g- and y-stems*

Look at the examples below to see other samples of unusual lower loops and stems.

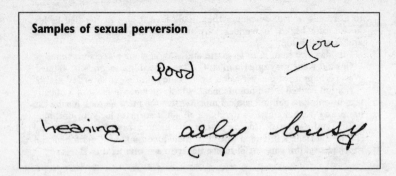

Samples of sexual perversion

Sometimes people have sexual perversions but they are constrained, so they do not act them out. You know for sure that people do act out their perversions if, in addition to usual g-stems, they have writing that has a heavy, muddy look or uneven pressure.

Homosexuality

As with all sexual behaviour, homosexuality is a very sensitive and private matter.

There are a number of handwriting experts who believe that it is possible to assess homosexuality in writing. However, even for the professional graphologist, homosexuality is very difficult to analyse. This is due to a number of different reasons.

First, there are so many different signs to look for in the writing. Only a very experienced analyst would be competent to say definitively whether or not the writer has a homosexual bias. Second, just because someone may be homosexually, heterosexually or bisexually inclined does not mean that they actually practise it. And third, some gay people do not display any homosexual signs in their writing. Often these are the types of people who are not overtly gay in behaviour and who are comfortable with their homosexuality.

Unlike other personality traits, in the opinion of the author handwriting analysis is *not* a foolproof method of assessing whether a person is heterosexual, homosexual or bisexual. There are a number of publications in print you may find of interest if you wish to explore this matter further. For the purposes of this introductory book, the traits are listed below.

However, it is vital to emphasize that just because you see homosexual traits in someone's writing that does not mean that person is a practising gay.

What to look for?

There are some major and some minor signs of homosexuality in writing. If one or all of the major signs are evident, then it is likely that the writer has homosexual leanings, whether practising or not. If all the minor signs are evident, then the writer is also likely to have gay inclinations. However, if only one or two of the minor signs are evident, then it is very *unlikely* that the writer is homosexual.

Major signs
1. Rounded and loopy letters in the middle zone with sharp sticks and angles in the lower zone.
2. The letters g and y have stems that look like big balloons being pulled towards the left of the page.
3. Capital J's have lower loops that are balloon-like and look as if they are being pulled towards the left.
4. Many of the letters f, g, j, q and y have figure-eight type signs drawn in their lower loops.

Minor signs
1. The lower g-stem is made of four or more different-type endings within one sample of writing.
2. The lower g-stem comes down from the baseline and then returns back upwards moving in the reverse direction from normal.
3. The lower g-stem is drawn like a felon's claw.
4. The letter d is written backwards, starting at the top of the stem and moving downwards.
5. The letter m has its second hump dented inwards or sideways.
6. The dots on the letters i and j are made with circles.
7. Small reversed ticks are placed on the top of letters in the upper zone.
8. The writing slants strongly to the left, and the letter g has a long stick-like lower ending.

9

Sample Compatibility Chart

On this page are handwriting samples belonging to Lara and Jake. These are followed by a compatibility chart outlining how well the couple are likely to get along. You may wish to copy the format of the chart when you prepare your own analyses. To give some background information, Lara and Jake are recently married and are both in their thirties. They were educated in the United Kingdom and both write with their right hands.

Lara's writing

existing concrete and pari

Start from Scratch . New

brought through the house

Jake's writing

teaches as Such, but our gardne
had worked for the family since
years old and Sloved my love

I. Emotional Slant	LARA'S WRITING **Slant** *Upright/Left with some far right*
Measure slant with the slant tool to decide if the writing is:	*Lara is predominantly a cool and objective individual, at times excessively cautious, reserved and careful to protect her own feelings*
• far left • left • upright • right • far right • very far right • varied	JAKE'S WRITING **Slant** *Right/Far right* *Jake reacts to emotional situations, but is not unduly swayed by them. His writing shows a warm, sympathetic nature, although he will rarely over-react due to emotion.*
	Compatibility *The couple will appreciate each other's emotional differences. Most of the time, Lara will bring objectivity and caution to the relationship, whereas Jake will bring emotionality. Problems could arise, should Jake become frustrated by Lara's caution and she in turn could be perturbed by his more relaxed attitude. Lara's occasional dramatic display of emotion will surprise and even unsettle Jake, who himself has a more consistent emotional nature.*
2. Emotional depth	LARA'S WRITING **Depth** *Heavy*
Look at the pressure of the writing on the page to decide if it is:	*Lara feels with intensity, remembering emotions for a long time. However she will often conceal the intensity of her feelings from others.*
• heavy • light • moderate • varied	JAKE'S WRITING **Depth** *Moderate/heavy* *Jake also feels strongly, but finds it easier to let go of his feelings, forgiving and forgetting, more easily moving on to the next emotional experience.*
	Compatibility *With their similar emotional depth, the couple will have an intense and generally secure relationship. Jake appreciates the strong emotion that lies beneath Lara's reserved front. He will need her to express her feelings to him.*

3. Thought processes

Look at connections between the letters and decide if they are rounded, needle-like, formed like upward-pointing v's or downward-pointing v's or coil-like.

Decide if the major thinking pattern is:

- slow and careful thinking
- quick thinking
- curious thinking
- questioning thinking
- superficial thinking

LARA'S WRITING

Predominant thought processes
Slow and careful with superficial and a little questioning

Lara approaches problems carefully and methodically. Although at times she may apppear slow in making decisions, she will invariably come to the correct conclusion. At times she will get mentally lazy, preferring to skim along the surface, due perhaps to her needing to reach conclusions faster than her normal slow and careful thinking pattern allows.

JAKE'S WRITING

Predominant thought processes
Curious with some quick and questioning

Jake likes to know the whys, wheres, and hows and he enjoys quick analytical thought. Quick thinking may occasionally mean that the wrong conclusions are reached because all the facts have not been sufficiently evaluated.

Compatibility
Lara's mind works in a contrasting way to that of her husband, who is much more likely to question things, be less accepting of others and faster in coming to decisions. Although Lara and Jake complement each other mentally, their very different thought processes may cause them problems, for they will have to make much more effort than most couples to understand how each other ticks. Patience and understanding, particularly on Jake's side, will be vital.

4. Optimism or pessimism	LARA'S WRITING	Optimism/pessimism *Evidence of pessimism*

For optimism, look for writing that slants upwards. For pessimism, look for writing that slants downwards.

Lara's writing shows a degree of pessimism or perhaps tiredness or slight depression. She may well be currently lacking enthusiasm or fearing the worst.

JAKE'S WRITING — Optimism/pessimism — *Neither evident*

The more strongly the writing slopes, the stronger the evidence of optimism. Decide if it is:

Jake's writing shows no evidence of either optimism or pessimism.

Compatibility
Communication between the two should help to reverse Lara's low state of mind.

- strong
- evident
- occasional
- not evident

---

5. Broad- or narrow-mindedness

LARA'S WRITING — Broad/narrow-mindedness — Occasional narrow-mindedness

Look for wide e loops in proportion to the rest of the middle zone, and wide circle parts to letters a, o, etc. The wider the e loops the stronger the broad-mindedness. Narrow-mindedness is seen in tightly drawn e loops and narrow circle letters. Decide if broad- or narrow-mindedness is:

Lara is slightly predisposed to narrow-mindedness.

JAKE'S WRITING — Broad/narrow-mindedness — Occasional narrow-mindedness

Jake is slightly predisposed to narrow-mindedness.

Compatibility
At times, they will both lean towards preconceived judgements and occasionally they may be unwilling to accept other people's points of view. Although for the majority of the time they will have similar views, when they have opposing views, this may result in arguments between them, as neither Lara nor Jake will be prepared to give way to the other. As neither shows this trait particularly strongly, it is unlikely to cause undue problems in their relationship.

- strong
- evident
- occasional
- not evident

6. Decisiveness or indecision

Look at letter and word endings to see if they have been finished with thick, firm, blunt endings which are as heavy in weight as the rest of the letters, indicating decisiveness. Or endings that taper out weakly with dwindling pressure. The firmer the endings the stronger the decisiveness. Decide if it is:

● strong
● evident
● occasional
● not evident

| LARA'S WRITING | Decisiveness/indecision
Averagely decisive |

Lara is quite decisive, although she may seem to take longer to come to decisions because she is predominantly a slow and careful thinker.

| JAKE'S WRITING | Decisiveness/indecision
Decisive |

Jake is decisive.

Compatibility
Both Lara and Jake see things in black and white and are unafraid of making decisions and sticking to them. This means that they are able to commit to their relationship and that both will be prepared to make decisions for the other.

7. Extrovert or introvert

Measure the slant with the measuring slant chart to decide if the writing slants to the left, indicating introversion, or slants to the right, indicating extrovertism. Decide if the writer is:

● introvert
● extrovert
● neither in particular

| LARA'S WRITING | Extrovert or Introvert
Varying extrovert/introvert |

Lara draws energy from being alone as well as from being around others.

| JAKE'S WRITING | Extrovert or Introvert
More extrovert |

Jake is averagely extrovert for an English national.

Compatibility
Similar in this respect, Lara and Jake are likely to be socially compatible.

8. Social adeptness

Check to see how closely together the letters are written. The more closely spaced, the more reserved the writer. The more widely spaced, the more relaxed and sharing the writer. Decide if the writer is:

- reserved and socially inept
- averagely socially adept
- relaxed and very socially adept

LARA'S WRITING	**Social adeptness**
	Quite socially adept

Lara finds it easy to be relaxed among people, sharing with others.

JAKE'S WRITING	**Social adeptness**
	Averagely socially adept

Jake feels averagely comfortable surrounded by people.

Compatibility
Compatible in this respect, both Lara and Jake find it easy to make friends and they no doubt tend to integrate well socially and have similar levels of social adeptness.

9. Closeness to others

Check spacing between words. Even spacing shows respect for social boundaries; uneven spacing shows unreliability in friendship; narrow spacing indicates the writer likes to be close to people; wide spacing indicates a preferred distance from people; very wide spacing shows isolation. Decide if the word spacing shows:

- respect for social boundaries
- unpredictability in friendship
- liking of closeness to others
- preference for distance from others
- social isolation

LARA'S WRITING	**Closeness to others**
	Quite distant

Lara likes to keep friends and acquaintances at a distance, emotionally and physically.

JAKE'S WRITING	**Closeness to others**
	Quite distant

Jake similarly prefers not to get too close to others.

Compatibility
Similar in this respect, they both need space, even though they like to be sociable

10. Expressiveness

Look at the middle zones of the letters and compare them to the upper and lower zones. If the middle zone is large the writer tends to be expressive and outgoing. If small he tends to be reserved and if varied in size, moody. Decide if the writer is:

- socially expressive
- reserved and non-expressive
- moody
- socially well adjusted

LARA'S WRITING **Expressiveness** *Quite expressive*

Lara is able to express herself well in group situations.

JAKE'S WRITING **Expressiveness** *Average*

Jake tends to be slightly more reserved when in social settings but on the whole is comfortable.

Compatibility
Once again Lara and Jake are similarly socially well adjusted.

11. Selection of friends

Look at the lower loops in the writing and decide if most are long and wide, indicating a wide variety of friends; narrow, indicating choosiness in friends; loops well below the baseline, indicating few friends; no lower loops, indicating solitude; a variety of loops and sticks indicating friendliness. Decide if the writer has:

- a wide group of friends
- a few select friends
- superficial friendships
- a preference for solitude
- a naturally friendly disposition

LARA'S WRITING **Selection of friends**
Wide group of friends

Lara relishes a wide circle of friends, particularly people with similar interests and backgrounds to herself.

JAKE'S WRITING **Selection of friends**
Naturally friendly disposition

Jake has a naturally friendly disposition and also likes to have many friends.

Compatibility
Lara and Jake's criteria with regard to friendship and sociability are very similar. They are likely to enjoy the company of each other's friends.

12. Talkative or reticent

Check the circle letters of a, b, d, g, o to see if the majority of circles are open, indicating talkativeness, or closed, indicating reticence. Decide if any show:

- talkativeness
- reticence
- mixture of talkativeness and reticence

LARA'S WRITING   **Talkativeness** *Quite talkative*

Lara likes to talk, but still retains some selectivity over what she says, and is unlikely to blurt out secrets. Nevertheless, she enjoys a bit of gossip. Her talkativeness will overcome the fact that she is quite emotionally reserved.

JAKE'S WRITING   **Talkativeness** *Reticent*

Jake is the reticent type and will not talk unless he really has something relevant to say.

Compatibility
Jake will need to feel confident that his wife is not discussing their personal affairs with others.

13. Sense of humour

Look at the letter m and the beginning of capital letters to see if there are any initial, smooth-flowing flourishes leading into the main letters. Decide if evidence of humour is:

- strong
- medium
- weak
- not evident

LARA'S WRITING   **Sense of humour** *Not evident*

As with most people, Lara's writing shows no evidence of humour.

JAKE'S WRITING   **Sense of humour** *Not evident*

Similarly, Jake's writing shows no evidence of humour.

Compatibility
This does not mean that neither appreciates a sense of humour, it simply implies that it is not a prominent trait in either of their personalities.

14. Jealousy

Check for small flattened loops drawn anti-clockwise at the beginning of letters. Decide if jealousy is:

- strong
- medium
- weak
- not evident

LARA'S WRITING   **Jealousy** *Not evident*

There is no evidence of jealousy in Lara's writing.

JAKE'S WRITING   **Jealousy** *Not evident*

There is no evidence of jealousy in Jake's writing.

Compatibility
Good news! Neither is jealous!

15. Self-consciousness

Check the letters m and n to see if the final hump is taller than the rest of the letter. Decide if self-consciousness is:

- strong
- medium
- weak
- not evident

LARA'S WRITING   **Self-consciousness** *Not evident*

Lara's handwriting shows no evidence of self-consciousness.

JAKE'S WRITING   **Self-consciousness** *Weak*

Jake can be a little self-conscious at times, uncomfortable about what others may think of him.

Compatability
Lara needs to be sensitive to Jake's self-consciousness.

16. Sensitivity to criticism

Check for looped t- and d-stems. Decide if sensitivity to criticism is:

- strong
- medium
- weak
- not evident

LARA'S WRITING   **Sensitivity to criticism**
Not evident

There is no evidence of sensitivity to criticism in Lara's writing.

JAKE'S WRITING   **Sensitivity to criticism**
Not evident

There is no evidence of sensitivity to criticism in Jake's writing.

Compatibility
Neither is unnecessarily upset by the other's criticism.

17. Suppression or repression

For suppression check for retraced letters in the middle zone. For repression check for frequent retracing in the letters m and n and a general look of squeezed letters. Decide if suppression or repression is:

- strong
- medium
- weak
- not evident

LARA'S WRITING   **Suppression or repression**
Not evident

There is no evidence of suppression or repression in Lara's writing.

JAKE'S WRITING   **Suppression or repression**
Not evident

There is no evidence of suppression or represion in Jake's writing.

Compatibility
As neither banishes unpleasant thoughts from their conscious minds into the unconscious, thus not facing up to problems, these personality traits will have no impact on their relationship.

18. Self-underestimation	LARA'S WRITING **Self-underestimation** *Weak*
Check for t-bars placed very low on the t-stems, below the top of the middle-zone letters. Decide if self-underestimation is:	*Lara has a tendency to underestimate her own worth and to shy away from looking towards the future, preferring to stick with the familiar, perhaps due to a slight fear of the unknown.*
	JAKE'S WRITING **Self-underestimation** *Not evident*
• strong • medium • weak • not evident	*Jake's writing shows no evidence of self-underestimation.*
	Compatibility *Both of them need to be aware of Lara's self-underestimation so that it is dealt with. If it grows, it could ultimately cause problems within the relationship.*
19. Argumentativeness	LARA'S WRITING **Argumentativeness** *Not evident*
Check to see if the initial stroke of the small letter p is higher than the circle part of the letter. Decide if argumentativeness is:	*There is no evidence of argumentativeness in Lara's writing.*
	JAKE'S WRITING **Argumentativeness** *Not evident*
	There is no evidence of argumentativeness in Jake's writing.
• strong • medium • weak • not evident	**Compatibility** *As neither partner enjoys arguing for the sake of it, their relationship is unlikely to be one of constant fights. They no doubt both prefer not to get embroiled in arguments.*
20. Violence	LARA'S WRITING **Violence** *Not evident*
Check for variations in slant, size, muddy and smeary pressure, angular slashing writing, argumentative p with a looped lower stem, larger letters in the middle of words. Decide if violence is:	*There is no evidence of violence in Lara's writing.*
	JAKE'S WRITING **Violence** *Not evident*
	There is no evidence of violence in Jake's writing.
• strong • medium • weak • not evident	**Compatibility** *Violence is unlikely to pose a problem in their relationship.*

21. Temper

Check to see if there are temper ticks, short jabs at the beginning of letters. Decide if temper is:

- strong
- medium
- weak
- not evident

LARA'S WRITING   **Temper** *Not evident*

There is no evidence of temper in Lara's writing.

JAKE'S WRITING   **Temper** *Weak*

There is little evidence of temper in Jake's writing and it is unlikely that his irritability will develop into a temper tantrum.

Compatibility
Temper is unlikely to be a problem for these two.

22. Irritability

Check for jabbed or distorted i or j dots that fly across the page. Decide if irritability is:

- strong
- medium
- weak
- not evident

LARA'S WRITING   **Irritability** *Not evident*

Lara is unlikely to be irritable

JAKE'S WRITING   **Irritability** *Quite strong*

Jake's writing shows irritability. He may become restless or impatient and at times be short with himself and others. Much of the time Jake will not display his irritability to others, but when he does express it, it is likely to be in the form of sarcasm.

Compatability
Jake's irritability, which could be due to tiredness or stress, will make life somewhat harder for Lara, who is not predisposed to irritability and has a placid nature.

23. Procrastination

Check for t-bars and i and j dots flying to the left of the stem. Decide if procrastination is:

- strong
- medium
- weak
- not evident

LARA'S WRITING   **Procrastination** *Not evident*

There is no evidence of procrastination in Lara's writing.

JAKE'S WRITING   **Procrastination** *Not evident*

There is no evidence of procrastination in Jake's writing.

Compatibility
Neither is predisposed to putting things off, both tend to face up to whatever needs to be done.

24. Bluff

Check for heavy, long, blunt lower strokes out of proportion with the rest of the writing. Decide if bluff is:

- strong
- medium
- weak
- not evident

LARA'S WRITING	**Bluff** *Weak*

Lara's writing shows a very slight tendency towards bluff. From time to time she may be more talk than action.

JAKE'S WRITING	**Bluff** *Not evident*

Jake's writing shows no evidence of bluff.

Compatibility
Jake may find Lara's bluff quite amusing. It is unlikely to be the cause of any problems in their relationship.

25. Stubbornness

Check to see if there are straight rigid downstrokes, sloping backwards, following upstrokes like a large inverted v. Decide if stubbornness is:

- strong
- medium
- weak
- not evident

LARA'S WRITING	**Stubbornness** *Not evident*

There is no evidence of stubbornness in Lara's writing.

JAKE'S WRITING	**Stubbornness** *Not evident*

There is no evidence of stubbornness in Jake's writing.

Compatibility
Lara and Jake both tend to be reasonable people and will not be difficult for the sake of being so. They will be prepared to listen to each other, and this should aid communication in the relationship.

26. Sarcasm

Check for t-bars and i and j dots made of lines that taper to needle-like points. Decide if sarcasm is:

- strong
- medium
- weak
- not evident

LARA'S WRITING	**Sarcasm** *Not evident*

There is no evidence of sarcasm in Lara's writing.

JAKE'S WRITING	**Sarcasm** *Quite strong*

Jake has a sharp tongue and the ability to use words to jibe at, tease or, in the extreme, even hurt others.

Compatibility
Sarcasm is not something that comes naturally to Lara, and she may get tired and even emotionally wounded by her husband's caustic words. Sarcasm can be the cause of amusement, but it can also be the cause of misery.

27. Goals

Check to see if the goals are:

- very low – t-bar below the top of the middle-zone letters
- low – t-bar level with the top of the middle-zone letters
- average – t-bar just above the top of the middle-zone letters
- high – t-bar within the top third of the t-stem, well above the middle-zone letters
- visionary – t-bar floating above the top of the t-stem

LARA'S WRITING **Goals** *Low*

Lara sets herself low, easy-to-achieve goals, preferring the day-to-day and the familiar, ensuring that she is always easily able to attain her goals. She underestimates her own abilities.

JAKE'S WRITING **Goals** *High/average*

Jake sets himself very high goals, reaching out, eager to take on great challenges, and planning into the future. His writing shows plenty of ambition, and he is willing to stretch himself and take risks.

Compatibility
Jake and Lara differ widely with regard to their ambitions and goal setting. Jake may find it hard to understand his wife's lack of confidence in her own abilities. Although their expectations for themselves are quite different, they should, nevertheless, be able to support each other.

28. Will power

Check the weight and pressure of the t-bar in relation to the rest of the writing. The stronger the pressure the stronger the will power. Decide if the will power is:

- strong
- medium
- weak
- not evident

LARA'S WRITING **Will power** *Medium/weak*

Lara's average will power means that she will easily achieve all of her aims.

JAKE'S WRITING **Will power** *Medium/strong*

In support of his higher goals, Jake is self-motivated. His strong will power will stand him in good stead in achieving most of his goals.

Compatibility
Both have the ability to choose a course of action for themselves, allowing them to maintain an element of independence within their relationship.

29. Enthusiasm

Check the length of the t-bar. Enthusiasm is present if it is twice the width of a middle-zone letter. Decide if enthusiasm is:

- strong
- medium
- weak
- not evident

LARA'S WRITING **Enthusiasm** *Weak*

Lara is not feeling particularly enthusiastic at the moment. This should not detract from her success, as she will not need to bring enthusiasm in order to achieve her low goals.

JAKE'S WRITING **Enthusiasm** *Strong*

Jake is feeling full of energy and enthusiasm, and this will add to his chances of success. All the same, his enthusiasm does tend to wane when projects are long and the obstacles high.

Compatibility
Their differing levels of enthusiasm could be a source of annoyance as Jake is currently on an up and Lara on a down.

30. Determination

Check the length and weight of the downstrokes, especially the lower stems of letters g, p and y. The longer and heavier they are in comparison to the rest of the writing, the stronger the evidence of determination. Decide if determination is:

- strong
- medium
- weak
- not evident

LARA'S WRITING **Determination** *Strong*

In contrast to her lack of enthusiasm, Lara is extremely determined. Once she decides on a course of action, she will stick with it, overcoming obstacles until the project is completed.

JAKE'S WRITING **Determination** *Medium*

Jake's determination is medium and he is more likely to give up if faced by too many obstacles, but then he is likely to have taken on greater challenges in the first place.

Compatibility
Although their ambitions and goal-setting are quite different, this means that there is little competition in the relationship, thus potentially leading to greater harmony. It is vital that they both appreciate each other's aims and ambitions in order to fully understand and support each other.

31. Self-confidence

Check high t-bars, underscored signatures and large capital letters. Decide if self-confidence is:

- strong
- medium
- weak
- not evident

LARA'S WRITING   **Self-confidence** *Medium/weak*

Lara's low t-bars are compensated by an underscoring of her signature. She underestimates her own worth.

JAKE'S WRITING   **Self-confidence** *Strong*

Jake's writing demonstrates a healthy self-confidence.

Compatibility
Lara's lack of confidence is not strong enough to affect their relationship adversely. Jake's strong self-confidence should have a positive effect on their partnership.

32. Materialism

Check the size of the middle-zone letters in relation to the upper and lower zones. If the writing exists predominantly within the middle zone, this indicates strong materialism. Decide whether the writer is:

- materialistic
- non-materialistic
- neither in particular

LARA'S WRITING   **Materialism**
                      Neither in particular

Lara is neither particularly materialistic nor non-materialistic.

JAKE'S WRITING   **Materialism**
                      Neither in particular

Compatibility
Their similar approach should help strengthen their relationship.

33. Organizational Abilities

Check the letter f to see if the top and bottom halves are well balanced. If not, there is no organizational ability. If they are balanced, check for:

- balanced f with no loops – organized but not flexible
- balanced f with upper loop only – can envisage plans but not action them
- balanced f with lower loop only – can't come up with plans, but can action them
- balanced f with upper and lower loops – can envisage and action plans

LARA'S WRITING **Organizational abilities**
No evidence

Lara's writing does not show evidence of organizational abilities.

JAKE'S WRITING **Organizational abilities**
Organized, but not very flexible

Jake is organized and will no doubt be tidy and like to live an orderly life.

Compatibility
Being organized is not something that Lara is likely to be concerned about. Jake is probably the organizer in their household.

34. Confusion

Check whether the writing looks messy and whether the upper and lower loops intermingle and cross over with lines above and below. Decide if confusion is:

- strong
- medium
- weak
- not evident

LARA'S WRITING **Confusion** *Not evident*

There is no evidence of confusion in Lara's writing

JAKE'S WRITING **Confusion** *Weak*

Although generally organized, Jake occasionally may take on too much and be unable to give full attention to one or more projects.

Compatibility
Confusion is unlikely to have an impact on their relationship.

35. Conservatism

Check the size of the middle-zone letters. If the writing looks compressed widthways, so that the letters look taller than they are wide, and the letters m and n look squeezed and a and o are narrow, the writer is conservative. Decide if the writer is:

● conservative
● ultra-conservative
● neither in particular

LARA'S WRITING   **Conservatism** *No evidence*

Lara's handwriting shows no evidence of conservatism.

JAKE'S WRITING   **Conservatism** *A little*

Jake has a slightly more conservative approach to life.

Compatability
Jake's slight conservatism or traditionalism is insufficient to affect their relationship.

36. Desire for variety

Check the lower loops. They need to be at least two and a half times the length of middle-zone letters to indicate a desire for variety. Long lower sticks indicate desire for variety within similar environments. Long lower loops indicate a desire for variety by new experiences. Decide if the desire for variety is:

● strong
● medium
● weak
● not evident

LARA'S WRITING   **Desire for variety** *Medium*

Lara's writing shows a desire for variety but within a familiar environment.

JAKE'S WRITING   **Desire for variety** *Weak*

Jake is comfortable with change but, being more conservative, will not seek it out.

Compatibility
Lara and Jake are quite similar in this respect, neither particularly comfortable in unfamiliar situations.

37. Deceit

Check the circle letters of a, d, e, g, o and q to see if there is a loop at the start and end of the circle formation. Also check the other deceit signs. Evaluate the strength of deceit in the writing by how often the sign appears. Decide if deceit is:

● strong
● medium
● weak
● not evident

LARA'S WRITING **Deceit** *Not evident*

Lara's writing shows no evidence of deceit.

JAKE'S WRITING **Deceit** *Not evident*

Jake's writing shows no evidence of deceit.

Compatibility
It is unlikely that either is being knowingly deceitful with the other.

38. Self-deceit

Check the circle letters of a, d, e, g, o and q to see if an initial loop has been drawn inside the circle part of the letters. The larger the size of the initial loop, and the more frequently it occurs, the greater the degree of self-deceit. Decide if it is:

● strong
● medium
● weak
● not evident

LARA'S WRITING **Self-deceit** *Weak*

There is no evidence of self-deceit in Lara's writing.

JAKE'S WRITING **Self-deceit** *Weak*

Occasionally Jake will push unpleasant or difficult thoughts out of his mind, not wanting to face reality head-on. This is not a strong trait and is something that the majority of people do to cope with difficulties.

Compatibility
Self deceit is unlikely to be a problematic factor in the relationship.

39. Secretiveness

Check the circle letters of a, d, e, g, o to q to see if there are any final loops coming out of the circle formation. The larger the loop, the greater the secrecy. Decide if it is:

- strong
- medium
- weak
- not evident

LARA'S WRITING   **Secretiveness** *Not evident*

Lara is very straightforward and frank, and one generally knows where one stands with her.

JAKE'S WRITING   **Secretiveness** *Weak*

Jake is more reserved with words, so from time to time he will keep information to himself.

Compatibility
Lara needs to be aware that Jake tends to reveal feelings and facts selectively and is generally quite a private person.

40. Honesty

Check the circle letters of a, d, e, g, o and q. Honesty is evident when the circles have no initial or final loop within them. The letters are made of a single circle with no embellishments. The more circle letters that are made in this formation, the greater the degree of honesty and frankness. Decide if it is:

- strong
- medium
- weak
- not evident

LARA'S WRITING   **Honesty** *Strong*

Lara's writing indicates she is a very frank type of person.

JAKE'S WRITING   **Honesty** *Quite strong*

Jake's writing shows quite a lot of honesty and frankness.

Compatibility
As both are likely to have high integrity, they will know where they stand with each other and will normally be honest about their feelings to each other.

41. Pride

Check the height of the t- and d-stems. Pride is evident if the stems are two to two and a half times the height of the middle-zone letters. The greater the number of letters t and d drawn like this, the greater the evidence of pride. Decide if it is:

- strong
- medium
- weak
- not evident

LARA'S WRITING	**Pride** *Weak*

Lara's writing shows a little pride – she has some desire to be approved of by both herself and others.

JAKE'S WRITING	**Pride** *Not evident*

Jake's writing does not show pride.

Compatibility
This will not be a contentious area in their relationship.

42. Vanity

Check the length of the t- and d-stems. Vanity is evident if the stems are over two and a half times the height of the middle zone letters. The greater the number of letters t and d drawn like this, the greater the evidence of vanity. Decide if it is:

- strong
- medium
- weak
- not evident

LARA'S WRITING	**Vanity** *Not evident*

Lara's writing shows no vanity.

JAKE'S WRITING	**Vanity** *Not evident*

Jake's writing shows no vanity.

Compatibility
Vanity is not an issue in their relationship.

43. Dignity

Check the t- and d-stems. For dignity to exist they must be totally retraced, looking like a single line. If the stem consists of a loop, then dignity is not present. The more stems retraced, the more dignity is evident. Decide if it is:

● strong
● medium
● weak
● not evident

LARA'S WRITING **Dignity** *Strong*

Lara's writing indicates she is a very dignified person.

JAKE'S WRITING **Dignity** *Quite strong*

Jake's writing shows quite a lot of dignity.

Compatibility
Both have dignity. They understand each other in this respect, both wanting to live their lives adhering to the conventional standards of society. No doubt they are a well respected couple, neither of them wishing to rock the boat. This dignity will stem much outward expression of emotion and irritability, as neither partner will want others to see them out of control.

44. Independence

Check the length of the t- and d- stems. The stems should be short, less than twice the height of the middle-zone letters. Check to see how many letters t and d are drawn like this and decide if independence is:

● strong
● medium
● weak
● not evident

LARA'S WRITING **Independence** *Quite strong*

Lara is willing and able to think for herself, coming to her own conclusions without being too concerned about what others think.

JAKE'S WRITING **Independence** *Strong*

Jake is similarly independent in his thinking.

Compatibility
With these similar standards, Lara and Jake should understand each other well.

45. Generosity

Check the length of the final strokes of letters and words. Generosity is present if the finals are long, at least the width of the preceding letter. Plenty of space should also be evident on the page. The greater the number of long finals, the greater the evidence of generosity. Decide if it is:

- strong
- medium
- weak
- not evident

LARA'S WRITING **Generosity** *Medium*

Generosity for the purpose of graphology is generosity without any ulterior motive. It is rare to find this in writing. Lara's writing shows some of this precious generosity.

JAKE'S WRITING **Generosity** *Not evident*

Jake's does not show generosity, but this does not imply that he is mean or stingy.

Compatibility
Lara's generosity will ease the relationship, as she will tend to be kind and forgiving in circumstances in which most people would not be so generous.

46. Meanness

Check the finals on letters and words. Meanness is evident if they are short and the writing looks cramped and squeezed with lines close together and few open circles. The stronger these traits, the more meanness is evident. Decide if it is:

- strong
- medium
- weak
- not evident

LARA'S WRITING **Meanness** *Not evident*

As her writing shows generosity, it dows not show meanness.

JAKE'S WRITING **Meanness** *Not evident*

Jake is not mean by nature.

Compatibility
Meanness should not be an issue for this couple.

47. Loyalty

Check the dots on the letters i and j. They should be round (not drawn in a circle) and neat. Also check for honesty, pride, decisiveness, generosity and positiveness (strong downstrokes). The greater the evidence of these traits, the stronger the signs of loyalty. Decide if it is:

- strong
- medium
- weak
- not evident

LARA'S WRITING **Loyalty** *Weak*

Loyalty is slightly present in Lara's writing.

JAKE'S WRITING **Loyalty** *Not evident*

Loyalty is not evident in Jake's writing.

Compatibility
Loyalty, or the desire to belong to causes, institutions, etc. is not of significance in this relationship.

48. Reliability

Check for evidence of honesty, loyalty, pride and consistent emotions. If there is evidence of fears, deceit or confusion, reliability will not be present. The greater the strength of the 'positive' traits, the greater the evidence of reliability. Decide if it is:

- strong
- medium
- weak
- not evident

LARA'S WRITING **Reliability** *Medium*

Lara's changes in emotional reactions indicate that she is probably only averagely reliable.

JAKE'S WRITING **Reliability** *Medium/strong*

Jake's writing indicates that he is likely to be reliable.

Compatibility
The couple are unlikely to face problems through lack of reliability in their relationship.

49. Sexual energy

Check the lower loops and stems of the letters g and y for pressure and width. Feel the reverse of the page. The heavier the pressure in comparison to the rest of the writing, the more sexually energetic the writer is. Averagely energetic writers have stems with the same pressure as the rest of the writing and unenergetic writers have stems lighter than the rest of the writing. Decide if sexual energy is:

- energetic
- averagely energetic
- unenergetic

LARA'S WRITING   **Sexual energy** *Average/strong*

Lara has plenty of energy.

JAKE'S WRITING   **Sexual energy** *Average*

Jake has a similar appetite for sex.

Compatibility
Lara and Jake's similarity in this respect is vital for their sexual compatibility.

50. Sensuality

Look at the lines of the writing. The thicker the lines and the wider they are, the more important the senses are to the writer. Decide if sensuality is:

- strong
- medium
- weak
- not evident

LARA'S WRITING   **Sensuality** *Medium*

Lara has an average to strong liking of the good things in life.

JAKE'S WRITING   **Sensuality** *Strong*

Jake's writing shows strong sensuality. He particularly relishes anything regarding the senses of sight, sound, taste, smell and touch.

Compatibility
They are likely to share similar interests in this respect.

51. Sensuousness

Look for writing that has a smudgy or bleary appearance, lines that are heavier in some places than others, and letters that look clogged up with ink. Decide if sensuousness is:

- strong
- medium
- weak
- not evident

LARA'S WRITING   **Sensuousness** *Not evident*

Lara's writing shows no evidence of sensuousness.

JAKE'S WRITING   **Sensuousness** *Medium*

Jake veers towards sensuousness, wanting to gratify the senses perhaps occasionally just for the sake of it. He will be a passionate and exciting love-maker.

Compatibility
Jake will need his partner to enjoy sensory gratification in the same way as he does himself.

52. Sexual disinterest

Check the lower loops and stems of the letters g and y. Look for sexual disinterest due to:

- Illness/anxiety – g and y stems large but with breaks, tremors or uneven pressure.
- Work pressure – g and y stems have short sticks pulled to the right
- Boredom – g and y stems have short endings with a rigid, monotonous look
- Self-interest – writing is predominantly within the middle zone, with little upper or lower zone stems.

Decide if sexual disinterest is

- strong
- medium
- weak
- not evident

LARA'S WRITING   **Sexual disinterest** *Not evident*

There is no evidence of sexual disinterest in Lara's writing.

JAKE'S WRITING   **Sexual disinterest** *Not evident*

There is no evidence of sexual disinterest in Jake's writing.

Compatibility
Sexual disinterest is not a problem for this couple.

53. Impotence

Check for the following signs of impotency:

- the lower g stem is lighter in pressure than the middle zone.
- the letter g looks broken, wobbly, shaky or varying in pressure
- the lower g stem is retraced
- the lower g stem is very short

Decide whether evidence of impotency is:

- strong
- medium
- weak
- not evident

LARA'S WRITING   **Impotence** *Not evident*

Lara's writing shows no indication of impotency.

JAKE'S WRITING   **Impotence** *Not evident*

Jake's writing shows no indication of impotency.

Compatibility
The lack of signs of impotency is to be expected as their writing indicates that they both have healthy libidos.

54. Sexual guilt

Check for sexual repression, evident when the lower loops of the letters g and y are very narrow or retraced. Check for guilt, evidenced by felon's claws on the letters g and y and by drooping middle-zone letters. Decide whether sexual guilt is:

- strong
- medium
- weak
- not evident

LARA'S WRITING   **Sexual guilt** *Not evident*

Lara's writing shows no evidence of sexual guilt.

JAKE'S WRITING   **Sexual guilt** *Not evident*

Jake's writing shows no evidence of sexual guilt.

Compatibility
Their love life is likely to be free of hang-ups!

55. Promiscuity

Check the lower loops and stems of the letters g and y. Promiscuity is evident if the g stems look like over-inflated balloons, three and a half times the length of the middle-zone letters. Supporting evidence is clogged up, muddy-looking letters. Decide if evidence of promiscuity is:

- strong
- medium
- weak
- not evident

LARA'S WRITING   **Promiscuity** *Weak*

Lara's writing shows a slight tendency towards promiscuity.

JAKE'S WRITING   **Promiscuity** *Not evident*

There is no evidence of promiscuity in Jake's writing.

Compatibility
Lara's need for sex will be matched by her husband's energy and sensuality.

56. Sexual experimentation

Check the g stems and look for the following signs of sexual experimentation:

- Unusually formed lower g-stems
- Reversed or distorted lower loops
- Downward-pointing lower g-stem loops
- Felon's claw-like structures on g-stems

Decide if evidence of sexual experimentation is:

- strong
- medium
- weak
- not evident

LARA'S WRITING   **Sexual experimentation**
                  Not evident

Lara's writing shows no evidence of sexual experimentation.

JAKE'S WRITING   **Sexual experimentation**
                  Medium

Jake's unusual reversed direction g-stems indicate an interest in sexual experimentation.

Compatibility
As Lara's writing does not share this trait, it may be that Jake's erotic desires remain within the realm of his imagination and are not actually carried out. It is useful for Lara to be aware of her husband's fantasies so that he does not feel compelled to act them out elsewhere.

Further Information

If you would like further information on graphology, such as how to have your handwriting professionally analysed for personal, career or recruitment purposes, please write to:

Miranda Cahn
PO Box 2007
Pulborough
West Sussex RH20 3FL
England

Please enclose a stamped addressed envelope.

For further information on the study course that leads to a professional qualification in graphology, please write to:

International Graphology Association (Ref: MC2007)
Stonedge
Dunkerton
Bath BA2 8AS
England

Index